Early praise for *Pragmatic Scala*

A well-paced, easy-to-read, and practical guide to Scala for Java programmers. Covers important aspects of this powerful multi-paradigm language, ensuring that you can become productive with Scala right away.

➤ **Ramnivas Laddad**
    Author of *AspectJ in Action*, speaker, and consultant

In *Pragmatic Scala*, Venkat provides a solid foundation to help you get started with Scala in a thorough yet succinct book that you can (and should) read cover to cover. He explores the most important topics you'll need to get comfortable with Scala, starting with the REPL and progressing through functional programming in Scala, handling concurrency with actors, and Java interoperability. You will definitely want to fire up your editor or IDE and code along with the book's numerous, interesting, and fun examples!

➤ **Scott Leberknight**
    Software architect, Fortitude Technologies

In a world of tweets, blogs, and bite-sized videos, there is still a place for the long-form narrative. It gives a teacher the time necessary to introduce challenging and complex topics. And, if we're being honest, Scala is a challenging and complex topic. Take this opportunity for Venkat to guide you through the Scala language, functional programming, concurrency, testing strategies, and more.

➤ **Brian Sletten**
    President, Bosatsu Consulting, Inc.

There are two reasons why I recommend this book for all my Scala classes. It covers the basics without insulting your intelligence and escalates you to advanced topics without going over your head. A must-have for anyone learning Scala.

➤ **Daniel Hinojosa**

Programmer, instructor, presenter, and author of *Testing in Scala*

Pragmatic Scala

Create Expressive, Concise, and Scalable Applications

Venkat Subramaniam

The Pragmatic Bookshelf

Dallas, Texas • Raleigh, North Carolina

Many of the designations used by manufacturers and sellers to distinguish their products are claimed as trademarks. Where those designations appear in this book, and The Pragmatic Programmers, LLC was aware of a trademark claim, the designations have been printed in initial capital letters or in all capitals. The Pragmatic Starter Kit, The Pragmatic Programmer, Pragmatic Programming, Pragmatic Bookshelf, PragProg and the linking *g* device are trademarks of The Pragmatic Programmers, LLC.

Every precaution was taken in the preparation of this book. However, the publisher assumes no responsibility for errors or omissions, or for damages that may result from the use of information (including program listings) contained herein.

Our Pragmatic courses, workshops, and other products can help you and your team create better software and have more fun. For more information, as well as the latest Pragmatic titles, please visit us at *https://pragprog.com*.

The team that produced this book includes:

Jacquelyn Carter (editor)
Potomac Indexing, LLC (index)
Liz Welch (copyedit)
Dave Thomas (layout)
Janet Furlow (producer)
Ellie Callahan (support)

For international rights, please contact *rights@pragprog.com*.

Printed in the United States of America.
ISBN-13: 978-1-68050-054-7
Printed on acid-free paper.
Book version: P1.0—September 2015

Contents

Part II — Diving Into Scala

Part III — Concurrency in Scala

Part IV — Applying Scala

Acknowledgments

When I signed up to write this book, little did I know about the challenges ahead. Daily routines became unbearable due to a neck injury. After spending months fighting that issue, I decided to back out of this book. Instead of responding as publishers, the Pragmatic Programmers came together as friends and family would. I went looking for a publisher—now I know I found real friends. Thanks to Susannah Pfalzer, Dave Thomas, Andy Hunt, and the rest of the crew who helped with this book.

I sincerely thank the technical reviewers of this book. Thanks to Scott Leberknight for his constructive reviews—whenever he reviews one of my books, my deepest learning happens. I thank Daniel Hinojosa, Rahul Kavale, Anand Krishnan, Ted Neward, Rebecca Parsons, Vahid Pazirandeh, and Ian Roughley for their valuable time and input in the making of this book—I really appreciate what you've done. Any errors in the book are solely mine.

Thanks to everyone who purchased a copy of this book in the beta form. Thanks to David Dieulivol and Chris Searle for submitting errata.

I greatly benefited from Jackie Carter's encouragement, support, advice, and suggestions. She is an absolute pleasure to interact with and such a guiding force. Thank you, Jackie, for all you've done. You made writing this book a pleasurable task.

I could not have done any of this without the support of my wife Kavitha and sons Karthik and Krupa—thank you, folks.

Introduction

Glad to see your interest in Scala. Thank you for choosing this book to learn and exercise the combined power of two programming paradigms—object-oriented and functional—fused together in one language.

The Java ecosystem is one of the most powerful platforms to develop and deploy enterprise applications. It's ubiquitous and versatile; it has a rich set of libraries and runs on multiple types of hardware; and there are well over 200 languages to program on it.

I've had the privilege to learn and work with a dozen languages and have written books on a few. Languages are like vehicles—they come with different capabilities and help us navigate the platform. It's quite heartwarming to see that programmers today have the liberty to choose from, and also intermix, multiple languages to program their applications.

Typical enterprise applications suffer from multiple issues—verbose code is hard to maintain, mutability increases bugs, and shared mutability turns the pleasurable task of programming concurrency into hell. We've repeatedly fallen prey to accidental complexities that arise from poor abstractions offered by mainstream languages.

Scala is one of the most powerful languages that compiles down to bytecode. It's statically typed, concise, and expressive, and it's being used to develop performant, scalable, responsive, and resilient applications by many organizations.

The right set of features have come together in this language to remove a number of traps. The Scala language and its libraries let us focus on the problem domain rather than being bogged down by low-level infrastructure details like threads and synchronization.

Scala has been designed to create applications that require high performance, faster response, and greater resilience. It's a language created to meet the high frequency and volume of data processing that large corporations and social media demand.

Scala has been used to build applications in various domains, including telecommunications, social networking, semantic web, and digital asset management. Apache Camel uses Scala for its DSL to create routing rules. Play and Lift are powerful web development frameworks built using Scala. Akka, built using Scala, is a prominent library for creating highly responsive concurrent and reactive applications. These libraries and frameworks take full advantage of Scala features such as conciseness, expressiveness, pattern matching, and concurrency.

Scala is a powerful language, but to get productive with it we need to focus on the essential parts of the language that provide the most value. This book will help you learn the essentials of Scala, so you can quickly get productive, get your work done, and create practical applications.

And, to help you create practical applications, Scala offers two different styles of programming.

Programming Styles in Scala

Scala does not limit us to one programming style. We can program with objects, or in functional style, and also mix the two to get the best of both worlds.

Java programmers are familiar and comfortable with OOP. Scala is object-oriented and statically typed—a notch more than Java on both fronts. That's good news since our investment over the years in OOP is not wasted but earns dividends as we begin to program in Scala. When creating traditional applications we can lean toward the OO style provided by Scala. We can write code much like the way we're used to in Java, leveraging the power of abstraction, encapsulation, inheritance, and above all, polymorphism. At the same time, we're not restricted to this model when our needs stretch beyond its strengths.

The functional style of programming is gaining traction, and Scala readily supports that as well. We can lean more easily toward immutability, create pure functions, reduce accidental complexities, and apply function composition and lazy evaluations. With the full benefit of the functional style we can create high-performant—single-threaded and multithreaded—applications in Scala.

Scala and Other Languages

Scala has drawn a good number of features from other languages, most notably Erlang. The actor-based concurrency in Scala was inspired by the success of that model in Erlang. Likewise, static typing and type inference in Scala was influenced by languages like Haskell. Functional style capabilities came from several languages that came before.

With the introduction of lambda expressions and the powerful streams API in Java 8 (see *Functional Programming in Java: Harnessing the Power of Java 8 Lambda Expressions [Sub14]*) we can write functional style code in Java. This is not a threat to Scala or any of the other languages on the JVM; instead it closes the gap between these languages, making it less difficult for programmers to adopt or switch between languages.

Scala nicely fits into the Java ecosystem, and we can readily use Java libraries from Scala. We can build full applications entirely in Scala or intermix it with Java and other languages on the JVM. So, Scala code could be as small as a script or as large as a full-fledged enterprise application.

Who Is This Book For?

This book is for experienced Java programmers. I assume you know the Java language syntax and the Java API. I also assume you have strong object-oriented programming skills. These assumptions will allow you to quickly get into the essence of Scala and make use of it on real applications.

Developers who are familiar with other languages can use this book as well but will have to supplement it with good Java books.

Programmers who are somewhat familiar with Scala can use this book to learn some language features that they may not otherwise have had the opportunity to explore. Those already familiar with Scala can use this book for training fellow programmers in their organizations.

What's in This Book?

My objective in writing this book is to get you up to speed on Scala so you can use it to write scalable, responsive, and resilient applications. There is a lot you need to learn to do that, but there is a lot more you don't need to know as well. If your objective is to learn everything that there is to learn about Scala, you will not find that in this book. There are other books on Scala that do a great job of introducing the language in great depth. What you will see in this book are essential concepts that you need to know to start using Scala.

I assume you are quite familiar with Java. So, you will not learn basic concepts of programming from this book. However, I do not assume you have knowledge of functional programming or the Scala language itself—you will learn that in this book.

I have written this book for a busy Java developer, so my objective is to make you comfortable with Scala quickly so you can start building parts of your application with it really soon. You will see that the concepts are introduced fairly quickly but with lots of examples.

There is no better way to learn a language than trying out examples—a lot of them. As you follow along with the book, key in the examples, run them, see the output, modify them with your own ideas, experiment, break the code, and put it back together. That's the most fun way to learn.

Scala Version Used in This Book

Using automated scripts, the examples in this book have been tried out with the following version:

```
Scala code runner version 2.11.7 -- Copyright 2002-2013, LAMP/EPFL
```

Take a few minutes to download the appropriate version of Scala for your system. This will help you follow along with the examples in this book.

Online Resources

You can download all the example source code for the book from the Pragmatic Bookshelf website for this book.[1] You can also provide feedback by submitting errata entries or posting your comments and questions in the forum.

If you're reading the book in PDF form, you can click on the link above a code listing to view or download the specific examples.

A number of web resources referenced throughout the book are collected in Appendix 2, *Web Resources*, on page 253. Here are a few that will help you get started with this book:

To download Scala visit the official website for the language.[2] You can find documentation for the Scala library at the documentation page.[3]

Let's ascend Scala.

---

1. http://www.pragprog.com/titles/vsscala2
2. http://www.scala-lang.org/download
3. http://www.scala-lang.org/api

Part I

Getting Your Feet Wet

*This part of the book will help Java programmers
ease into Scala. You'll learn:*
- *what Scala offers*
- *to create classes, tuples, and more*
- *to use REPL*
- *how Scala differs from Java*
- *about types and type inference*

CHAPTER 1

Exploring Scala

Scala is a great language for writing highly expressive and concise code without sacrificing the power of static typing.

You can use Scala to build anything from small utility programs to entire enterprise applications. You can program in the familiar object-oriented style, and transition, when you like, to the functional style of programming. Scala does not force developers down a single path; you can start on familiar grounds and, as you get comfortable with the language, make use of features that can help you become more productive and your programs more efficient.

Let's quickly explore some of the features of Scala, and then take a look at a practical example in Scala.

Scala Features

Scala, short for Scalable Language, is a hybrid functional programming language. It was created by Martin Odersky and was first released in 2003 (for more information, see "A Brief History of Scala" in Appendix 2, *Web Resources*, on page 253). Here are some of the key features of Scala:

- It supports both an imperative style and a functional style.
- It is purely object-oriented.
- It enforces sensible static typing and type inference.
- It is concise and expressive.
- It intermixes well with Java.
- It is built on a small kernel.
- It is highly scalable, and it takes less code to create high-performing applications.
- It has a powerful, easy-to-use concurrency model.

You'll learn more about each of these features throughout this book.

More with Less

One of the first differences you'll find as you ease into Scala is that you can do more with a lot less code in Scala than in Java. The conciseness and expressiveness of Scala will shine through every line of code you write. You'll start applying Scala's key features and soon they'll make your routine programing quite productive—Scala simplifies everyday programming.

To get a taste of Scala's power and its benefits, let's look at a quick example where we make use of many of the features. Even though the syntax may appear unfamiliar at this time, key in the code and play with it as you read along. The more you work with the code, the quicker it becomes familiar.

If you've not installed Scala yet, please see Appendix 1, *Installing Scala*, on page 251 for the steps. Now to the first code example:

```
Introduction/TopStock.scala
Line 1  val symbols = List("AMD", "AAPL", "AMZN", "IBM", "ORCL", "MSFT")
     2  val year = 2014
     3
     4  val (topStock, topPrice) =
     5    symbols.map { ticker => (ticker, getYearEndClosingPrice(ticker, year)) }
     6          .maxBy { stockPrice => stockPrice._2 }
     7
     8  printf(s"Top stock of $year is $topStock closing at price $$$topPrice")
```

If this is your first look at Scala, don't be distracted by the syntax. Focus on the big picture for now.

Given a list of symbols, the code computes the highest priced stock among them. Let's tear apart the code to understand it.

Let's look at the main parts of the code first. On line 1, symbols refers to an immutable list of stock ticker symbols and, on line 2, year is an immutable value. On lines 5 and 6, we use two powerful, specialized iterators—the map() function and maxBy() function. In Java we're used to the term *method*, to refer to a member of a class. The word *function* is often used to refer to a procedure that's not a member of a class. However, in Scala we use the words *method* and *function* interchangeably.

Each of the two iterators take on two separate responsibilities. First, using the map() function, we iterate over the ticker symbols to create another list with pairs or tuples of tickers and their closing price for the year 2014. The resulting list of tuples is of the form List((symbol1, price1), (symbol2, price2), ...).

The second iterator works on the result of the first iterator. maxBy() is a specialized iterator on the list that picks the first highest value. Since the list is a collection of tuples (pairs) of values, we need to tell maxBy() how to compare the values. In the code block attached to maxBy() we indicate that given a tuple, we're interested in its second property (represented by _2): the price value. That was very concise code, but quite a bit is going on there. Let's visualize the actions in the following figure:

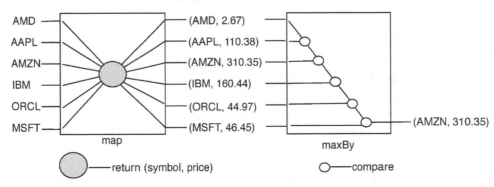

As we see in the figure, map() applies the given function or operation—fetching price—for each symbol to create the resulting list of symbols and their prices. maxBy() then works on this subsequent list to create a single result of the symbol with the highest price.

The previous code is missing the getYearEndClosingPrice() function; let's take a look at that next:

```
Introduction/TopStock.scala
def getYearEndClosingPrice(symbol : String, year : Int) = {
  val url = s"http://ichart.finance.yahoo.com/table.csv?s=" +
    s"$symbol&a=11&b=01&c=$year&d=11&e=31&f=$year&g=m"

  val data = io.Source.fromURL(url).mkString
  val price = data.split("\n")(1).split(",")(4).toDouble
  price
}
```

Even though the syntax may not yet be familiar, this code should be easy to read. In this short and sweet function, we send a request to the Yahoo Finance web service and receive the stock data in CSV format. We then parse the data, to extract and return the year-end closing price. Don't worry about the format of the data received right now; that's not important for what we're focusing on here. In Chapter 15, *Creating an Application with Scala*, on page 227, we'll revisit this example and provide all the details about talking to the Yahoo service.

To run the previous example, save the two pieces of code in a file named TopStock.scala and type the command

```
scala TopStock.scala
```

You'll see a result like this:

```
Top stock of 2014 is AMZN closing at price $310.35
```

Spend a few minutes tracing through the code to make sure you understand how this is working. While you're at it, see how the method computed the highest price without ever explicitly changing any variable or object. The entire code is totally dealing with only immutable state; no variable or object was tortured, err...changed, after it was created. As a result, you wouldn't have to be concerned about any synchronization and data contention if you were to run it in parallel.

We've fetched data from the web, done some comparisons, and yielded the desired result—nontrivial work, but it took only a few lines of code. This Scala code will stay concise and expressive even if we ask some more of it. Let's take a look.

In the example, we're fetching data for each symbol from Yahoo, which involves multiple calls over the network. Assume the network delay is d seconds and we're interested in analyzing n symbols. The sequential code will take about n * d seconds. Since the biggest delay in the code will be network access to fetch the data, we can reduce the time to about d seconds if we execute the code to fetch data for different symbols in parallel. Scala makes it trivial to turn the sequential code into parallel mode, with only one small change:

```
symbols.par.map { ticker => (ticker, getYearEndClosingPrice(ticker, year)) }
     .maxBy { stockPrice => stockPrice._2 }
```

We inserted a call to par; that's pretty much it. Rather than iterating sequentially, the code will now work on each symbol in parallel.

Let's highlight some nice qualities of the example we wrote:

- First, the code is concise. We took advantage of a number of powerful Scala features: function values, (parallel) collections, specialized iterators, values, immutability, and tuples, to mention a few. Of course, I have not introduced any of these yet; we're only in the introduction! So, don't try to understand all of that at this moment, because we have the rest of the book for that.

- We used functional style—function composition, in particular. We transformed the list of symbols to a list of tuples of symbols and their prices using the map() method. Then we transformed that into the desired value using the maxBy() method. Rather than spending effort on controlling the iteration—as we'd do in imperative style—we ceded control to the library of functions to get the job done.

- We employed concurrency without pain. There was no need for wait() and notify() or synchronized. Since we handled only immutable state, we did not have to spend time or effort (and sleepless nights) with data contention and synchronization.

These benefits have removed a number of burdens from our shoulders. For one, we did not have to struggle to make the code concurrent. For an exhaustive treatise about how painful threads can be, refer to Brian Goetz's *Java Concurrency in Practice [Goe06]*. With Scala, we can focus on application logic instead of worrying about the low-level concerns.

We saw a concurrency benefit of Scala. Scala concurrently (pun intended) provides benefits for single-threaded applications as well. Scala provides the freedom to choose and mix two styles of programming: the imperative style and the assignment-less pure functional style. With the ability to mix these two styles, in Scala we can use the style that's most appropriate in the scope of a single thread. For multithreading or safe concurrency, we would lean toward the functional style.

What we treat as primitives in Java are objects in Scala. For example, 2.toString() will generate a compilation error in Java. However, that is valid in Scala— we're calling the toString() method on an instance of Int. At the same time, in order to provide good performance and interoperability with Java, Scala maps the instances of Int to the int representation at the bytecode level.

Scala compiles down to bytecode. We can run it the same way we run programs written using the Java language or we can also run it as a script. We can also intermix it well with Java. We can extend Java classes from Scala classes, and vice versa. We can also use Java classes in Scala and Scala classes in Java. We can program applications using multiple languages and be a true Polyglot Programmer—see "Polyglot Programming" in Appendix 2, *Web Resources*, on page 253.

Scala is a statically typed language, but, unlike Java, it has sensible static typing. Scala applies type inference in places it can. Instead of specifying the type repeatedly and redundantly, we can rely on the language to learn the type and enforce it through the rest of the code. We don't work for the compiler; instead, we let the compiler work for us. For example, when we define var i = 1, Scala immediately figures that the variable i is of type Int. Now, if we try to assign a String to that variable as in i = "haha", Scala will give an error, like this:

```
sample.scala:2:
error: type mismatch;
 found   : String("haha")
 required: Int
i = "haha" //Error
    ^
one error found
```

Later in this book we'll see how type inference works beyond such simple definitions and transcends further to function parameters and return values.

Scala favors conciseness. Placing a semicolon at the end of statements is second nature to Java programmers. Scala provides a break for your right pinky finger from the years of abuse it has taken—semicolons are optional in Scala. But, that is only the beginning. In Scala, depending on the context, the dot operator (.) is optional as well, and so are the parentheses. Thus, instead of writing s1.equals(s2);, we can write s1 equals s2. By losing the semicolon, the parentheses, and the dot, code gains a high signal-to-noise ratio. It becomes easier to write domain-specific languages.

One of the most interesting aspects of Scala is *scalability*. We can enjoy a nice interplay of functional programming constructs along with the powerful set of libraries, to create highly scalable, concurrent applications and take full advantage of multithreading on multicore processors.

The real beauty of Scala is in what it does not have. Compared to Java, C#, and C++, the Scala language has a very small kernel of rules built into it. The rest, including operators, are part of the Scala library. This distinction has a far-reaching consequence. Because the language does not do more, we can do a lot more with it. It's truly extensible, and its library serves as a case study for that.

The code in this section showed how much we can get done with only a few lines of code. Part of that conciseness comes from the declarative style of functional programming—let's take a closer look at that next.

Functional Programming

Functional programming (FP) has been around for decades, but it's finally gaining much needed traction. If you've mostly done OOP it'll take some effort to get comfortable with FP, but Scala eases the burden quite a bit.

The nature of Scala being a hybrid language—we can write in both imperative and functional style—can be a blessing and a curse. It's a blessing because when writing code in Scala, we can make it work and make it better. Programmers new to FP can initially write code in imperative style and refactor it to functional style. Also, if a particular algorithm will truly benefit from an imperative implementation, we can easily code that in Scala. However, it could be a curse if teams use this flexibility to arbitrarily mix the paradigms. A good oversight by lead developers may be necessary to help maintain a consistent coding style that's desirable for the team.

Functional programming honors immutability, and favors higher-order functions and function composition. These features collectively make the code concise, expressive, easier to understand, and easier to modify. Immutability also helps to reduce errors that often creep in due to state change.

Let's take a few minutes to get a sense of functional programming by contrasting it with the imperative style.

Here's a Java version of the imperative code to find the maximum temperature from among values for a given day:

```
public static int findMax(List<Integer> temperatures) { //Java code
  int highTemperature = Integer.MIN_VALUE;
  for(int temperature : temperatures) {
   highTemperature = Math.max(highTemperature, temperature);
  }
  return highTemperature;
}
```

Scala supports imperative style as well; here's a Scala version of the code:

Introduction/FindMaxImperative.scala
```
def findMax(temperatures : List[Int]) = {
  var highTemperature = Integer.MIN_VALUE
  for(temperature <- temperatures) {
   highTemperature = Math.max(highTemperature, temperature)
  }
  highTemperature
}
```

We created the mutable variable highTemperature and continually modified it in the loop. We have to ensure that we initialize mutable variables properly and that we're changing them in the right place to the right values.

Functional programming is a declarative style in which we say what to do instead of how something should be done. XSLT, rules engines, and ANTLR are some of the tools where declarative style is prevalent. Let's rewrite the previous code in functional style with no mutable variables:

Introduction/FindMaxFunctional.scala
```scala
def findMax(temperatures : List[Int]) = {
  temperatures.foldLeft(Integer.MIN_VALUE) { Math.max }
 }
```

That's a nice interplay of Scala conciseness and functional programming style.

We created the function findMax() that accepts an immutable collection of temperature values as its parameter. The = symbol between the parentheses and the curly brace told Scala to infer the return type of this function, in this case an Int.

Within the function, the foldLeft() method of the collection exercises the function Math.max() for each element of the collection. The max() method of the java.lang.Math class takes two parameters, which are the values we want to determine the maximum of. Those two parameters are being sent implicitly in the previous code. The first implicit parameter to max() is the previous high value, and the second parameter is the current element in the collection that foldLeft() is navigating or iterating over. foldLeft() takes the result of the call to max, which is the current high value, and sends it to the subsequent call to max() to compare with the next element. The parameter to foldLeft() is the initial value for the high temperature.

The following figure helps us visualize the functioning of the findMax() function in this example, with some sample values for temperatures.

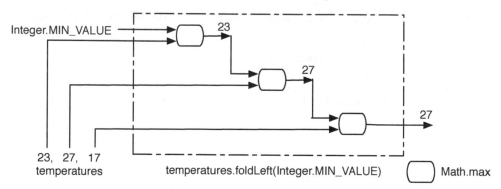

The figure shows that the findMax() function invokes the foldLeft() method on the temperatures list. The foldLeft() method first applies the given function Math.max() with the initial value Integer.MIN_VALUE and the first element in the list 23. The greater of those two, 23, is then passed again to the Math.Max() method, along with the second value of the list. The subsequent result of that computation, 27, which is the greater of the two values, is then compared with the final element in the list, again using the Math.max() method. The sequence of these operations, within the boxed rectangle, is totally the inner working of the foldLeft() method. The findMax() finally returns the result that the foldLeft() method yields.

The code in the example is quite dense; take a few minutes to let it sink in.

The foldLeft() method takes effort to grasp—let's work through another mental exercise to understand. Assume for a minute that the elements in the collection are people who form a line and that we want to find the age of the oldest person. We write 0 on a note and give it to the first person in the line. The first person discards the note (because he's older than age 0); creates a new note with his age, 20; and hands the slip to the next person in line. The second person, who is younger than 20, simply passes the note to the person next to him. The third person, who is 32, discards the note and creates a new one to pass along. The note we get from the last person will contain the age of the oldest person in the line. Visualizing this sequence will help you understand what foldLeft() does under the hood.

The previous code may feel like taking a shot of Red Bull. Scala code is highly concise and can be intense. You have to put in some effort to learn the language. But once you do, you will be able to take advantage of its power and expressiveness.

Let's take a look at another example of functional style. Suppose we want a list whose elements are double the values in an original list. Rather than loop through each element to realize that, simply instruct that the elements be doubled and let the language do the looping, as shown here:

Introduction/DoubleValues.scala

```
val values = List(1, 2, 3, 4, 5)

val doubleValues = values.map(_ * 2)
```

Read the keyword val as *immutable.*It tells Scala that the variables values and doubleValues can't be changed once created.

Although it may not look like it, _*2 is a function. It is an anonymous function, which means it's a function with only a body but no name. The underscore (_) represents the argument passed to this function. The function itself is passed as an argument to the map function. The map() function iterates over the collection and, for each element in the collection, invokes the anonymous function given as a parameter. The overall result is a new list consisting of elements that are double those in the original list.

Functions are first-class citizens in Scala, which is why we can treat functions, in this case the one that doubles a number, just like regular parameters and variables.

Although we obtained a list with double the values of elements in the original list, we did so without modifying any variable or object. This immutable approach is a key concept that makes functional programming a desirable style for concurrent programming. In functional programming, functions are pure. The output they produce is based solely on the input they receive, and they are not affected by or affect any state, global or local.

Programming with immutability has clear benefits, but wouldn't making copies of objects, instead of changing them, result in poor performance and increased memory usage? It can, if we're not careful. Scala relies on some special data structures to provide good performance and efficient memory usage. For example, Scala List is immutable, and so a copy of the list with an additional element in the first position can share an existing list. Thus, making a copy of a list to insert an element in the beginning is a O(1) operation both in time and space. Likewise, Scala's Vector is an implementation of a special immutable data structure named *Tries*. It's designed to make copying the collection highly efficient, with constant time and space complexity to effect change to an arbitrary element in the collection.

Wrapping Up

We got a good glimpse of the highly concise and expressive nature of Scala using a few practical examples in this chapter. The short examples serve as a whirlwind tour of several features, including functional style, effortless concurrency, use of collections, fancy iterators, programming with immutability, and using tuples. We learned about defining variables and values, about the static type checking, and about type inference. Above all, we also saw how concise and expressive Scala is.

While we quickly touched on a number of things, we have the rest of the book to dive into each of those, and more, in depth. Let's get started with ways to compile and run Scala code in the next chapter.

CHAPTER 2

Taking Scala for a Ride

Surprisingly, it's very easy to get Scala code up and running, whether you're creating a short script or a full-fledged enterprise application. You can use any of the available IDEs or just a lightweight editor.

In this chapter, you'll learn how to quickly run your Scala scripts from the command line and how to compile multiple files containing Scala code. If, at any time, you're curious what Scala's thinking—what the inferred types of variables are—you can quickly jump into the REPL where Scala interactively reveals valuable details. There's no better way to learn Scala than by trying out some examples, so type the code and run them as you read along. Let's get started with the most fun and interactive tool—the REPL.

Using the REPL

Quite a few languages provide a REPL—*read-eval-print loop*—a tool that's a convenient way to key in snippets of code and interactively see the code come to life immediately. In addition to executing code snippets, REPLs often provide details that are not easily accessible at runtime. That makes REPL a special tool for experimentation and also to learn how the language infers types for variables and functions.

The command-line shell named scala is the REPL for Scala and it's the quickest way to try out the language. Using this tool we can start playing with small code snippets. This is not simply a learning tool; it comes in handy during development of large applications as well. You can quickly try out some code ideas—micro prototyping—in the REPL and then use the world's best technology of copy and paste to get the code from the REPL into your application.

To start the REPL, on the command line (in a terminal window or command prompt), type scala. That should print an introductory message followed by a prompt:

```
Welcome to Scala version 2.11.7 (Java HotSpot(TM) 64-Bit Server VM, Java
1.8.0_45).
Type in expressions to have them evaluated.
Type :help for more information.

scala>
```

At the prompt, type val number = 6, and hit Return. The Scala shell responds to indicate that it inferred the variable number to be an Int based on what's assigned to it, the value 6:

```
scala> val number = 6
number: Int = 6
```

Now try reassigning number, and Scala will respond with this error:

```
scala> number = 7
<console>:11: error: reassignment to val
       number = 7
              ^
```

Scala complains that we can't reassign the constant number. In the console, however, we can redefine constants and variables. For example, the shell will quietly accept the following:

```
scala> val number = 7
number: Int = 7
```

Redefining constants and variables within the same scope is possible only in the interactive shell, and not in real Scala code or script—this flexibility makes it easier to experiment within the shell and, at the same time, prevents errors in application code.

We saw how Scala inferred the type as Int. Let's try another example where it infers a variable as List.

```
scala> val list = List(1, 2, 3)
list: List[Int] = List(1, 2, 3)
```

Any time while writing application code, if you're not sure what an expression will be inferred as, quickly try it in the shell.

In the shell, use the up arrow to bring back commands typed previously. The shell can even bring back commands from a previous invocation of the shell.

While typing a line of command, press Ctrl+A to go to the beginning of the line or Ctrl+E to go to the end of the line.

The shell tries to execute what's typed as soon it receives the Return key. If we type something incomplete and press Return, for example in the middle of writing a method definition, the shell will prompt for more code with a vertical bar (|). For example, let's define a method isPalindrome() on two lines, then call the method twice and view the results:

```
scala> def isPalindrome(str: String) =
     |    str == str.reverse
isPalindrome: (str: String)Boolean

scala> isPalindrome("mom")
res0: Boolean = true

scala> isPalindrome("dude")
res1: Boolean = false

scala> :quit
```

Type :quit to exit the shell.

Rather than keying in all the code, we can load code from a file into the shell using the :load option. For example, to load a file named script.scala, type :load script.scala. This option is useful to load and experiment with prewritten functions and classes while remaining in the interactive mode.

Although the shell is a convenient way to experiment with small pieces of code, you'll soon want to find a way to easily run code saved in files—you'll learn how to do that next.

Scala on the Command Line

The scala command can run in two modes, as an interactive shell or in batch mode. If we don't provide any arguments, as we saw, the command brings up the interactive shell. However, if we provide a filename then it runs the code in it within a stand-alone JVM.

The file we provide may be a script file or an object file—that is, a compiler-generated .class file. By default, we can let the tool guess the type of the given files. Alternately, use the -howtorun option to tell it to treat the file as a script file or as an object file. Finally, to send Java properties, use the -Dproperty=value format. Let's create a file and run it using the command.

Here's a file named HelloWorld.scala with the following contents:

FirstStep/HelloWorld.scala

```
println("Hello World, Welcome to Scala")
```

Execute this script with the command scala HelloWorld.scala, as you see here along with the output:

```
>scala HelloWorld.scala
Hello World, Welcome to Scala
```

Follow the filename with any arguments you want to send to the program.

The ability to run code in a file as a script, without the extra steps of compilation, is quite convenient. Use this to write code related to system maintenance or administrative tasks, for example, and easily run them from your favorite IDEs, from the command line, or as part of a continuous integration chain of scripts.

Even though we don't explicitly invoke the compiler when using the scala command, the code goes through rigorous compilation and type checking. The scala tool compiles the given script into bytecode in memory and then executes it.

Recall that in Java any stand-alone program is required to have a class with the static void main method. That rule applies to Scala programs also since they run on the JVM. However, Scala does not force us to implement the main() method. Instead, it takes the trouble to roll the script into the traditional main() method of a Main class. So, when we run the script, we're running in an instance of the JVM main() method of this synthesized Main class. You can view the bytecode generated during the execution of the scala command using the -savecompiled option before the filename, and the tool will save it to a JAR file.

Now that you know how to run Scala code stored in a file through the scala tool, let's look at how to cut out that explicit usage of the command and directly run a stand-alone script.

Running Scala Code as a Stand-alone Script

Most operating systems support the *shebang* syntax to run arbitrary scripts. We can use that approach to run stand-alone files with Scala code in it. This eliminates the needs to explicitly invoke the scala command and works seamlessly as long as Scala is installed on the system.

Running as a Stand-alone Script on Unix-like Systems

On Unix-like systems, set the shebang preamble in the script like this:

FirstStep/hello.sh
```
#!/usr/bin/env scala
println("Hello " + args(0))
```

Make sure the file hello.sh has executable permission by typing chmod +x hello.sh. Then to run it, type the following command on the command line:

```
./hello.sh Buddy
```

Buddy is the argument that is passed to the script. Here's the output from the call:

```
Hello Buddy
```

Running as a Stand-alone Script on Windows

You can configure Windows to invoke Scala directly on a double-click of a stand-alone .scala file. To do that, within Windows Explorer, double-click a Scala script file with the .scala extension. Windows will complain that it can't open the file and will ask you to select a program from a list of installed programs. Browse to the location where Scala is installed, and select scala.bat. Now you can run the program by simply double-clicking it in Windows Explorer, or you can run it from the command prompt without adding the .scala extension to the filename.

When you double-click the program within Windows Explorer, you will notice that a window pops up, displays the result of execution, and quickly shuts down. To keep that window open, you can point the file to a .bat file that will run Scala and pause. To do this, right-click the Scala program, select "Open With...," and browse to and select the .bat file.

Here's an example:

FirstStep/RunScala.bat
```
echo off
cls
call scala %1
pause
```

If you double-click HelloWorld.scala, our setup will now automatically run the RunScala.bat file, and you should see the following output appear:

```
C:\Windows\system32\cmd.exe
Hello World, Welcome to Scala
Press any key to continue . . .
```

So far we've looked at running Scala from the command line, but you can also run it from an IDE.

IDE Support for Scala

Java developers make heavy use of IDEs to develop applications. All major IDEs—Eclipse, IntelliJ IDEA, NetBeans—have plug-ins to assist with Scala development. They provide facilities similar to what we're used to when programming in Java—syntax highlighting, code completion, debugging, proper indentation, and so on. Furthermore, we can mix and reference Scala and Java code in the same project.

Depending on your favorite IDE, simply install the appropriate plug-in. If you're using lightweight editors such as Sublime Text and TextMate, look for builders or bundles for Scala.

We have run Scala code as script so far and avoided explicit compilation. As a program grows in size to more than one file or into multiple classes, you'll want to compile it. Let's take a look at the steps.

Compiling Scala

You want to compile the code explicitly if you have multiple files or want to distribute the bytecode instead of the source code. Here's how to write a piece of Scala code and compile it using the scalac compiler. In the following example, we define a small executable code in an object named Sample that extends the App trait—you'll soon learn about Scala singleton objects and traits. App instructs the compiler to generate the necessary main() method to make Sample the starting class.

FirstStep/Sample.scala

```
object Sample extends App {
  println("Hello Scala")
}
```

Compile the code with the command scalac Sample.scala, and then run it using either the scala tool or the java command. To use the scala tool, type scala Sample. To use the java tool, specify the classpath for scala-library.jar. Here's an example of compiling with the scalac tool and running the program first with the scala tool and then with the java tool on my Mac:

```
> scalac Sample.scala
> scala Sample
Hello Scala
> java -classpath /opt/scala/current/lib/scala-library.jar:. Sample
Hello Scala
```

Here's a small trick: name current as a symbolic link to the current version of Scala installed on your machine. The symbolic link will help switch Scala versions easily without having to change the *PATH* and classpath settings. To change versions, simply change the symbolic link. You could create a similar symbolic link on your machine, or you could replace the word current with the appropriate directory name for the current version of Scala you're using.

On Windows, we'd set the classpath to the full path of the scala-library.jar file.

Wrapping Up

In this chapter we picked up the commands to run Scala—ran some sample code in the shell, learned how to run a stand-alone script, and learned how to compile Scala code. We're all set to dive into Scala; in the next chapter we'll start on familiar Java grounds and transition into Scala.

CHAPTER 3

From Java to Scala

With Scala, you can build on your Java skills. Scala is similar to Java in several ways and yet different in so many others. Scala favors pure object orientation, but it maps types to Java types where possible. Scala supports the familiar imperative coding style and at the same time supports the functional style. Thanks to this facility, you can start coding right away with the style you're familiar with without incurring a steep learning curve.

In this chapter, we'll start on familiar ground—with Java code—and then move toward Scala. Crank up your favorite editor; we're ready to write some Scala code.

Scala as Concise Java

Java code often has a lot of boilerplate code—getters, setters, access modifiers, code to deal with checked exceptions.... The growing list bloats the code. As you'll see here, the Scala compiler walks a few extra miles so you don't have to expend efforts to write and maintain code that can be generated.

Less Boilerplate

Scala has very high code density—you type less to achieve more. To contrast, let's start with an example of Java code:

FromJavaToScala/Greetings.java
```java
//Java code
public class Greetings {
  public static void main(String[] args) {
    for(int i = 1; i < 4; i++) {
      System.out.print(i + ",");
    }
    System.out.println("Scala Rocks!!!");
  }
}
```

Here's the output:

```
1,2,3,Scala Rocks!!!
```

Scala makes quite a few things in this code optional. First, it does not care whether you use semicolons. Second, there's no real benefit for the code to live within the class Greetings in a simple example like this, so you can get rid of that. Third, there's no need to specify the type of the variable i. Scala is smart enough to *infer* that i is an integer. Finally, you can use println without the System.out. prefix. Here's the Java code simplified to Scala:

FromJavaToScala/Greet.scala

```scala
for (i <- 1 to 3) {
  print(s"$i,")
}

println("Scala Rocks!!!")
```

To run this script, type scala Greet.scala on the command line, or run it from within your IDE.

You should see this output:

```
1,2,3,Scala Rocks!!!
```

Rather than concatenating the print message using the + operator, we used string interpolation (using the syntax s"...${expression}..."), which makes code more expressive and concise—we'll discuss string interpolation in *String Interpolation*, on page 34.

Scala's loop structure is pretty lightweight. We simply indicated that the value of the index i goes from 1 to 3. The left of the arrow (<-) defines a val and its right side is a generator expression. On each iteration, a new val is created and initialized with a consecutive element from the generated values.

Scala reduces boilerplate code. It offers some syntactical conveniences too.

More Convenience

In the previous code we used a val. You can define a variable using either a val or a var. The variables defined using val are immutable and can't be changed after initialization. Those defined using var—aka *keyword of shame*—however, are mutable and can be changed any number of times.

The immutability applies to the variable and not the instance to which the variable refers. For example, if we write val buffer = new StringBuffer(), we can't change what buffer refers to. However, we can modify the state of the referred instance using StringBuffer's methods like append(). Don't assume that an object with only val references is entirely immutable.

On the other hand, if we define an instance of an immutable class like String using, for example, val str = "hello", then we can modify neither the reference nor the state of the referred instance.

You can make an instance of a class immutable by defining all of its fields using val and providing only methods that allow reads and not changes to the state of the instance.

In Scala, prefer val over var as much as possible since that promotes immutability, which leads to fewer errors, and functional style.

In the Greet.scala code, the range that was generated included both the lower bound (1) and the upper bound (3). You can exclude the upper bound from the range via the until() method instead of the to() method:

FromJavaToScala/GreetExclusiveUpper.scala
```
for (i <- 1 until 3) {
  print(s"$i,")
}

println("Scala Rocks!!!")
```

Run the code to see this output:

```
1,2,Scala Rocks!!!
```

It's easy to miss that to() is a *method*. to() and until() are actually methods on RichInt—we'll discuss rich wrappers in *Scala Classes for Java Primitives*, on page 24. The variable I, which is of type Int, is implicitly converted to RichInt so this method could be called on the variable. These two methods return an instance of Range. So, calling 1 to 3 is equivalent to 1.to(3), but the former is more elegant.

In Scala you can drop both the dot and the parentheses if a method takes either zero or one parameter. If a method takes more than one parameter, you must use the parentheses, but the dot is still optional.

We already saw a benefit of this flexibility: a + b is really a.+(b), and 1 to 3 is really 1.to(3).

You can take advantage of this lightweight syntax to create code that reads fluently. For example, assume we have a turn() method defined on a class Car:

```
def turn(direction: String) //...
```

We can call the previous method in a lightweight syntax as follows:

```
car turn "right"
```

By dropping the dots and parentheses you can reduce noise in code.

In the previous example, it appears that we've reassigned i as we iterated through the loop. However, i is not a var; it is a val. Each time through the loop we're creating a different val named i. We can't inadvertently change the value of i within the loop because i is immutable. Quietly, we've already taken a step toward functional style here; let's take it further.

Leaning Toward Functional Style

We can also perform the loop in a more functional style using foreach():

FromJavaToScala/GreetForEach.scala
```
(1 to 3).foreach(i => print(s"$i,"))

println("Scala Rocks!!!")
```

Here's the output:

```
1,2,3,Scala Rocks!!!
```

The previous example is concise, and there are no assignments. We used the foreach() method of the Range class. This method accepts a function value as a parameter. So, within the parentheses, we're providing a body of code that takes one argument, named in this example as i. The => separates the parameter list on the left from the implementation on the right.

Scala infers types and is fully object-oriented, but it does not deal separately with primitives. This leads to a consistent handling of all data types; however, Scala does this without compromising performance.

Scala Classes for Java Primitives

Java presents a split view of the world—it treats primitives, such as int and double, differently from objects. Since Java 5, to a limited extent, we can treat primitives like objects using autoboxing. However, Java doesn't permit method calls like 2.toString() on primitives. Plus autoboxing involves casting overhead and has a few negative consequences.

Unlike Java, Scala treats all types as objects. This means you can call methods on literals, just like you can call methods on objects. In the following code, we create an instance of Scala's Int and send it to the ensureCapacity() method of java.util.ArrayList, which expects a Java primitive int.

```
FromJavaToScala/ScalaInt.scala
class ScalaInt {
  def playWithInt() {
    val capacity : Int = 10
    val list = new java.util.ArrayList[String]
    list.ensureCapacity(capacity)
  }
}
```

Here, Scala quietly treated Scala.Int as the primitive Java int. This is done by pure compile-time translation and as a result there is no performance loss at runtime for type conversions. You could have defined val capacity = 10 and let Scala infer the type, but we specified it explicitly to illustrate the compatibility with Java int.

There is similar magic that you can use to call methods like to() on Int, as in 1.to(3) or 1 to 3. Since Int can't directly handle that request, Scala quietly applies the intWrapper() method to convert the Int to scala.runtime.RichInt and then invokes the to() method on it. We will explore implicit type conversions in *Implicit Type Conversions*, on page 86.

Classes like RichInt, RichDouble, RichBoolean, and so on are called *rich wrapper* classes. They provide convenience methods that can be used for classes in Scala that represent the Java primitive types and String.

The implicit conversions and type mapping to primitives makes Scala code concise. That's just the beginning—Scala's Tuple and multiple assignments capability take the niceties further.

Tuples and Multiple Assignments

In Java, while methods can take multiple arguments, they can only return one result. Returning more than a single value needs clumsy workarounds in Java. For example, to return a person's first name, last name, and email address we'd have to employ a Person class and return an array of Strings or an ArrayList. Scala's Tuple, combined with multiple assignments, makes returning multiple values a simple task.

A *tuple* is an immutable object sequence created as comma-separated values. For example, the following represents a tuple with three objects: ("Venkat", "Subramaniam", "venkats@agiledeveloper.com").

You can assign the elements of a tuple into multiple vals or vars in parallel, as we see here:

```
FromJavaToScala/MultipleAssignment.scala
def getPersonInfo(primaryKey : Int) = {
  // Assume primaryKey is used to fetch a person's info...
  // Here response is hard-coded
  ("Venkat", "Subramaniam", "venkats@agiledeveloper.com")
}

val (firstName, lastName, emailAddress) = getPersonInfo(1)

println(s"First Name: $firstName")
println(s"Last Name: $lastName")
println(s"Email Address: $emailAddress")
```

Here's the output from executing this code:

```
First Name: Venkat
Last Name: Subramaniam
Email Address: venkats@agiledeveloper.com
```

If you assign the result of the method to fewer variables or to more variables Scala will keep an eye out and report an error. This error reporting is done at compile time for source code or during the compilation phase if run as a script. For example, in the following we're assigning the result of the method call to fewer variables than in the tuple:

```
FromJavaToScala/MultipleAssignment2.scala
def getPersonInfo(primaryKey : Int) = {
  ("Venkat", "Subramaniam", "venkats@agiledeveloper.com")
}

val (firstName, lastName) = getPersonInfo(1)
```

Scala will report this error:

```
MultipleAssignment2.scala:5: error: constructor cannot be instantiated to
expected type;
 found   : (T1, T2)
 required: (String, String, String)
val (firstName, lastName) = getPersonInfo(1)
    ^
one error found
```

Instead of assigning the values, you can also access individual elements of a tuple. For example, if we execute val info = getPersonInfo(1), then we can access the first element using the syntax info._1, the second element using info._2, and so on.

The underscore paired with a number, like _1, represents the index or position of the element we'd like to access in a tuple. Unlike collections, tuples are accessed using a 1-based index. Also, unlike collections, if you specify an index out of range, you get a compilation error instead of runtime error—pretty nifty, eh?

Some programmers complain about the underscore being used to index tuples. They say that the dot-underscore is unwieldy and hard to read. If you don't like underscores there's an easy way to deal with it—get over it (just kidding).

Tuples are useful not only for multiple assignments. They're useful to pass a list of data values as messages between actors in concurrent programming, and their immutable nature comes in handy here. Their concise syntax helps keep the code on the message sender side very concise. On the receiving side, you can use pattern matching to concisely receive and process the message, as you'll see in *Matching Tuples and Lists*, on page 145.

Returning multiple values from methods and functions is quite convenient, Scala also has some things for passing arguments.

Flexible Parameters and Arguments

Defining parameters and passing arguments are among the most common tasks we perform when programming in any language. Scala offers some nice facilities and conveniences to define variable numbers of arguments, declare default values for parameters, and define named arguments.

Passing Variable Arguments (Varargs)

Methods like println() take a variable number of parameters. You can pass zero, one, or more arguments to such methods. In Scala you can create your own functions that can take a variable number of parameters.

We can design methods to take a variable number of arguments—*varargs*. However, if we have more than one parameter, only the trailing parameters can take a variable number of arguments. To indicate that a parameter can take a variable number of arguments, use an asterisk after the last parameter's type. Here's an example max() function:

FromJavaToScala/Parameters.scala
```
def max(values: Int*) = values.foldLeft(values(0)) { Math.max }
```

Here's an example of invoking the max() function:

FromJavaToScala/Parameters.scala
```
max(8, 2, 3)
```

We passed three arguments to the function. However, we can pass a different number of arguments—for example:

FromJavaToScala/Parameters.scala
```
max(2, 5, 3, 7, 1, 6)
```

When a parameter's type is declared with a trailing *, Scala defines the parameter as an array of that type. Let's confirm that with an example:

FromJavaToScala/ArgType.scala
```
def function(input: Int*) = println(input.getClass)

function(1, 2, 3)
```

When we run the code, the output shows the type of the parameter:

```
class scala.collection.mutable.WrappedArray$ofInt
```

We invoked the max() function with an arbitrary number of arguments. The parameter is of type array, so we can use iterators to process the collection of arguments received. It may be tempting to pass an array as an argument, instead of discrete values, but that won't work, as we see in the next example:

```
val numbers = Array(2, 5, 3, 7, 1, 6)
max(numbers) // type mismatch error
```

The previous code will produce the following compilation error:

```
CantSendArray.scala:5: error: type mismatch;
 found   : Array[Int]
 required: Int
max(numbers) // type mismatch error
    ^
one error found
```

This error is mainly due to type incompatibility; the parameter is more array-like than literally being an array type. Nevertheless, if we have an array of values, we surely would like to pass that. We can, using the array explode notation, like this:

```
val numbers = Array(2, 5, 3, 7, 1, 6)
max(numbers: _*)
```

The series of symbols after the argument name tells the compiler to explode the array into the necessary format, to send as a variable number of arguments.

Now that you know how to pass a variable number of arguments to methods, let's look at another nice related feature—default values.

Providing Default Values for Parameters

Scala makes it convenient to skip most common or sensible default values when calling methods or constructors.

In real life, if we assume first-class postage is the most common postage option, we'd like to ask an assistant to "mail this, please" instead of "mail this, please, by first class." A request to mail with no particular mention of postage would be inferred as a desire to send by first class.

In Java we can design the flexibility to skip one or more parameters using overloading. While it works quite well from the caller's point of view, overloading takes more effort and more code, and may lead to duplication—hence, it is error prone. In Scala you can achieve that easily with default values for parameters.

Here's an example of a method with default values for its parameters:

FromJavaToScala/DefaultValues.scala
```
def mail(destination: String = "head office", mailClass: String = "first") =
  println(s"sending to $destination by $mailClass class")
```

Both parameters of the mail() method have default values. If a parameter is skipped in the call, the attached default value will kick in.

Here are the options to call the mail() method:

FromJavaToScala/DefaultValues.scala
```
mail("Houston office", "Priority")
mail("Boston office")
mail()
```

In the first call we provided arguments for both parameters. In the second call we skipped the second parameter, and in the third we skipped both parameters. We can see the result of the compiler filling in values for the skipped parameters in the output:

```
sending to Houston office by Priority class
sending to Boston office by first class
sending to head office by first class
```

The substitution of the default value for a skipped parameter is done at compile time. Exercise caution when overriding methods. If a method in the base class uses one default and the corresponding overridden method in the derived class uses a different default, you can easily get confused as to which value will get used.

For multiparameter methods, if you choose to skip the value for one of the parameters, you have to use the default for all parameters that follow it in the parameter list. For instance, you can't use a default value for the destination and provide an explicit value for the mailClass in the previous example. The reason for this restriction is that the value to substitute for the skipped parameters is determined based on the position. The flexibility of default values for parameters can interplay with another fluency that Scala offers to ease this restriction, as you'll see next.

Using Named Arguments

Scala's type checking will prevent you from sending the wrong type of arguments to methods. However, for methods that take multiple parameters of the same type, passing arguments—for example, power(2, 3)—may cause some involuntary head-scratching; is 2 the exponent or the base?

Thankfully, in cases like this, you can make the code expressive and fluent by naming the arguments in the call—for example, power(base = 2, exponent = 3).

Let's use named arguments when calling the mail() method we saw in the previous section:

```
FromJavaToScala/Named.scala
mail(mailClass = "Priority", destination = "Bahamas office")
```

In the call we explicitly identified the arguments using the names of the intended parameters. With named arguments, the order in which we specify the arguments does not matter—to make the point, in the previous example, we've first provided the value for the second parameter of the mail() method.

You have to be aware of a few caveats when working with named arguments:

- You're required to provide values for all parameters with no default values.

- For parameters with a default value, you can optionally provide a named argument.

- You can provide a value for a parameter at most once.

- When overriding methods of a base class, you should keep the parameter names consistent. If you don't, the compiler may use the parameter names in the methods of the base class when your intention may be otherwise.

- If there are overloaded methods with the same parameter names but different types, it's possible that the call is ambiguous. In that case the compiler will give a stern error and you'd have to fall back on positional arguments.

Note that the order is not enforced. For methods with multiple parameters with default values, the restriction of using default values for trailing parameters is removed when naming arguments; for example, we can write this call:

```
mail(mailClass = "Priority")
```

In general, to invoke the mail() function, the compiler will require the value for the destination parameter since we're specifying the value for the second parameter mailClass. However, as in the previous code, we can get around that restriction by naming the argument. Thus, we get more flexibility when mixing default values with named arguments than when using default values with positional arguments.

Implicit Parameters

In *Providing Default Values for Parameters*, on page 29 you learned about default values for parameters—if you don't pass an argument for a parameter, Scala will give it a default value. That's nice; we don't have to give values that are intuitively obvious or that can be inferred by default. But the default value that's given is decided by the creator of the function and not the caller. Scala provides an alternative, so the caller can decide what value to send—by default —instead of the function definer deciding that.

Let's consider an example that will benefit from this feature. With smartphones and mobile devices that we all carry around, we constantly have to connect to different networks: one network at home, another at the office, yet another at the airline lounge... The operation we perform is the same—connecting to a network—but the network we connect to, by default, depends on the context. We don't want to specify the network each and every time; that becomes tiring. At the same time, we don't want one default value to take effect all the time either. We can solve this problem using a special type of parameter called an implicit parameter.

The function definer should first mark the parameter as implicit. For this, Scala insists that implicit parameters are in a separate parameter list than regular parameters—Scala supports multiple parameter lists as you'll learn in *Currying*, on page 107. If a parameter is defined as implicit, an argument for that parameter is optional, just like default valued parameters. However, if the argument is not passed, Scala will look for an implicit variable in the scope of the call. The implicit variable is required to have the same type as the implicit parameter—thus there can be at most one implicit variable for each type within a scope.

Let's create an example to use this feature.

FromJavaToScala/ImplicitParameters.scala

```scala
class Wifi(name: String) {
  override def toString = name
}

def connectToNetwork(user: String)(implicit wifi: Wifi) {
  println(s"User: $user connected to WIFI $wifi")
}

def atOffice() = {
  println("--- at the office ---")
  implicit def officeNetwork = new Wifi("office-network")
  val cafeteriaNetwork = new Wifi("cafe-connect")

  connectToNetwork("guest")(cafeteriaNetwork)
  connectToNetwork("Jill Coder")
  connectToNetwork("Joe Hacker")
}

def atJoesHome() = {
  println("--- at Joe's home ---")
  implicit def homeNetwork = new Wifi("home-network")

  connectToNetwork("guest")(homeNetwork)
  connectToNetwork("Joe Hacker")
}

atOffice()
atJoesHome()
```

The connectToNetwork() function has two parameter lists, one with a regular parameter of type String and the other with an implicit parameter of type Wifi.

In the atOffice() function we've defined two instances of the Wifi class, one of them marked implicit. We make three calls to the connectToNetwork() function, but we provide an argument for the wifi parameter only on the first call. The other two calls expect the compiler to fill in the argument. If the parameter has a default value, the compiler would go looking for the value in the function definition. However, since this is an implicit parameter, the compiler looks for the value defined as implicit in the scope of the function call.

In the atJoesHome() function we've defined only one instance of Wifi but marked it as implicit. Passing this parameter to the connectToNetwork() method is optional. For example, a guest user would want to know what network to connect to, but it may be the same one that the resident uses implicitly. In this case, it's okay to explicitly specify the parameter that is defined as implicit.

If a parameter is defined as implicit, then the caller should pass an argument for it or skip it if there is an implicit variable of the appropriate type in scope; otherwise, the compiler will raise an error.

Run the script and observe the output:

```
--- at the office ---
User: guest connected to WIFI cafe-connect
User: Jill Coder connected to WIFI office-network
User: Joe Hacker connected to WIFI office-network
--- at Joe's home ---
User: guest connected to WIFI home-network
User: Joe Hacker connected to WIFI home-network
```

The output shows that when the arguments were skipped, the implicit variables in the respective scope were used. Even though it's the same function that's called from different functions, the missing arguments passed in were not the same. While both default valued parameters and implicit parameters let the caller skip the argument, the value that the compiler binds the argument to is quite different.

Strings and Multiline Raw Strings

String in Scala is simply java.lang.String. You can use String just like you do in Java. However, Scala does provide a few additional conveniences when working with String.

Scala can automatically convert a String to scala.runtime.RichString. This brings a few useful methods like capitalize(), lines(), and reverse() to String.

It's really simple in Scala to create a string that runs multiple lines—no more of those messy +=. Place the multiple lines of strings within three double quotes ("""..."""). That's Scala's support for the so-called here documents, or *heredocs*. To see it in action, let's create a string that runs a few lines long:

FromJavaToScala/MultiLine.scala

```
val str = """In his famous inaugural speech, John F. Kennedy said
        "And so, my fellow Americans: ask not what your country can do
        for you-ask what you can do for your country." He then proceeded
        to speak to the citizens of the World..."""
println(str)
```

The output is as follows:

```
In his famous inaugural speech, John F. Kennedy said
        "And so, my fellow Americans: ask not what your country can do
        for you-ask what you can do for your country." He then proceeded
        to speak to the citizens of the World...
```

You can embed double quotes within the multiline strings as we saw in the previous example. Scala took the content within triple double quotes as is; this is called a *raw string* in Scala. In fact, Scala took the string too literally; the indentations in the code were carried into the string. We can trim the leading spaces using the method stripMargin() of RichString, like this:

FromJavaToScala/MultiLine2.scala

```
val str = """In his famous inaugural speech, John F. Kennedy said
        |"And so, my fellow Americans: ask not what your country can do
        |for you-ask what you can do for your country." He then proceeded
        |to speak to the citizens of the World...""".stripMargin
println(str)
```

stripMargin() removes all blanks or control characters before the leading pipe (|). If the pipe symbol appears anywhere else other than the leading position on any line, it's retained. If for some reason that symbol is sacred in an application, we can use a variation of the stripMargin() method that accepts another preferred margin character. Here's the output for the previous code:

```
In his famous inaugural speech, John F. Kennedy said
"And so, my fellow Americans: ask not what your country can do
for you-ask what you can do for your country." He then proceeded
to speak to the citizens of the World...
```

Raw strings are also useful when creating regular expressions. For example, it's easier to type and to read """\d2:\d2""" than "\\d2:\\d2".

Heredocs help to create multiline strings, but we also often concatenate strings when creating messages for use, such as with println(). You can remove that clutter using string interpolation.

String Interpolation

Creating a string form of output or messages is a chore in Java. For example, it takes effort to create a message "A discount of 10% has been applied" where the value 10 comes from a variable named discount. You may write:

```
String message = "A discount of " + discount + "% has been applied"
```

In addition to the effort, the code is hard to read. Alternately, you could write:

```
String message = String.format("A discount of %d% has been applied", discount);
```

But that's verbose too. Scala provides a fluent and concise syntax to create string literals with expressions. Here's the Scala equivalent that produces the desired message:

```
val message = s"A discount of $discount% has been applied"
```

That leading s before the double quote refers to the *s*-interpolator—it hunts down expressions in the string and replaces with their values. Any variable that is in scope at the point of the string declaration can be used within the expression.

The string literal may have zero or more embedded expressions. If an expression is a simple variable, prefix it with a dollar sign ($). For more complex expressions, place them in curly braces, as in the next example:

```
var price = 90
val totalPrice = s"The amount of discount is ${price * discount / 100} dollars"
```

The dollar sign is used as a delimiter for an expression, but it's also used as an escape symbol if the string should have a $ sign. Here's a rewrite of the previous message to illustrate that:

```
val totalPrice = s"The amount of discount is $$${price * discount / 100}"
```

In the previous example the variable price was immutable. You may wonder about the consequence of that variable being mutable. Let's dig in.

```
val discount = 10
var price = 100
val totalPrice =
  s"The amount after discount is $$${price * (1 - discount/100.0)}"
println(totalPrice)

price = 50
println(totalPrice)
```

We changed the value of price after the string literal interpolation. The value of the expression was captured at the time of interpolation and any change to the variables will not affect or change the string, as we see in the output:

```
The amount after discount is $90.0
The amount after discount is $90.0
```

Use caution when dealing with mutable variables and string interpolation. You can remove the confusion here by avoiding mutability of the variable or by re-creating an interpolated string after the change.

The *s*-interpolator only replaces the expressions with their variables but does not perform any formatting. For example, you may key the following code in the Scala REPL to see the behavior:

```
val product = "ticket"
val price = 25.12
val discount = 10
println(s"On $product $discount% saves $$${price * discount/100.00}")
```

The expressions were evaluated, but the output has the amount in three decimal places:

```
On ticket 10% saves $2.512
```

To format the output, in addition to interpolating, use the *f*-interpolator. The formatting of the string follows the same convention as the printf function in Java, except that you can embed the expressions like we did in the examples so far. Let's change the previous string to use formatting:

```
println(f"On $product $discount%% saves $$${price * discount/100.00}%2.2f")
```

We followed the last expression with the format 2.2f to constrain the output to two decimal places. Also, we had to escape the percent symbol with an additional %. We did not place any formatting after the product or the discount variable, though we could have placed a %s and %d, respectively. If you don't specify a format, the *f*-interpolator will assume the format as %s—convert to string—which worked out as a good default for the string on hand, as you can see in the output:

```
On ticket 10% saves $2.51
```

Scala comes with a third *raw*-interpolator, which replaces expressions with values but leaves out any nonprintable characters like line breaks. In addition to the three built-in interpolators, you can create custom interpolators, but for that you have to know about implicit classes, so we'll revisit this topic in *Implicit Classes*, on page 89.

The string interpolation is yet another way Scala makes code concise. But concise comes from quite a number of places. Next, we will see how sensible defaults reduce code and clutter.

Sensible Defaults

Scala has some defaults that make code concise and easier to read and write. Here are a few of these features:

- It has support for scripts. Not all code needs to be within a class. If a script is sufficient for your needs, put the executable code directly in a file without the clutter of an unnecessary class.

- return is optional. The last expression evaluated is automatically returned from method calls, assuming it matches with the return type declared for the method. Not having to put in that explicit return makes code concise, especially when passing closures as method parameters.

- Semicolons (;) are optional. You don't have to end each statement or expression with a semicolon—see *Semicolon Is Semi-optional*, on page 42 —and this reduces noise in the code. To place multiple statements in the same line, use semicolons to separate them. In the absence of a semicolon, Scala will smartly figure out whether a statement or expression is complete, and, if not, will continue to the following line for the rest of the code.

- Classes and methods are public by default, so you don't explicitly use the keyword public.

- Scala provides lightweight syntax to create JavaBeans—it takes less code to create variables and final properties (see *Creating Classes*, on page 50).

- You're not forced to catch exceptions that you don't care about—see *Exceptions in Scala*, on page 161—which reduces the code size and also avoids improper exception handling.

- Parentheses and dots are also optional, as we discussed in *More Convenience*, on page 22.

In addition, by default Scala imports two packages, the scala.Predef object, and their respective classes and members. You can refer to classes from these preimported packages simply by using their class names. Scala imports the following, in order:

- java.lang
- scala
- scala.Predef

Since java.lang is automatically imported, you can use common Java types in scripts without any imports. So, you can use String, for example, without prefixing it with the package name java.lang or importing it.

You can also use Scala types easily since everything in the package scala is imported.

The Predef object contains types, implicit conversions, and methods that are commonly used in Scala. So, since it is imported by default, you're able to use those methods and conversions without any prefix or import. They become so convenient that you'll begin to believe that they are part of the language, when they are actually part of the Scala library.

The object Predef also provides aliases to things like scala.collection.immutable.Set and scala:collection.immutable.Map. So, when you refer to Set or Map, for instance, you're referring to their definitions in Predef, which in turn refers to their definitions in the scala.collection.immutable package.

Scala's sensible defaults help make code concise. Next we will see how some of the defaults interplay with operator symbols.

Operator Overloading

Technically, Scala has no operators, so *operator overloading* means overloading symbols like +, +-, and so on. In Scala, these are method names. Operators take advantage of Scala's lenient method invocation syntax—Scala does not require a dot (.) between the object reference and method name.

These two features combined give the illusion of operator overloading. So, when you call ref1 + ref2, you're actually writing ref1.+(ref2), and invoking the +() method on ref1.

Let's look at an example of providing the + operator on a Complex class that represents complex numbers. Complex numbers, as we know, have a real part and an imaginary part, and they're useful in computing complex equations that involve the square root of negative numbers. Here's the Complex class:

FromJavaToScala/Complex.scala
```scala
class Complex(val real: Int, val imaginary: Int) {
  def +(operand: Complex) : Complex = {
    new Complex(real + operand.real, imaginary + operand.imaginary)
  }

  override def toString : String = {
    val sign = if(imaginary < 0) "" else "+"
    s"$real$sign${imaginary}i"
  }
}

val c1 = new Complex(1, 2)
val c2 = new Complex(2, -3)
val sum = c1 + c2
println(s"($c1) + ($c2) = $sum")
```

If we execute the previous code, we'll see this:

```
(1+2i) + (2-3i) = 3-1i
```

In the first statement, we created a class named Complex and defined a constructor that takes two parameters. We used Scala's expressive syntax to create a class, as we'll explore further in *Creating Classes*, on page 50.

Within the + method, we created a new instance of the Complex class. The real part and the imaginary part of the result is the sum of the real and imaginary parts of the two operands, respectively. The statement c1 + c2 resulted in a call to the +() method on c1 with c2 as an argument to the method call—that is, c1.+(c2).

The fact that Scala does not have operators is intriguing. However, not having operators does not waive the need for dealing with operator precedence. Although it appears that since Scala doesn't have operators it also can't define operator precedence, fear not—an expression like 24 - 2 + 3 * 6 evaluates correctly to 40 in both Java and Scala. Scala doesn't define precedence on operators; it defines precedence on methods.

The first character of methods is used to determine their priority. If two characters with same priority appear in an expression, then the method on the left takes higher priority. Here is the priority of the first letter listed from low to high:[1]

```
all letters
|
^
&
< >
= !
:
+ -
* / %
all other special characters
```

Let's look at an example of operator/method precedence. In the following code, we have defined both an add method and a multiply method on Complex:

FromJavaToScala/Complex2.scala
```scala
class Complex(val real: Int, val imaginary: Int) {
  def +(operand: Complex) : Complex = {
    println("Calling +")
    new Complex(real + operand.real, imaginary + operand.imaginary)
  }

  def *(operand: Complex) : Complex = {
    println("Calling *")
    new Complex(real * operand.real - imaginary * operand.imaginary,
        real * operand.imaginary + imaginary * operand.real)
  }
  override def toString : String = {
    val sign = if(imaginary < 0) "" else "+"
    s"$real$sign${imaginary}i"
  }
}
```

---

1. See "Scala Language Reference" in Appendix 2, *Web Resources*, on page 253.

```
val c1 = new Complex(1, 4)
val c2 = new Complex(2, -3)
val c3 = new Complex(2, 2)
println(c1 + c2 * c3)
```

Let's take a look at the effect of overloading of operators in the output:

```
Calling *
Calling +
11+2i
```

In the last line we're calling +() first on the left before calling *(), but since *() takes precedence, it is executed first.

Coming from a Java background, we have seen so far how concise and expressive Scala code can be. Scala, however, has some surprises in store. Learning about these early on will help you cope with these nuances, so let's take a look at them next.

Scala Surprises for the Java Eyes

As you start to appreciate Scala's design elegance and conciseness, you should be aware of some nuances—for example, Scala differs semantically from Java in the way it handles assignment, equality check, and return from functions. Since the way these are handled is a significant departure from what we're used to in Java, it's easy to make mistakes. Take the time to learn these to avoid surprises.

Result of Assignment

In Java, the result of the assignment operation, like a = b, is the value of a, so multiple assignments like x = a = b; can appear in series, but not so in Scala. The result of assignment operation in Scala is a Unit—a rough equivalent of Void. As a consequence, assigning that result to another variable may result in a type mismatch. Take a look at the following example:

FromJavaToScala/SerialAssignments.scala
```
var a = 1
var b = 2

a = b = 3
```

When we attempt to execute the previous code, we'll get this compilation error:

```
SerialAssignments.scala:4: error: type mismatch;
 found    : Unit
 required: Int
```

```
a = b = 3
      ^
one error found
```

This behavior is at the least a minor annoyance.

Scala's ==

Java handles == differently for primitive types vs. objects. For primitive types, == means value-based comparison, whereas for objects it's identity-based comparison. So, if a and b are int, then a == b results in true if both the variables have equal values. However, if they're references to objects, the result is true only if both references are pointing to the same instance—that is, the same identity. Java's equals() method provides value-based comparison for objects, provided it is overridden correctly by the appropriate class.

Scala's handling of == is different from Java; however, it is consistent across all types. In Scala, == represents value-based comparison, no matter what the type is. This is ensured by implementing ==() as final in the class Any (the class from which all types in Scala derive). This implementation uses the good old equals() method.

To provide your own implementation of equality for a class, you must override the equals() method. However, this is easier said than done. Implementing equals() correctly in an inheritance hierarchy requires not only overriding the equals() method to compare relevant fields, but also overriding the hashCode() method, as discussed in Joshua Bloch's *Effective Java [Blo08]*.

For value-based comparison, in Scala, you can use a concise == instead of the equals() method. To perform the identity-based comparison on references, a new eq() method is available. Let's look at using these two methods of comparison in an example:

FromJavaToScala/Equality.scala
```scala
val str1 = "hello"
val str2 = "hello"
val str3 = new String("hello")

println(str1 == str2) // Equivalent to Java's str1.equals(str2)
println(str1 eq str2) // Equivalent to Java's str1 == str2
println(str1 == str3)
println(str1 eq str3)
```

str1 and str2 are referring to the same instance of String, because Java interned the second "hello". However, str3 is referring to another newly created instance of String. All three references are pointing to objects that hold equal values, "hello." str1 and str2 are equal in identity and so are also equal in value. However, str1 and str3 are equal only in value, but not in identity. The following output illustrates the semantics of the == and eq methods/operators used in the previous code:

```
true
true
true
false
```

Scala's handling of == is consistent for all types and avoids the common confusion of using == in Java. However, you must be aware of this departure from the Java semantics to avoid any surprises.

Semicolon Is Semi-optional

Scala is lenient when it comes to statement/expression termination—semicolons (;) are optional, and that reduces noise in code. You can place a semicolon at the end of a statement/expression, particularly if you want to place multiple statements or expressions on the same line. Be careful, though. Placing multiple statements or expressions on the same line may reduce readability, as in the following:

```
val sample = new Sample; println(sample)
```

Scala infers a semicolon if a line does not end with an infix notation, like +, *, or ., that is not within parentheses or square brackets. It also infers a semicolon at the end of a line if the next line starts with something that can start a statement or an expression.

Scala, however, demands a semicolon in front of a { in some contexts. The effect of not placing it may surprise you. Let's look at an example:

```
FromJavaToScala/OptionalSemicolon.scala
val list1 = new java.util.ArrayList[Int];
{
  println("Created list1")
}

val list2 = new java.util.ArrayList[Int]
{
  println("Created list2")
}

println(list1.getClass())
println(list2.getClass())
```

That gives this output:

```
Created list1
```

```
Created list2
class java.util.ArrayList
class Main$$anon$2$$anon$1
```

We placed a semicolon when we defined list1. So, the { that followed it started a new code block. However, since we did not place a semicolon when we defined list2, Scala assumes we are creating an anonymous inner class that derives from ArrayList[Int]. So, list2 is referring to an instance of this anonymous inner class and not a direct instance of ArrayList[Int]. If your intent is to start a new code block after creating an instance, place a semicolon.

Java requires semicolons but Scala gives you the freedom to opt out of using semicolons—make use of that. The code is concise and less noisy without those semicolons. By dropping them, you can begin to enjoy an elegant lightweight syntax. Reserve the use of semicolon for cases like the previous one, when you have to resolve potential ambiguity.

Avoid Explicit return

In Java we use return to give results from methods. That's not a good practice in Scala; returns are implicit in Scala and placing an explicit return command affects Scala's ability to infer the return type. Let's see this in an example:

FromJavaToScala/AvoidExplitReturn.scala
```
def check1 = true
def check2 : Boolean = return true
def check3 : Boolean = true
println(check1)
println(check2)
println(check3)
```

In the previous code, Scala was quite happy to infer the return type of the method check1(). On the other hand, since we used an explicit return in the method check2(), Scala did not infer the type. In this case, we were forced to provide the return type Boolean.

It's better to avoid the explicit return commands, even if you chose to provide the return types, like for the method check3()—it's less noisy, and you get used to the Scala idiom that the results of last expressions are automatically returned.

Scala is also packed with some pleasant surprises in the area of encapsulation —it provides fine-grained control over the access boundaries, far beyond what's offered in Java.

Default Access Modifier

Scala's access modifier is different from Java:

- Java defaults to package internal visibility if you don't specify any access modifier. Scala, on the other hand, defaults to public.

- Java provides an all-or-nothing proposition. Either it's visible to all classes in the current package or it's not visible to any. Scala gives fine-grained control over visibility.

- Java's protected is generous. It includes derived classes in any package plus any class in the current package. Scala's protected is akin to C++ and C#—only derived classes can access it. However, you can also ask Scala for quite a liberal and flexible interpretation of protected.

- Finally, Java encapsulation is at the class level. You can access the private fields and methods of any object of a class from within its instance method. This is the default in Scala as well; however, you can customize it to access only within the current instance's methods, similar to what Ruby provides.

Let's explore these variations from Java using some examples.

Customizing Access Modifiers

By default, Scala treats classes, fields, and methods as public if you don't use an access modifier. If you want to make a member private or protected, simply mark it with the respective keyword like this:

FromJavaToScala/Access.scala
```
class Microwave {
  def start() = println("started")
  def stop() = println("stopped")
  private def turnTable() = println("turning table")
}
val microwave = new Microwave
microwave.start()                  // OK
```

In this code, by default the methods start() and stop() are public. We can access those two methods on any instance of Microwave. On the other hand, we've defined turnTable() explicitly as private. We can't access that method from outside the class. If we try, as in the previous example, we will get this error:

```
Access.scala:9: error: method turnTable in class Microwave cannot be
accessed in this.Microwave
microwave.turnTable() //ERROR
          ^
one error found
```

Leave out access modifiers for public fields and methods. For other members, make the access as restrictive as desired with an explicit access modifier.

Scala's Protected

In Scala, protected makes the decorated members visible to the class and its derived classes only. Other classes that belong to the same package, of the defining class, can't access these members. Furthermore, the derived class can access the protected members only on its own type. Let's examine these with an example:

FromJavaToScala/Protected.scala

```
Line 1  package automobiles

        class Vehicle {
          protected def checkEngine() {}
     5  }
        class Car extends Vehicle {
          def start() { checkEngine() /*OK*/ }
          def tow(car: Car) {
            car.checkEngine() //OK
    10    }
          def tow(vehicle: Vehicle) {
            vehicle.checkEngine() //ERROR
          }
        }
    15  class GasStation {
          def fillGas(vehicle: Vehicle) {
            vehicle.checkEngine() //ERROR
          }
        }
```

By compiling the code we can see, in the compiler error message, these access controls taking effect:

```
Protected.scala:12: error: method checkEngine in class Vehicle cannot be
accessed in automobiles.Vehicle
 Access to protected method checkEngine not permitted because
 prefix type automobiles.Vehicle does not conform to
 class Car in package automobiles where the access take place
    vehicle.checkEngine() //ERROR
            ^
Protected.scala:17: error: method checkEngine in class Vehicle cannot be
accessed in automobiles.Vehicle
 Access to protected method checkEngine not permitted because
 enclosing class GasStation in package automobiles is not a subclass of
 class Vehicle in package automobiles where target is defined
    vehicle.checkEngine() //ERROR
            ^
two errors found
```

In the previous code, checkEngine() of Vehicle is protected and is accessible from any instance method of Vehicle. We can access that method from within an instance method, like start(), of the derived class Car. We can also access it on an instance of Car from within an instance method, like tow(), of Car. However, we can't access that method on an instance of Vehicle from within Car and also from within another arbitrary class, like GasStation, even if it belongs to the same package as Vehicle. This behavior is different from how Java treats protected access. Scala is a lot more stringent about access to protected members.

Fine-Grained Access Control

On one hand, Scala is more restrictive than Java in how it treats the protected modifier. On the other hand, it gives a far greater flexibility and also fine-grained control over setting access visibility.

You can specify additional parameters for private and protected modifiers. So, instead of simply decorating a member with private, you can decorate it as private[AccessQualifier], where AccessQualifier may be any enclosing class name, an enclosing package name, or this—meaning instance-only visibility.

The qualifier in the access modifier may tell Scala to treat the member as private for all classes except in these cases:

- If no AccessQualifier is given—this is the default—then the member is accessible only from the current class and its companion object (we'll look at companion objects in Chapter 4, *Working with Objects*, on page 49).

- If the AccessQualifier is a class name, then the member is accessible from the class, its companion objects, plus the class and the companion objects of the enclosing class whose name is given as the AccessQualifier.

- If the AccessQualifier is an enclosing package name, then the member is accessible from the class, its companion object, plus within any class nested under the mentioned package.

- If the AccessQualifier is this, then the access to the member is restricted to the instance and is not visible to other instances of the same class—this is the most restrictive of all the options.

That's quite a few combinations that can set heads spinning. An example of the fine-grained access control can help make things clear:

```
FromJavaToScala/FineGrainedAccessControl.scala
Line 1  package society  {

          package professional {
            class Executive {
     5          private[professional] var workDetails = null
                private[society] var friends = null
                private[this] var secrets = null

                def help(another : Executive) = {
    10            println(another.workDetails)
                  println(secrets)
                  println(another.secrets) //ERROR
                }
              }
    15
            class Assistant {
              def assist(anExec: Executive) = {
                println(anExec.workDetails)
                println(anExec.friends)
    20          }
              }
            }

          package social {
    25      class Acquaintance {
              def socialize(person: professional.Executive) {
                println(person.friends)
                println(person.workDetails) // ERROR
              }
            }
    30      }
          }
        }
```

Compiling the code produces the following errors:

```
FineGrainedAccessControl.scala:12: error: value secrets is not a member of
society.professional.Executive
        println(another.secrets) //ERROR
                        ^
FineGrainedAccessControl.scala:28: error: variable workDetails in class
Executive cannot be accessed in society.professional.Executive
        println(person.workDetails) // ERROR
                       ^
two errors found
```

The example illustrates quite a few Scala nuances. In Scala we can define nested packages, akin to C++ and C# nested namespaces. We can either follow the Java style to define packages—using dots, as in package society.professional; —or use the C++ or C# nested namespace style. If we decide to place multiple small classes belonging to a hierarchy of packages all in one file—again a departure from Java—the latter style is convenient.

In the previous code, we gave visibility for Executive's private field workDetails to any class within the enclosing package professional. Scala thus permits access to this field from a method of the class Assistant, which is in that package. However, the class Acquaintance from another package can't touch the field.

For the private field friends, on the other hand, we gave access to any class within the enclosing package society. This gives permission to access the field friends from the class Acquaintance, which is located in a subpackage of society.

The default visibility of private is class level—from an instance method of a class we can access the members decorated as private on *any instance* of the same class. However, Scala gives a finer control over private and protected with the this qualifier. For instance, in the previous example, since secrets is decorated private[this], instance methods can access this field only on implicit instances, that is, on this instance—that field can't be accessed on other instances. That's the reason why we can access secrets but not another.secrets from within the help() instance method. Likewise, a field decorated with protected[this] is accessible from within an instance method of a derived class but only on the current instance.

Wrapping Up

In this chapter, we took a quick drive through Scala from the perspective of Java programmers. We saw ways in which Scala is similar to Java and how, at the same time, it sets itself apart.

At first glance, Scala appears to be lighter Java—you can do everything you do in Java, but with less verbose and more expressive syntax. Beyond that, Scala provides a number of things that's not supported in Java: tuples, multiple assignments, named arguments, default values, implicit parameters, multiline strings, string interpolation, and more flexible access modifiers.

While we only scratched the surface of Scala in this chapter, it brought out some key strengths of the language. In the next chapter, you'll learn how Scala supports the OO paradigm.

CHAPTER 4

Working with Objects

Scala is fully object-oriented and provides concise syntax for creating classes and working with objects. You can achieve everything that's possible in Java, and in addition, Scala provides some more powerful features to help with OO programming. Also, even though Scala is a pure object-oriented language, it still has to support Java's not-so-pure OO concepts like static methods. Scala tackles that in a fairly interesting way using companion objects. Companion objects are singletons that accompany a class and are quite common in Scala.

We're going to start on familiar ground and quickly dive into the OO aspects of Scala. We'll port a simple Java class to Scala, and then we'll dig into Scala's capabilities. Constructors may look a little funny at first because Scala code tends to be more concise than Java code, but soon you'll see the benefits the language offers for creating objects.

Creating and Using Classes

Creating classes in Scala is shockingly expressive and highly concise. We're going to explore how to create instances first, then how to create classes, and finally how to define fields and methods.

Creating Instances

Creating an instance of a class in Scala is not much different from creating instances in Java. For example, let's create an instance of StringBuilder:

```
new StringBuilder("hello")
```

That's pretty much like in Java, except for the missing semicolon. We used new followed by the class name and the argument(s) for its constructor. The class StringBuilder has another overloaded constructor that doesn't take any parameters. Let's use that next:

```
new StringBuilder()
```

That worked, but Scala programmers view the empty parentheses as noise. Incidentally, Scala does not require () when using new if the constructor takes no parameters. Let's rewrite the code:

```
new StringBuilder
```

As you can see, creating instances is simple, but the real fun is in creating our own abstractions.

Creating Classes

Let's start with a Java example for creating a class that follows the bean convention for properties:

WorkingWithObjects/Car.java
```java
//Java example
public class Car {
  private final int year;
  private int miles;

  public Car(int yearOfMake) { year = yearOfMake; }

  public int getYear() { return year; }
  public int getMiles() { return miles; }

  public void drive(int distance) {
    miles += Math.abs(distance);
  }
}
```

The class Car has two properties, year and miles, and the corresponding getter methods, called getYear() and getMiles(). The drive() method manipulates the miles property, whereas the constructor initializes the final field year. In short, we have a couple of properties, as well as methods to initialize and manipulate them.

In Scala we don't create a class; instead we write a constructor—much like in JavaScript. Think of the constructor as an object factory—it tells how an object should be constructed. Scala directs our focus on creating objects from the get-go.

Here's Scala's way to do the same thing as the Java code:

WorkingWithObjects/UseCar.scala
```scala
class Car(val year: Int) {
 private var milesDriven: Int = 0

 def miles = milesDriven
```

```
 def drive(distance: Int) {
  milesDriven += Math.abs(distance)
 }
}
```

In the Java version, we explicitly defined the field and method for the property year and wrote an explicit constructor. In Scala, the parameter to the class constructor—we refer to this informally as *class*—took care of defining that field and writing the accessor method. Here's how we would use the Scala class:

WorkingWithObjects/UseCar.scala
```
val car = new Car(2015)
println(s"Car made in year ${car.year}")
println(s"Miles driven ${car.miles}")
println("Drive for 10 miles")
car.drive(10)
println(s"Miles driven ${car.miles}")
```

And here's the result of running the command scala UseCar.scala:

```
Car made in year 2015
Miles driven 0
Drive for 10 miles
Miles driven 10
```

Since Scala's access control is public by default, the class Car is accessible from any package or file. Using the val keyword we defined year to be immutable, or final in Java. The field milesDriven is mutable—we used var instead of val to define it—however, it's private since we explicitly decorated its access control. Let's explore the details of defining members further.

Defining Fields, Methods, and Constructors

The conciseness that Scala offers continues when defining methods and constructors. As you learn to write Scala code, take a minute to look under the hood into the bytecode that Scala generates. This is a great way to learn what's going on and nail some of the concepts firmly.

Scala rolls the class definition into the primary constructor and provides a concise way to define fields and corresponding methods. Let's look at a few examples.

Let's start with the following concise class definition:

WorkingWithObjects/CreditCard.scala
```
class CreditCard(val number: Int, var creditLimit: Int)
```

There's no need for curly braces ({}) if the class definition has no body.

That's it. That's a full definition of a class with two fields, one constructor, a getter for the immutable number field, and both a getter and a setter for the mutable creditLimit field. That one line of Scala code is equivalent to well over ten lines of Java code. Oh dear, you may wonder, if the code's so concise, what would programmers do with the time saved from not having to type all that extra code? Go home—no need to waste time writing silly code that the compiler can generate.

To examine how the Scala compiler transformed the concise code into a full-blown class, compile the previous code using the command scalac CreditCard.scala, and run the command javap -private CreditCard to see what the compiler generated:

```
Compiled from "CreditCard.scala"
public class CreditCard {
  private final int number;
  private int creditLimit;
  public int number();
  public int creditLimit();
  public void creditLimit_$eq(int);
  public CreditCard(int, int);
}
```

Let's examine the code synthesized by the compiler. First, Scala automatically made the class public—the default access control in Scala.

We declared number as val, so Scala defined number as a private final field and created a public method number() to help fetch that value. Since we declared creditLimit as var, Scala defined a private field named creditLimit and gave us a public getter and setter for it. The default generated getters and setters do not follow the JavaBean conventions; we'll soon see how to control that.

We declared one of the constructor parameters as val and the other as var. If you declare a constructor parameter without either of those keywords, then the compiler will create a private final field for internal access within the class. Fields generated from such parameters don't get any accessors and are not accessible from outside the class.

Scala will execute as part of the primary constructor any expression or executable statement directly placed into the class definition. Let's take a look at an example to see this:

WorkingWithObjects/Construct.scala
```
class Construct(param: String) {
  println(s"Creating an instance of Construct with parameter $param")
}
```

```
println("Let's create an instance")
new Construct("sample")
```

The call to println() directly appears in the class definition in the previous code. We can see in the output that this code is executed as part of the constructor call:

```
Let's create an instance
Creating an instance of Construct with parameter sample
```

In addition to the fields declared using the primary constructor's parameters, you can define other fields, methods, and zero or more auxiliary constructors. In the following code, the this() method is an auxiliary constructor. We are also defining the variable position and overriding the toString() method:

WorkingWithObjects/Person.scala
```
class Person(val firstName: String, val lastName: String) {
  var position: String = _

  println(s"Creating ${toString}")

  def this (firstName: String, lastName: String, positionHeld: String) {
    this (firstName, lastName)
    position = positionHeld
  }
  override def toString : String = {
    s"$firstName $lastName holds $position position"
  }
}

val john = new Person("John", "Smith", "Analyst")
println(john)
val bill = new Person("Bill", "Walker")
println(bill)
```

The primary constructor that's combined with the class definition takes two parameters, firstName and lastName. You can easily make the primary constructor private if you desire; see *Stand-alone and Companion Objects*, on page 62.

In addition to the primary constructor, we have an auxiliary constructor, defined using the method named this(). It takes three parameters: the first two are the same as in the primary constructor, and the third is positionHeld. From within the auxiliary constructor, we're calling the primary constructor to initialize the name-related fields. Scala strictly enforces a rule that the first statement within an auxiliary constructor is required to be a call to either the primary constructor or another auxiliary constructor.

Here's the output from the previous code:

```
Creating John Smith holds null position
John Smith holds Analyst position
Creating Bill Walker holds null position
Bill Walker holds null position
```

In Scala fields are given special treatment. Any var defined within a class is mapped to a private field declaration followed by the definition of corresponding getter and setter accessor methods. The access privilege you mark on the field is actually used for accessor methods. That's the reason, in the previous example, that even though we marked the position field as public, the default accessor in Scala, the compiler created a private field and public accessors. You can see this in the following excerpt of running javap on the compiled bytecode:

```
private java.lang.String position;
public java.lang.String position();
public void position_$eq(java.lang.String);
```

The declaration of position turned into a field definition plus a special getter method named position() and a setter method named position_=().

In the previous definition of position, we could have set the initial value to null. Instead, we used an underscore (_). Scala provides the convenience of initializing var to its default value using the underscore—this can save some keystrokes since Scala requires variables to be initialized before use. In the context of the previous example, the _ stands for the default value for the type —so, for Int, it will evaluate to 0 and for Double, it would be 0.0. For a reference type, it evaluates to null, and so on. This convenience of initialization using an underscore is not available for variables declared using val, however, since they can't be modified after creation. Therefore, you're required to give appropriate values when initializing.

We explored how concise defining methods and constructors are in Scala and also looked under the hood to get a grasp of the actual code that Scala generated. Although concise code gets converted to full-blown classes during compilation, the names of the generated accessor methods don't follow the JavaBean convention—that may raise some eyebrows. Thankfully, it's easy to fix.

Following the JavaBean Convention

The accessors that the Scala compiler generates by default don't conform to the JavaBean method naming conversion. This is not a big deal if your classes are used only from Scala. But, it's rather undesirable if the classes are used from Java. That's because, since both Java programmers and Java IDEs are so used to the JavaBean convention, the Scala style accessors would be confusing and hard to use from Java. Furthermore, most Java frameworks assume the JavaBean convention and not following that would make it hard to use Scala classes with those frameworks. No sweat—it's an easy fix with an annotation.

Simply mark the desired field declarations with the scala.beans.BeanProperty annotation. Upon seeing this annotation the Scala compiler will faithfully generate the JavaBean-like accessors in addition to the Scala style accessors. And the Scala syntax for using annotations is much the same as in Java.

For example, we've marked one constructor parameter and the field declaration with the annotation in the following code:

WorkingWithObjects/Dude.scala
```
import scala.beans.BeanProperty

class Dude(@BeanProperty val firstName: String, val lastName: String) {
  @BeanProperty var position: String = _
}
```

Using the annotation we instructed Scala to create the accessor methods getFirstName(), getPosition(), and setPosition(), in addition to the Scala style accessors for the two parameters and the declared field. Since we did not mark the parameter lastName with the annotation, it does not get the JavaBean style accessor. We can see this by taking a peek at the generated code by running the commands:

```
scalac Dude.scala
javap -private Dude
```

Look at the output of javap to confirm your understanding of the effects of the annotation and how to create code that follows the JavaBean convention:

```
Compiled from "Dude.scala"
public class Dude {
  private final java.lang.String firstName;
  private final java.lang.String lastName;
  private java.lang.String position;
  public java.lang.String firstName();
  public java.lang.String lastName();
  public java.lang.String position();
  public void position_$eq(java.lang.String);
  public void setPosition(java.lang.String);
  public java.lang.String getFirstName();
  public java.lang.String getPosition();
  public Dude(java.lang.String, java.lang.String);
}
```

If you mark all the primary constructor parameters and the fields with the BeanProperty annotation, then from Java you can use the JavaBean convention to access the properties of the class. This will make your fellow Java developers happy due to pleasant interoperability. At the same time, you can use either the JavaBean convention or—preferably—the Scala style to access the properties from Scala, as that's more idiomatic and less noisy.

Type Aliasing

When working with a large library you may come across a class name that simply does not work for you. The name is either long or unwieldy, or you simply feel there is a better name that captures the abstraction. You have the freedom to alias, and give the class the name that will make you feel good.

Here's a class with a rather long name:

```
WorkingWithObjects/PoliceOfficer.scala
class PoliceOfficer(val name: String)
```

Cop says it all and is easier to type as well. Here's how we can alias the PoliceOfficer class without losing its identity:

```
WorkingWithObjects/CopApp.scala
object CopApp extends App {
  type Cop = PoliceOfficer

  val topCop = new Cop("Jack")
  println(topCop.getClass)
}
```

Compile and run the code to see this output:

```
class PoliceOfficer
```

The type of the instance still reflects its true identity, but the conversational name Cop is aliased to that class name only within the scope of our file.

In the Scala library a variety of classes have been aliased. Sometimes the alias is used to give better names and at other times it's used to refer to certain classes in select packages. For instance, Set is an alias that refers to the version of Set in the immutable package instead of the version in the mutable package.

Extending a Class

Extending a base class in Scala is similar to extending in Java except for two good restrictions: method overriding requires the override keyword, and only the primary constructor can pass parameters to a base constructor.

The Override annotation was introduced in Java 5 but its use is optional in Java. Scala insists that the keyword override is used when overriding a method. By requiring that keyword, Scala will help minimize errors that often arise from typos in method names. You can avoid either accidentally overriding a method unintentionally or writing a new method when your intent was to override a base method.

In Scala, auxiliary constructors have to call either the primary constructor or another auxiliary constructor. In addition, you can pass parameters to a base constructor only from the primary constructor. At first this may appear to be an unnecessary restriction, but Scala imposes this rule for a good reason —it reduces errors that often creep in due to duplication of logic among constructors of a class.

In essence, the primary constructor acts as the gateway to initialize an instance of a class, and the interaction with the base class for initialization is controlled through this.

As an example, let's extend a class:

WorkingWithObjects/Vehicle.scala
```scala
class Vehicle(val id: Int, val year: Int) {
  override def toString = s"ID: $id Year: $year"
}

class Car(override val id: Int, override val year: Int, var fuelLevel: Int)
  extends Vehicle(id, year) {
  override def toString = s"${super.toString} Fuel Level: $fuelLevel"
}

val car = new Car(1, 2015, 100)
println(car)
```

Take a look at the output of running this code:

```
ID: 1 Year: 2015 Fuel Level: 100
```

Since the properties id and year in Car are derived from Vehicle, we indicate that in the Car class by using the keyword override before the respective parameters of the primary constructor. Seeing this keyword, the Scala compiler will not generate fields for these two properties. Instead, it will route the accessor methods for these properties to the appropriate methods of the base class. If you forget to put in the override keyword for these two parameters, you'll get a compiler error.

Also, since we're overriding the toString() method of java.lang.Object in Vehicle and in Car, we had to prefix the definitions of toString() with override as well.

When extending a class you must pass the parameters from the derived class to one of the base class constructors. Since only the primary constructor can invoke a base constructor, place this call right after the base class name is mentioned, following the extends declaration.

Parameterized Types

As we've seen, not only is extending a class concise in Scala, but it's also streamlined to alleviate some common programming errors. Generic or parameterized types further help to create classes and functions that can work with multiple different types. The types can be specified at compile time instead of code writing time, making the code more extensible without losing type safety.

Since in Scala you can create stand-alone functions, you can create parameterized functions as well. Let's create one:

WorkingWithObjects/Parameterized.scala
```
def echo[T](input1: T, input2: T) =
  println(s"got $input1 (${input1.getClass}) $input2 (${input2.getClass})")
```

Rather than specifying the echo() function's parameter types to be some type like Int or String, we left them open as parametric type T for the programmer to decide. The notation [T] signals to the compiler that the type T that follows is not some existing, poorly named, single-letter class but is a parameterized type.

You'd call this function much like any function, but the types of the parameters are decided at this time. Let's call the echo() function using two different types of arguments:

WorkingWithObjects/Parameterized.scala
```
echo("hello", "there")
echo(4, 5)
```

We passed Strings in the first call, and then Ints in the second call. The compiler accepts these with no complaint and synthesizes the function, tailored to the type of the argument. Let's see the output:

```
got hello (class java.lang.String) there (class java.lang.String)
got 4 (class java.lang.Integer) 5 (class java.lang.Integer)
```

Since we used the same type T for both the parameters, Scala will require that the arguments be of the same type. There is one gotcha, however. All types in Scala derive from Any, which we'll see in Chapter 5, *Making Use of Types*, on page 71. The following call will, unfortunately, work:

```
echo("hi", 5)
```

The result of this call shows:

```
got hi (class java.lang.String) 5 (class java.lang.Integer)
```

If you want to prevent fellow programmers from mixing arguments of different types during refactoring, you can place a directive, like so:

```
echo[Int]("hi", 5) //error: type mismatch
```

In this case the compiler will insist that both the arguments are of type Int. This shows that it's hard to reliably enforce that the two parameters are of the same type.

If your intention was to receive two different types of arguments, then you can express that more clearly, like in the following example:

```
def echo2[T1, T2](input1: T1, input2: T2) =
  println(s"received $input1 and $input2")


echo2("Hi", "5")
```

Creating parameterized classes is just as easy as creating parameterized functions. Let's create a Message class that again postpones the type of its field:

```
class Message[T](val content: T) {
  override def toString = s"message content is $content"

  def is(value: T) = value == content
}
```

The type of the field content is parameterized and will be decided per instance of the class. The same is true for the type of the parameter of the is() method. Unlike the stand-alone function, we did not have to place the notation [T] in the definition of the is() method. If the method were to receive a parameterized type other than the parameterized type T specified at the class level, then we'd have to use that notation for the same reasons as mentioned before.

Let's create a few instances of the Message class and invoke the is() method:

```
val message1 : Message[String] = new Message("howdy")
val message2 = new Message(42)

println(message1)
println(message1.is("howdy"))
println(message1.is("hi"))
println(message2.is(22))
```

We explicitly specified the type for the first variable message, but let Scala infer the type for message2. Unlike Java, Scala does not permit raw types; providing the type as Message instead of Message[String] in the definition of message1 will be an error. Either provide the full details of the parameterized type or let Scala infer it for you.

Once we created the two instances we implicitly call the toString() method in the println() call and also invoke the is() method a few times. Let's see the response:

```
message content is howdy
true
false
false
```

The parameterized type is specialized when the instances are created. If you try to send an incorrect type, you will receive a stern error, like in this example:

```
message1.is(22) //error: type mismatch
```

Sadly, the following code will not produce any error—the character input is quietly converted to the compatible Int type. Don't rely too much on the type checking; use caution:

```
message2.is('A') //No error!
```

The Message class is defined to take one parameterized type. In general, a class can accept multiple parameterized types, much like the echo2() method received two.

In Java angle brackets (<>) are used to specify the generic types. We saw how in Scala, square brackets ([]) are used instead. That's not the only difference, however. Unlike Java where type erasure make generics rather weak, Scala performs more rigorous type checking on parameterized types—we will see this in *Type Inference for Generics and Collections*, on page 74. Also, we can place constraints on the parameterized types—we will explore this in *Variance of Parameterized Type*, on page 82.

Singletons and Companions

Scala takes a significant departure from Java in how it deals with static fields and methods. Furthermore, it has first-class support for singleton objects. Let's explore singletons and companions, and see how static is handled in Scala.

Singleton Object

Singleton is a popular pattern discussed in *Design Patterns: Elements of Reusable Object-Oriented Software [GHJV95]* by Gamma et al. A singleton is a class that has only one instance. We use singletons to represent objects that act as a central point of contact for certain operations such as database access, object factories, and so on.

It turned out that the singleton pattern is easy to understand but hard to implement in Java—see Joshua Bloch's *Effective Java [Blo08]*. Thankfully, this problem is addressed in Scala at the language level. To create a singleton use the keyword object instead of class. Since you can't instantiate a singleton object, you can't pass parameters to the constructor.

Here's an example of a singleton called MarkerFactory along with a class named Marker:

WorkingWithObjects/Singleton.scala
```scala
import scala.collection.mutable._

class Marker(val color: String) {
  println(s"Creating ${this}")

  override def toString = s"marker color $color"
}

object MarkerFactory {
  private val markers = Map(
    "red" -> new Marker("red"),
    "blue" -> new Marker("blue"),
    "yellow" -> new Marker("yellow"))

  def getMarker(color: String) =
    markers.getOrElseUpdate(color, new Marker(color))
}

println(MarkerFactory getMarker "blue")
println(MarkerFactory getMarker "blue")
println(MarkerFactory getMarker "red")
println(MarkerFactory getMarker "red")
println(MarkerFactory getMarker "green")
```

Here's the result of running this code:

```
Creating marker color red
Creating marker color blue
Creating marker color yellow
marker color blue
marker color blue
```

```
marker color red
marker color red
Creating marker color green
marker color green
```

In the example, the class Marker represents color markers with some initial colors. MarkerFactory is a singleton that helps reuse precreated instances of Marker.

You can access the singleton—the only instance—of MarkerFactory by its name. Once you define a singleton, its name represents the single instance of the singleton object.

There is one problem in the previous code, however. We can directly create an instance of Marker without going through MarkerFactory. Let's look at how to restrict the creation of instances of a class to its singleton factory next.

Stand-alone and Companion Objects

The MarkerFactory we just saw is an example of a *stand-alone* object. It's not automatically connected to any class, even though we have used it to manage instances of Marker.

You can associate a singleton to a class if you like. Such a singleton will share the same name as a class name and is therefore called a *companion object*. The corresponding class is called a *companion class*. This romance leads to some very powerful capability as we'll see.

In the previous example, we wanted to regulate the creation of Marker instances. Classes and their companion objects have no boundaries between them—they can access the private fields and methods of each other. Also, constructors of a class, including the primary constructor, can be marked private. We can combine these two facilities to solve the problem highlighted at the end of the previous section. Here's a rewrite of the Marker example using a companion object:

WorkingWithObjects/Marker.scala
```scala
import scala.collection.mutable._

class Marker private(val color: String) {
  println(s"Creating ${this}")

  override def toString = s"marker color $color"
}

object Marker {
  private val markers = Map(
    "red" -> new Marker("red"),
```

```
    "blue" -> new Marker("blue"),
    "yellow" -> new Marker("yellow"))

  def getMarker(color: String) =
    markers.getOrElseUpdate(color, new Marker(color))
}

println(Marker getMarker "blue")
println(Marker getMarker "blue")
println(Marker getMarker "red")
println(Marker getMarker "red")
println(Marker getMarker "green")
```

Let's look at the output of running the previous code:

```
Creating marker color red
Creating marker color blue
Creating marker color yellow
marker color blue
marker color blue
marker color red
marker color red
Creating marker color green
marker color green
```

The constructor of Marker is declared private; however, the companion object can access it. Thus, we're able to create instances of Marker from within the companion object. If you try to create an instance of Marker outside the class or the companion object, you'll get an error.

Each class may have an optional companion object that can be placed in the same file as their companion classes. Companion objects are common in Scala and provide class-level convenience methods. They also serve as a nice workaround for the lack of static members in Scala, as we'll see next.

static in Scala

Scala does not have the static keyword; allowing static fields and static methods directly in a class would break the pure object-oriented model that Scala supports. At the same time, Scala fully supports class-level operations and properties through singletons and companion objects.

Let's revisit the previous Marker example. It would be nice to get the supported colors from Marker. However, it would not make sense to direct such a query on any specific instance of the class; it's a class-level operation. In other words, if we were coding in Java, we would've written that query method as a static method in the Marker class. But, Scala does not provide static. The language has been designed so that such methods reside as regular methods in singletons and companion objects. Let's modify the Marker example to create methods in the companion object:

WorkingWithObjects/Static.scala

```scala
import scala.collection.mutable._

class Marker private (val color: String) {
  override def toString = s"marker color $color"
}
object Marker {
  private val markers = Map(
    "red" -> new Marker("red"),
    "blue" -> new Marker("blue"),
    "yellow" -> new Marker("yellow"))

  def supportedColors = markers.keys
  def apply(color: String) = markers.getOrElseUpdate(color, new Marker(color))
}
println(s"Supported colors are : ${Marker.supportedColors}")
println(Marker("blue"))
println(Marker("red"))
```

This is the output from running the code:

```
Supported colors are : Set(yellow, red, blue)
marker color blue
marker color red
```

We wrote the method supportedColors() in the companion object—the parentheses in the method definition are optional if the method takes no parameters. We call it on the Marker companion object like we'd call static methods on classes in Java.

The companion object also provides another benefit: the ability to create instances of the companion class without the need for the new keyword. The special apply() method does this trick. In the previous example, when we invoke Marker("blue"), we're actually calling Marker.apply("blue"). This is a lightweight syntax to create or get instances.

Let's quickly look under the hood to see how the methods in singletons or companion objects get compiled into bytecode. Here's a singleton with a method:

WorkingWithObjects/Greeter.scala

```scala
object Greeter {
  def greet() = println("Ahoy, me hearties!")
}
```

To see the code generated by the Scala compiler, run the following commands:

```
scalac Greeter.scala
javap -private Greeter
```

The output from the call to javap is

```
Compiled from "Greeter.scala"
public final class Greeter {
  public static void greet();
}
```

The method in the singleton has been created as a static method at the bytecode level. This is good news from the Java interoperability point of view.

If you take a peek at the files created from the previous compilation, you'd notice, not one, but two class files created from Greeter.scala. We will discuss the details of the additional class and some of the challenges with interoperability that Scala may pose in Chapter 14, *Intermixing with Java*, on page 213.

Creating Enumerations

In Scala you can use Java enums. Alternately, you can create enumerations in Scala as well.

To create an enumeration in Scala you will start by creating an object—much like the syntax used to create a singleton. However, you can assign multiple named instances—after all, the singleton pattern doesn't force a single instance; it's simply a way to control the creation of select instances.

Let's create an enumeration to represent various currencies:

WorkingWithObjects/finance1/finance/currencies/Currency.scala
```
package finance.currencies

object Currency extends Enumeration {
  type Currency = Value
  val CNY, GBP, INR, JPY, NOK, PLN, SEK, USD = Value
}
```

An enumeration is an object that extends the Enumeration class. Use the keyword val to define the select instance of the enumeration, like CNY, GBP,... in the example. Assign these specialized names to a special Value, which represents the type of the enumeration within its definition—Value isn't directly accessible outside of the enumeration.

That sounds good, but there's a problem. Remember how the name of a singleton refers to an instance. For example, MarkerFactory in the previous example referred to the singleton instance defined using object. With enumerations, however, we do want to refer to the enumeration name as a general reference to any one of the values. For example, take a look at this Money class:

WorkingWithObjects/finance1/finance/currencies/Money.scala
```scala
package finance.currencies

import Currency._

class Money(val amount: Int, val currency: Currency) {
  override def toString = s"$amount $currency"
}
```

In the constructor of Money we want to receive a Currency as a parameter. It would make no sense to treat the word Currency in val currency: Currency as an instance. Instead it should be considered a *type*. Now you know the reason for the line type Currency = Value—this tells the compiler to treat the word Currency as a type instead of an instance. We see type aliasing from *Type Aliasing*, on page 56 being applied here.

We can iterate over the enumeration's values using the values property:

WorkingWithObjects/UseCurrency.scala
```scala
import finance.currencies.Currency

object UseCurrency extends App {
  Currency.values.foreach { currency => println(currency) }
}
```

Scala automatically creates meaningful methods like toString() that displays appropriate names for the enumerations as we see in the output:

```
CNY
GBP
INR
JPY
NOK
PLN
SEK
USD
```

In Java to create a singleton you create an enum, but in Scala to create an enum you create a singleton; weird, eh?

As you can see, there are significant departures from Java in the way Scala deals with static and singletons. Next we'll take a look at another departure from Java: packages can not only have classes, but—surprise—functions also.

Package Objects

By convention Java packages contain only interfaces, classes, enumerations, and annotation types. Scala goes a step further: packages can also have variables and functions. These are placed in special singleton objects called *package objects*.

If you find yourself creating a class only to hold a set of shared methods among other classes in a package, then a package object will remove that extra burden to create and then repeatedly reference that extra class. Let's explore this with an example.

First let's create an example using singleton and then convert it to a package class so we can get a good feel for its benefits.

In this example we will reuse the Currency enumeration and the Money class we created earlier. Here's a Converter singleton with a method convert() to help convert money from one currency to another.

WorkingWithObjects/finance1/finance/currencies/Converter.scala
```
package finance.currencies

import Currency._

object Converter {
  def convert(money: Money, to: Currency) = {
    //fetch current market rate... using mocked value here
    val conversionRate = 2
    new Money(money.amount * conversionRate, to)
  }
}
```

Let's use this method in a Charge class in the same package.

WorkingWithObjects/finance1/finance/currencies/Charge.scala
```
package finance.currencies

import Currency._

object Charge {
  def chargeInUSD(money: Money) = {
    def moneyInUSD = Converter.convert(money, Currency.USD)
    s"charged $$${moneyInUSD.amount}"
  }
}
```

In the chargeInUSD() method we prefixed the method convert() with the name of the singleton containing the method. Likewise, in a class CurrencyApp, which is outside of the finance.currencies package, we will reference the method with the same prefix.

WorkingWithObjects/finance1/CurrencyApp.scala
```scala
import finance.currencies._

object CurrencyApp extends App {
  var moneyInGBP = new Money(10, Currency.GBP)

  println(Charge.chargeInUSD(moneyInGBP))

  println(Converter.convert(moneyInGBP, Currency.USD))
}
```

Keenly observe the usage: the convert() operation is quite fundamental to the finance.currencies package, but the prefix Converter does not add any value. It's an artificial placeholder—a noise. We can get rid of it using package objects.

A package object is nothing but a singleton, much like the Converter is, with a special name and syntax. It takes the name of the containing package and is marked with the word package. Let's rewrite the Converter as a package object:

WorkingWithObjects/finance2/finance/currencies/package.scala
```scala
package finance

package object currencies {
  import Currency._

  def convert(money: Money, to: Currency) = {
    //fetch current market rate... using mocked value here
    val conversionRate = 2
    new Money(money.amount * conversionRate, to)
  }
}
```

We changed object Converter to package object currencies, where currencies is the subpackage name. We placed the file containing this code, package.scala, in the directory finance/currencies, much like how we will place classes belonging to this package. The package keyword serves two purposes in Scala: to define a package and also to define a package object.

With this change, we can drop the class/singleton prefix when referring to the convert() method, creating an impression that this method belongs to the package directly, as we see in the next code:

WorkingWithObjects/finance2/finance/currencies/Charge.scala
```scala
package finance.currencies

import Currency._
```

```
object Charge {
  def chargeInUSD(money: Money) = {
    def moneyInUSD = convert(money, Currency.USD)
    s"charged $$${moneyInUSD.amount}"
  }
}
```

Likewise, we can drop the prefix when referring to the method from a class outside this package:

WorkingWithObjects/finance2/CurrencyApp.scala
```
import finance.currencies._

object CurrencyApp extends App {
  var moneyInGBP = new Money(10, Currency.GBP)

  println(Charge.chargeInUSD(moneyInGBP))

  println(convert(moneyInGBP, Currency.USD))
}
```

The import financial.currencies._ brings both the singleton Charge and the method convert() into scope.

We placed one method in our package object. Package objects can have any number of methods—even zero. If you have traits in your package, you can expose the methods in any of the traits by merely extending the package object from the traits you desire—we'll look at traits in Chapter 7, *Traits*, on page 119.

You may be curious to find how the package object is implemented at the bytecode level. Scala compiles package objects into classes named package in the appropriate package. Thus, our singleton package object currencies is compiled to the finance.currencies.package class.

The Scala library makes extensive use of package objects. The package scala is automatically imported in every Scala code. Thus, the scala package object is also imported. This package object contains many type aliases and implicit type conversions. For example, anytime you use List[T] in code, it automatically refers to scala.collection.immutable.List[A] thanks to an alias defined in the scala package object.

Wrapping Up

We explored working with objects in this chapter. You saw how to concisely create classes and extend them. You also learned to alias types and to create parameterized types and enumerations. Finally, you saw singletons, companion objects, and Scala's package objects. That's a boatload of features. Take some time to practice with what you've learned so far. In the next chapter we'll move from creating classes to working with types and type inferences.

CHAPTER 5

Making Use of Types

One of the key strengths of Scala is static typing. With static typing, the compilers act as a first level of defense against errors. They can verify that the objects on hand are really of the types intended. It's a way to enforce interface contracts at compile time. Such verification can give us confidence that the compiled code *meets* certain expectations.

Sadly, in a number of mainstream statically typed languages, static typing means more typing—with fingers. However, good static typing should verify code without getting in your way. For example, Haskell, one of the languages that influenced Scala, does not force you to key in type information to make use of its superb static typing capabilities.

Scala is statically typed, but thankfully, it leans sensibly toward type inference. For the most part we don't have to mention types—Scala smartly deduces the necessary details from the context. At the same time, it does not go overboard with type inference to the extent where it's hard to understand or evolve code.

In this chapter, we'll explore Scala's static typing and type inference. We'll also look at three special types in Scala: Any, Nothing, and Option. Finally we'll take a look at some powerful type conversion tricks.

Type Inference

Like any statically typed language, Scala verifies types of objects at compile time. At the same time, it does not require you to state the obvious; it can infer types. You can use type inference for both simple types and generics.

Type Inference for Simple Types

We'll first explore type inference for simple types. Let's start with a piece of code where we indicate the type, as we're used to doing in languages like C++ and Java:

MakingUseOfTypes/DefiningVariableWithType.scala
```
val greet : String = "Ahoy!"
```

We defined a variable named greet, mentioned its type is String, and gave it a value. Unlike Java, where you specify the type and then the variable name, in Scala you do the reverse—for two reasons: First, by asking us to place the type after the name, Scala alludes that picking a good variable name is more important than mentioning type. Second, the type information is optional.

Let's take a look at the variable definition. From the value we assigned to the variable, the type of the variable is very clear. This is a case of no ambiguity, so mentioning the type is redundant. Since Scala can figure out the obvious type, let's rewrite the previous definition, without the type detail:

MakingUseOfTypes/DefiningVariable.scala
```
val greet = "Ahoy!"
```

At compile time Scala will determine the type of a variable if you did not specify it and if there's no ambiguity. In the previous example, the type of greet was inferred to be a String. We can check this in three ways. First, let's ask Scala for the type information, in code:

MakingUseOfTypes/DefiningVariable.scala
```
println(greet)
println(greet.getClass)
```

We printed the value in the variable as well as its type. Let's see what Scala reports:

```
Ahoy!
class java.lang.String
```

The output confirms that the type of the variable is the type we'd expect. However, the example does not confirm that Scala in fact inferred this at compile time and not runtime. A look at the bytecode generated by the compiler will be a sure way to tell. Let's place the code in a class and compile it:

MakingUseOfTypes/TypeInference.scala
```
class TypeInference {
  val greet = "Ahoy!"
}
```

Use the following commands to compile the code and view the details in the bytecode:

```
scalac -d bin TypeInference.scala
javap -classpath bin -private TypeInference
```

Here's the output from the javap tool, confirming that the variable is of the desired type:

```
Compiled from "TypeInference.scala"
public class TypeInference {
  private final java.lang.String greet;
  public java.lang.String greet();
  public TypeInference();
}
```

Viewing the bytecode is a sure way to check on what the Scala compiler generated, but that takes effort. If you want a quick confirmation of the type, Scala REPL is your friend—see *Using the REPL*, on page 13. Type the command scala on the command line to invoke the REPL and then type the definition. Let's key the example definition into the REPL:

```
scala> val greet = "Ahoy!"
greet: String = Ahoy!

scala> :quit
```

The REPL gives a quick feedback of the value and the type of the variable we created.

That's type inference in action. You can skip keying in the type details for the most part, but Scala requires type declaration in a few places. We have to specify types when

- defining class fields with no initial value

- defining parameters for functions/methods

- defining return type for a function/method, but only if we use an explicit return or use recursion

- defining a variable with a different type than the value may imply—for example, val frequency: Double = 1

Other than these situations, type information is optional and, if left out, Scala will infer it. It may take some getting used to—to undo some Java practices —before you get comfortable skipping the type information. As you make the transition, no worries, Scala will patiently accept the type information, albeit redundant. Start out by mentioning types and, as you get comfortable, leave out types where you feel it's not necessary. If Scala can't figure out the type, it will ask for it, loud and clear.

Type Inference for Generics and Collections

Scala provides type inference and type safety for the Java generics collections as well. In the following example we define instances of ArrayList, first with explicit type and then with type inferred.

MakingUseOfTypes/Generics.scala
```
import java.util._

var list1 : List[Int] = new ArrayList[Int]
var list2 = new ArrayList[Int]
```

Again, in this case, leaving out the type makes the code less noisy, especially since it's quite obvious from the context of the declaration. Scala is quite vigilant about the types of objects. It prohibits any conversions that may cause typing issues. Here's an example:

MakingUseOfTypes/Generics2.scala
```
import java.util._

var list1 = new ArrayList[Int]
var list2 = new ArrayList
list2 = list1 // Compilation Error
```

We created a variable, list1, that refers to an instance of ArrayList[Int]. Then we created another variable, list2, that refers to an instance of ArrayList with an unspecified parametric type—we'll soon find out what this manifests into. When we try to assign the first reference to the second, Scala gives this compilation error:

```
Generics2.scala:5: error: type mismatch;
 found    : java.util.ArrayList[Int]
 required: java.util.ArrayList[Nothing]
Note: Int >: Nothing, but Java-defined class ArrayList is invariant in
type E.
You may wish to investigate a wildcard type such as `_ >: Nothing`. (SLS
3.2.10)
list2 = list1 // Compilation Error
      ^
one error found
```

For the list2, behind the scenes, Scala actually created an instance of ArrayList[Nothing]. Nothing is a subtype of all classes in Scala. By treating the new ArrayList as an instance of ArrayList[Nothing], Scala rules out any possibility of adding an instance of any meaningful type to this collection. This is because we can't treat an instance of base as an instance of derived and Nothing is in the bottommost place in the type hierarchy.

Scala insists the collection types on either side of an assignment are the same —we'll see later in *Variance of Parameterized Type*, on page 82 how to alter this default behavior.

Here is an example using a collection of objects of type Any—Any is the base type of all types:

```
MakingUseOfTypes/Generics3.scala
import java.util._

var list1 = new ArrayList[Int]
var list2 = new ArrayList[Any]

var ref1 : Int = 1
var ref2 : Any = null

ref2 = ref1 //OK

list2 = list1 // Compilation Error
```

This time list1 refers to an ArrayList[Int], while list2 refers to an ArrayList[Any]. We also created two other references, ref1 of type Int and ref2 of type Any. Scala has no qualms if we assign ref1 to ref2. It's equivalent to assigning an Integer reference to a reference of type Object in Java. However, Scala doesn't allow, by default, assigning a collection of arbitrary type instances to a reference of a collection of Any instances—later we'll discuss covariance, which provides exceptions to this rule. Java generics enjoy an enhanced type safety in Scala.

When dealing with generics as well, you don't have to specify the type in order to benefit from Scala type checking. You can rely on type inference where it makes sense. The inference happens at compile time. You can be certain that the type checking takes effect right then when you compile the code, without incurring any runtime overhead.

Scala insists that a nonparameterized collection be a collection of Nothing and restricts assignment across types. These combine to enhance type safety at compile time—providing for a sensible, low-ceremony static typing.

In the previous examples, we used Java collections. Scala also provides a wealth of collections, as we'll see in Chapter 8, *Collections*, on page 129.

We've gotten a glimpse of Any and Nothing. Let's take a closer look at these types.

Fundamental Types

Even though you can use any Java type in Scala, you can also enjoy a few types native to Scala. Scala makes a clearer distinction between value types and reference types and also goes a few extra miles with type definitions to enhance type verification and inference. Let's get a grasp of these fundamental types since you'll encounter these types in Scala quite often.

The Any Type

Scala's Any type is a superclass of all types, as you can see here.

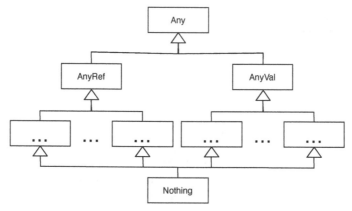

Any can serve as a common reference to objects of any type. Any is an abstract class with the following methods: !=(), ==(), asInstanceOf(), equals(), hashCode(), isInstanceOf(), and toString().

The direct descendants of Any are AnyVal and AnyRef. AnyVal stands as a base for all types in Scala—for example, Int, Double, and so on—that map over to the primitive types in Java. On the other hand, AnyRef is the base for all reference types. Although AnyVal does not have any additional methods, AnyRef contains the methods of Java's Object such as notify(), wait(), and finalize().

AnyRef directly maps to the Java Object, so you can pretty much use it in Scala like you'd use Object in Java. On the other hand, you can't call all the methods of Object on a reference of Any or AnyVal, even though internally Scala treats them as Object references when compiled to bytecode. In other words, while AnyRef directly maps to Object, Any and AnyVal are type erased to Object. This is much like the way generics are type erased in Java.

While Any is at the top of the hierarchy, the bottommost type is Nothing.

Something about Nothing

Nothing in Scala is everything. It's easy to see why we need Any, but Nothing seems rather odd at first, especially since it can stand in for any class.

Nothing is quite important to support the type verification mechanics of Scala. Scala's type inference works hard to determine the type of expressions and functions. If the type inferred is too broad, it won't help type verification. At the same time, we do want to infer the type of an expression or function where one branch returns, say, an Int and another branch throws an exception, like in the following example:

```
def someOp(number : Int) =
  if(number < 10)
    number * 2
  else
    throw new RuntimeException("invalid argument")
```

In this case, inferring the return type of the function as Any would be too broad and useless. It's more useful to infer the return type as Int. It's easy to see that the arithmetic expression evaluates as Int. Furthermore, the branch that throws the exception must be inferred, in this case, to return an Int or a sub-type of Int for it to be compatible with the inferred return type. However, throw can't be treated arbitrarily as an Int type since an exception may occur just about anywhere. Nothing comes to the rescue—it makes type inference work smoothly by acting as a subtype of all types. Since it's a subtype of all types, it is substitutable for anything. Nothing is abstract, so you won't ever have a real instance of it anywhere at runtime. It's purely a helper for type inference and verification purposes.

Let's explore this further with an example. Let's take a look at a method, named madMethod(), that throws an exception and see how Scala infers the type, using the REPL:

```
scala> def madMethod() = { throw new IllegalArgumentException() }
madMethod: ()Nothing

scala> :quit
```

The interactive REPL session reveals that Scala inferred the return type of an expression that throws an exception as Nothing. Scala's Nothing is actually quite something—it is a subtype of every other type. So, Nothing is substitutable for anything in Scala.

While Any is the mother of all classes, Nothing can stand in for anything.

Option Type

Remember the sage advice in Joshua Bloch's *Effective Java [Blo08]*, to return an empty collection instead of a null reference. If we follow that advice, we don't have to endure NullPointerException, and iteration becomes easy even when the resulting collection is empty. That's good advice to follow when working with collections, but we need something similar to follow when working with other return types.

When you perform pattern matching, for example, the result of the match may be an object, a list, a tuple, and so on, or it may be nonexistent. Returning a null quietly is problematic in two ways. First, the fact that there may not be a result is not expressed explicitly. Second, there is no way to force the caller of the function to check for nonexistence or null.

Scala goes a step further to specify nonexistence. With Scala's Option[T] you can program with intention, and specify that you do actually intend to return no result. Scala achieves this in a type-safe manner so the check can be enforced at compile time. Let's look at an example of using this special type:

```
MakingUseOfTypes/OptionExample.scala
def commentOnPractice(input: String) = {
  //rather than returning null
  if (input == "test") Some("good") else None
}

for (input <- Set("test", "hack")) {
  val comment = commentOnPractice(input)
  val commentDisplay = comment.getOrElse("Found no comments")
  println(s"input: $input comment: $commentDisplay")
}
```

Here, the method commentOnPractice() may return a comment of type String, or may not have any comments at all. If we were to return a null, we're at the mercy of the receiver to perform a null check. This is a burden; in addition the code would be smelly and error prone.

Instead of returning an instance of String, the method commentOnPractice() returns either an instance of Some[T] or a None. These two classes extend from the Option[T] class. The code that receives an instance of Option[T] would have to fetch the result, with a clear expectation that the result may be nonexistent. In the previous example, we used the getOrElse() method of Option[T], where we provide an alternative if the result did not exist. Let's exercise the previous code and take a look at the output:

```
input: test comment: good
input: hack comment: Found no comments
```

By making the type explicit as Option[String], Scala forces you to check for the nonexistence of an instance. Since this is enforced at compile time, you're less likely to get a NullPointerException because of unchecked null references. By calling the getOrElse() method on the returned Option[T], you can proactively indicate your intentions in case the result is nonexistent—that is, None.

Either

The Option type is useful when the result of a function call may or may not exist. Sometimes you may like to return one of two different values from a function. Scala's Either comes in handy for this purpose.

Suppose a compute() method performs some calculations for a given input, but it's valid only for positive integers. For invalid input, instead of throwing an exception, we could gracefully return an error message. Either has two values: the left value (which is considered an error) and the right value (which is considered a correct or expected value). Let's write the example compute() function.

MakingUseOfTypes/UsingEither.scala
```
def compute(input: Int) =
  if(input > 0)
    Right(math.sqrt(input))
  else
    Left("Error computing, invalid input")
```

The compute() method checks if the input is valid and if it is, returns a valid result wrapped into the right part of Either using the Right singleton. On the other hand, if the input is invalid, it returns the error details as the left part of Either using the Left singleton.

When you receive an Either you can extract the content using pattern matching, as in this displayResult() function:

MakingUseOfTypes/UsingEither.scala
```
def displayResult(result: Either[String, Double]) = {
  println(s"Raw: $result")
  result match {
    case Right(value) => println(s"result $value")
    case Left(err) => println(s"Error: $err")
  }
}
```

We first display the values in the result as is. Then we extract the value using pattern matching to display the right part or the left part, as appropriate.

Let's call the displayResult() function:

```
MakingUseOfTypes/UsingEither.scala
displayResult(compute(4))
displayResult(compute(-4))
```

The output from this code is shown here:

```
Raw: Right(2.0)
result 2.0
Raw: Left(Error computing, invalid input)
Error: Error computing, invalid input
```

If you want to convey the possible nonexistence of a value, use Optional, but to vary between possibly two different values, use Either.

Return Type Inference

In addition to inferring the types of variables, Scala tries to infer the return type of functions and methods. However, there is a catch—it depends on how you define a function. Scala's return type inference kicks in only if you use an equals sign (=) to separate a method declaration from its body. Otherwise, the method is considered to return a Unit, which is equivalent to Void in Java. Let's examine the return types of the following functions:

```
MakingUseOfTypes/functions.scala
def function1 { Math.sqrt(4) }
def function2 = { Math.sqrt(4) }
def function3 = Math.sqrt(4)
def function4 : Double = { Math.sqrt(4) }
```

We've defined function1() by providing a name and the function body within curly braces. Though syntactically correct, it's not idiomatic and it's better to avoid this style—the return type of this function will be inferred as Unit. Let's move to the next function, function2(), where we've used an equals (=) before the function body. That's the only structural difference between the functions function1() and function2(); however, that's significant in Scala. While Scala assumed that function1() is void, it infers function2() as returning a Double —Java's double—since the expression in the function body yields that type of result. The use of equals (=) between the function declaration and its body is the desired idiomatic style in Scala—use it even for void methods.

If a function has a single simple or compound expression, then you can drop the curly braces as we did when defining function3(). This reduces noise when the body is small—for example, with simple getters and setters that perform minimal checks.

> **\\//** **Joe asks:**
> **♂** **Should I Use () or Not?**
>
> When defining a function with zero parameters, should we place the () or not? What about when calling the function?
>
> If a method is merely an accessor to a field or a property, then don't place the () in the definition. In this case, you can't use the () in the call. Also, if a method performs some computation and returns the result, then drop the ()—toString, getClass, for example.
>
> On the other hand, if a function has a side effect—it mutates or makes a change to some data, writes to a file, updates a database, or even writes to the console using println()—then use () both in the declaration and in the call.
>
> Any method that returns a Unit will have to cause a side effect—if it returned nothing and did not cause a side effect, it would be useless and do nothing. So, you'd mark such a method with the () and also use parentheses when calling.

Instead of leaving out the type, as we did in the first three functions, you could explicitly specify the return type as in function4(). Here again, the curly braces can be dropped if the body is a single expression. Whether the return type is explicitly specified or inferred, the return types of all functions and methods are determined at compile time.

If you decide to specify the return type it has to be compatible with the type that is yielded by the last expression in the method body. If it's not compatible —for example, if you declare the return type of function4() as String—Scala will give a type-mismatch compile-time error.

You can confirm your understanding of the return type inference by running the previous functions declarations through Scala REPL:

```
scala> def function1 { Math.sqrt(4) }
function1: Unit

scala> def function2 = { Math.sqrt(4) }
function2: Double

scala> def function3 = Math.sqrt(4)
function3: Double

scala> def function4 : Double = { Math.sqrt(4) }
function4: Double

scala> :quit
```

The return types of each of the functions is displayed after the colon. While function1()'s return type is assumed to be Unit, all the other functions we defined in the previous example have a return type of Double. Use the REPL to try out your own examples, and experiment with various return types and syntax to see what's accepted and how it's inferred by Scala.

In general, for internal APIs, it's better to let Scala infer the type of functions and methods. You have one less thing to worry about, and you can let the well-built type inference do its job. For external, client-facing APIs, do mention the type so it's easier for users to readily see the type they can expect. When defining methods for interfaces (traits in Scala) you obviously have to specify the return type since there's no implementation.

Scala's type inference is convenient. Although its type checking is rigorous, Scala does offer some flexibility, as you'll see next.

Variance of Parameterized Type

Scala prevented us from assigning a reference of ArrayList[Int] to a reference of ArrayList[Any] in *Type Inference for Generics and Collections*, on page 74. That's a good thing; in general a collection of derived should not be assignable to a collection of base. However, there are times when we want some lenience to that rule. In those situations, we can ask Scala to permit otherwise invalid conversions. Tighten your seat belts—we're in for a fun, but intense, ride.

Covariance and Contravariance

Scala will stop at compile time any conversions that may potentially lead to runtime failures. Specifically, as an example, it prevents the following code from compiling:

```
var arr1 = new Array[Int](3)
var arr2: Array[Any] = null

arr2 = arr1 // Compilation ERROR
```

Here's the error reported by the compiler:

```
NotAllowed.scala:4: error: type mismatch;
 found    : Array[Int]
 required: Array[Any]
Note: Int <: Any, but class Array is invariant in type T.
You may wish to investigate a wildcard type such as `_ <: Any`. (SLS
3.2.10)
arr2 = arr1 // Compilation ERROR
       ^
one error found
```

The previous restriction is a good thing. Imagine if Scala—like Java—did not restrict that. Here is Java code that can get us into trouble:

```
Line 1  //Java code
   -    class Fruit {}
   -    class Banana extends Fruit {}
   -    class Apple extends Fruit {}
   5
   -    public class Trouble {
   -      public static void main(String[] args) {
   -        Banana[] basketOfBanana = new Banana[2];
   -        basketOfBanana[0] = new Banana();
  10
   -        Fruit[] basketOfFruits = basketOfBanana;
   -        basketOfFruits[1] = new Apple();
   -
   -        for(Banana banana : basketOfBanana) {
  15          System.out.println(banana);
   -        }
   -      }
   -    }
```

The previous code will compile with no errors. However, when we run it, it will give the following runtime error:

```
Exception in thread "main" java.lang.ArrayStoreException: Apple
        at Trouble.main(Trouble.java:12)
```

The reason for the error is, at runtime, we're trying to place an apple into a basket of bananas, under the pretext of using a basket of fruits. While the failure happened on line 12, the root cause is that the Java compiler did not stop us on line 11.

While the previous problem slipped through the Java compiler, to be fair, it doesn't allow the following:

```
//Java code
ArrayList<Integer> list = new ArrayList<Integer>();
ArrayList<Object> list2 = list; // Compilation error
```

Unfortunately, it's easy to bypass this in Java like this:

```
ArrayList list3 = list;
```

The ability to send a collection of subclass instances where a collection of base class instances is expected is called *covariance*. And the ability to send a collection of superclass instances where a collection of subclass instances is expected is called *contravariance*. By default Scala does not allow either one of them.

Supporting Covariance

Although the default behavior of Scala is good in general, there are genuine cases where we'd want to cautiously treat a collection of a derived type—say a collection of Dogs—as a collection of its base type—say a collection of Pets. Consider the following example:

```scala
class Pet(val name: String) {
  override def toString = name
}

class Dog(override val name: String) extends Pet(name)

def workWithPets(pets: Array[Pet]) {}
```

We've defined two classes—a Dog that extends a class Pet. We have a method workWithPets() that accepts an array of Pets but really does nothing. Now, let's create an array of Dogs:

```scala
val dogs = Array(new Dog("Rover"), new Dog("Comet"))
```

If we send the dogs to the previous method, we will get a compilation error:

```scala
workWithPets(dogs) // Compilation ERROR
```

Scala will complain at the call to workWithPets()—we can't send an array of Dogs to a method that accepts an array of Pets. But, the method is benign. However, Scala doesn't know that, and it's trying to protect us. We have to tell Scala that it's okay to let this happen. Here's an example of how we can do that:

```scala
def playWithPets[T <: Pet](pets: Array[T]) =
  println("Playing with pets: " + pets.mkString(", "))
```

We've defined the method playWithPets() with a special syntax. T <: Pet indicates that the class represented by T is derived from Pet. This syntax is used to define an upper bound—if you visualize the class hierarchy, Pet is the upper bound of type T—T can be any type Pet or lower in the hierarchy. By specifying the upper bound, we're telling Scala that the parameterized type T of the parameter array must be at least an array of Pet but can be an array of any class derived from Pet. So, now we are allowed to make the following call:

```scala
playWithPets(dogs)
```

Here's the corresponding output:

```
Playing with pets: Rover, Comet
```

If you try to send an array of Objects or an array of objects of some type that does not derive from Pets, you'll get a compilation error.

Supporting Contravariance

Now let's say we want to copy pets from one collection to another. We can write a method named copy() that accepts two parameters of type Array[Et]. However, that will not help us send an array of Dogs. Furthermore, we should be able to copy from an array of Dogs into an array of Pets. In other words, it's okay for the receiving array to be a collection of supertypes of the class of the source array in this scenario. What we need is a lower bound:

MakingUseOfTypes/PlayWithPets.scala
```
def copyPets[S, D >: S](fromPets: Array[S], toPets: Array[D]) = { //...
}

val pets = new Array[Pet](10)
copyPets(dogs, pets)
```

We've constrained the destination array's parameterized type (D) to be a supertype of the source array's parameterized type (S). In other words, S (for a source type like Dog) sets the lower bounds for the type D (for a destination type like Dog or Pet)—it can be any type that is type S or its supertype.

Customizing Variance on a Collection

In the previous two examples, we controlled the parameters of methods in the method definition. You can also control this behavior if you're the author of a collection—that is, if you assume that it's okay for a collection of derived to be treated as a collection of base. You can do this by marking the parameterized type as +T instead of T, as in the following example:

MakingUseOfTypes/MyList.scala
```
class MyList[+T] //...
var list1 = new MyList[Int]
var list2 : MyList[Any] = null
list2 = list1 // OK
```

Here, +T tells Scala to allow covariance; in other words, during type checking, it asks Scala to accept a type or its base type. So, we're able to assign a MyList[Int] to MyList[Any]. Remember, this was not possible for Array[Int]. However, this is possible for the functional list List implemented in the Scala library—we'll discuss this in Chapter 8, *Collections*, on page 129.

Similarly, you can ask Scala to support contravariance on your types using -T instead of T for parameterized types.

By default, the Scala compiler strictly enforces the variance. We can request lenience for covariance or contravariance. In any case, the Scala compiler will check for type soundness of variance.

Implicit Type Conversions

The compile-time type checking is quite rigorous in Scala. If you don't pass the type expected by a function or invoke an arbitrary method on an instance, you'll get a stern error at compile time. While this is good most of the time, occasionally you'd want to pass an instance of one type where another type is expected—mainly where such use will make code intuitive, more expressive, and easy to write. Likewise, you may want to invoke your own domain-specific convenient methods on third-party classes. This can give an illusion of greater power to open and add methods to existing third-party classes. All this is possible in Scala with just a few tricks by using type conversions.

There are two different ways to implement type conversions—writing implicit functions and creating implicit classes. The first approach has been around for a while in Scala, but the implicit classes are relatively new. Let's explore both.

Implicit Functions

By default, at the sight of an invalid method call, the Scala compiler gets ready to snicker. However, if it sees an implicit conversion in the current scope, it quietly transforms your object using that conversion and applies the method you ask for. Let's see how with a domain-specific language (DSL)—a fluent syntax—we'll implement such an example.

When working with date and time operations it'd be quite convenient and more readable to write code like this:

```
2 days ago
5 days from_now
```

That looks more like data input than code—one of the characteristics of DSLs. At the first glance, we took advantage of Scala's optional treatment of dot and parentheses. But there's more—we're calling a method days() on 2 and sending in a variable ago in the first expression. In the second expression, we're calling the method on 5 and sending in a variable from_now. Since Int does not have that method, it would appear like magic if that code works.

If we try to compile the previous code, Scala will complain that days() is not a method on Int. But, relentless programmers don't easily take no for an answer;

we'll get it working. We can ask Scala to quietly convert the Int to something that will help accomplish the previous operation.

With implicit type conversion you can extend the language to create your own vocabulary that's specific to your application/domain or to create your own domain-specific languages.

Let's start with some crufty code to first understand the concept and then refactor that into a nice class.

We need to define the variables ago and from_now and ask Scala to accept the days() method. Defining variables is easy, but for it to accept the method, let's create a class DateHelper that takes an Int as a constructor parameter:

```scala
import scala.language.implicitConversions
import java.time.LocalDate

class DateHelper(offset: Int) {
  def days(when: String) = {
    val today = LocalDate.now
    when match {
      case "ago" => today.minusDays(offset)
      case "from_now" => today.plusDays(offset)
      case _ => today
    }
  }
}
```

If you want to use implicit conversion functions, Scala will require import scala.language.implicitConversions. This readily warns the reader that type conversions are ahead in code.

The DateHelper class provides the days() method we want. The match() method used in that method is part of Scala's pattern matching facility—we'll look at that in Chapter 9, *Pattern Matching and Regular Expressions*, on page 143. Since DateHelper is a regular class we can create an instance and invoke the days() method. But, the real fun is in calling the days() method on an Int and letting Scala quietly convert the Int to an instance of DateHelper so the method can be called. The Scala feature that enables this trick comes in the form of a simple function prefixed with the implicit keyword.

If a function is marked as implicit Scala will automatically pick it up if it's present in the current scope, visible through current imports, or present in the current file. Let's create the implicit function and make our fluent calls:

```scala
implicit def convertInt2DateHelper(offset: Int) = new DateHelper(offset)

val ago = "ago"
```

```
val from_now = "from_now"

val past = 2 days ago
val appointment = 5 days from_now

println(past)
println(appointment)
```

If you run the code along with the definition of DateHelper, you'll see that Scala automatically converts the given numbers into an instance of DateHelper and invokes the days() method to produce this result:

```
2015-08-11
2015-08-18
```

Now that the code works, it's time to clean it up a bit. We don't want to write the implicit converter each time we need the conversion. By tucking away the converter into a separate singleton object, we get better reusability and ease of use. Let's move the converter to the companion object of DateHelper:

MakingUseOfTypes/DateHelper.scala

```scala
import scala.language.implicitConversions
import java.time.LocalDate

class DateHelper(offset: Int) {
  def days(when: String) = {
    val today = LocalDate.now
    when match {
      case "ago" => today.minusDays(offset)
      case "from_now" => today.plusDays(offset)
      case _ => today
    }
  }
}

object DateHelper {
  val ago = "ago"
  val from_now = "from_now"
  implicit def convertInt2DateHelper(offset: Int) = new DateHelper(offset)
}
```

When we import DateHelper, Scala will automatically find the converter for us. This is because Scala applies conversions in the current scope and in the scope of what we import.

Here's an example of using the implicit conversion we wrote in DateHelper:

```
MakingUseOfTypes/DaysDSL.scala
import DateHelper._

object DaysDSL extends App {
  val past = 2 days ago
  val appointment = 5 days from_now

  println(past)
  println(appointment)
}
```

Here's the result of compiling and running the code:

```
2015-08-11
2015-08-18
```

Scala has a number of implicit conversions already defined in the Predef object and the package object of the scala package, which are imported by default. For example, when we write 1 to 3, Scala implicitly converts 1 from Int to the rich wrapper RichInt and invokes its to() method.

If multiple conversions are visible, Scala will pick the one that's appropriate so the code compiles. However, Scala applies at most one implicit conversion at a time. If multiple conversions compete at the same method call, Scala will give an error.

The magic of calling 2 days ago is nice, but we had to write one class and one conversion function. What name should we give to that function, where do we put it, and how do programmers find it? We can get rid of the conversion function, and all those concerns, with implicit classes. You write an implicit class and Scala takes care of creating the necessary plumbing, as you'll see next.

Implicit Classes

Instead of creating a regular class and a separate implicit conversion method, you can tell Scala that the sole purpose of a class is to serve as an adapter or converter. To do this, mark a class as an implicit class. When using an implicit class Scala places a few restrictions. Most notably it can't be a stand-alone class—it has to be within a singleton object, a class, or a trait. Let's rework the fluent date example to use an implicit class.

```
MakingUseOfTypes/DateUtil.scala
object DateUtil {
  val ago = "ago"
  val from_now = "from_now"

  implicit class DateHelper(val offset: Int) {
```

```scala
  def days(when: String) = {
    import java.time.LocalDate
    val today = LocalDate.now
    when match {
      case "ago" => today.minusDays(offset)
      case "from_now" => today.plusDays(offset)
      case _ => today
    }
  }
 }
}
```

The singleton object DateUtil serves as a placeholder for the variables or constants and the modified class DateHelper, now declared implicit, in its new home. We also moved the import of LocalDate to within the class where it's needed. Scala does not require the implicitConversions import when implicit classes are used. This is because, unlike arbitrary conversion functions that can be pulled in, the implicit classes are more visible from the declaration and the import of their scope.

Using the implicit conversion is not much different from the previous example. Let's use the modified conversion:

MakingUseOfTypes/DateUtil.scala
```scala
object UseDateUtil extends App {
  import DateUtil._

  val past = 2 days ago
  val appointment = 5 days from_now

  println(past)
  println(appointment)
}
```

The definition of ago and from_now came from the singleton object DateUtil, as did the implicit conversion through the DateHelper that is also part of this housing object.

For providing fluency, ease of use, and extending existing classes with domain-specific methods, prefer implicit classes over implicit methods—implicit classes express the intention more clearly and also are easier to locate than arbitrary conversion methods. They can also remove object creation overhead when combined with value classes, which you'll see next.

Value Classes

Code like 2 days ago is charming, but what's the catch? Let's take a look under the hood to see what the Scala compiler actually did to that expression.

Compile the file DateUtil.scala using scalac and run javap -c UseDateUtil\$, the shadow inner class that Scala created for the singleton, and quickly search for the call to the days() method. Let's examine a few lines of bytecode around the method call:

```
     5: invokevirtual #73                      // Method
DateUtil$.DateHelper:(I)LDateUtil$DateHelper;
     8: getstatic     #69                      // Field
DateUtil$.MODULE$:LDateUtil$;
    11: invokevirtual #77                      // Method
DateUtil$.ago:()Ljava/lang/String;
    14: invokevirtual #83                      // Method
DateUtil$DateHelper.days:(Ljava/lang/String;)Ljava/time/LocalDate;
```

Here's the cost of the fluent code—an instance of DateHelper is created and then the method days() is called on it. Each time you call a fluent method you incur an object creation overhead. The result: The more implicit conversions you make, the more short-lived garbage objects you create.

Scala's value objects directly address this problem. These little garbage objects are eliminated and the compiler will directly compile the fluent method calls using a combination of functions without an intermediate object. To create a value object, simply extend your class from AnyVal. Let's modify our DateHelper to a value class.

```
implicit class DateHelper(val offset: Int) extends AnyVal {
```

Extending from AnyVal is the only change we made to DateHelper. The rest of the code in the previous example is unchanged. Now compile the code and take a peek at the bytecode like you did before:

```
     8: invokevirtual #78                      // Method
DateUtil$.DateHelper:(I)I
    11: getstatic     #74                      // Field
DateUtil$.MODULE$:LDateUtil$;
    14: invokevirtual #82                      // Method
DateUtil$.ago:()Ljava/lang/String;
    17: invokevirtual #86                      // Method
DateUtil$DateHelper$.days$extension:(ILjava/lang/String;)Ljava/time/LocalDate;
```

Examine the first lines of the two javap excerpts, one from before the change to DateHelper and the one after. Instead of returning an instance of DateHelper, the compiler has now synthesized the method to return the primitive shown as I for int. Furthermore, the last lines in the two excerpts show that the days() method is no longer called on an instance but is written as an extension method. In short, Scala has eliminated the short-lived garbage instance—there's no longer an instantiation toll to use fluent extension methods.

The implicit wrapper classes like RichInt and RichDouble in Scala are implemented as value classes. While you can write your own implicit classes as value classes, value classes are not limited to this use.

Value classes are useful anywhere a simple value or primitive is adequate but instead you want to use a class for better abstraction. In this case, a value class can give you the best of both worlds: better design and more expressive code without really using an explicit object. Let's dig into this further with an example.

We can better represent a pet's name using a class Name than a mere String. Let's create a Name and use it in a few contexts.

```
MakingUseOfTypes/NameExample.scala
class Name(val value: String) {
  override def toString = value
  def length = value.length
}

object UseName extends App {
  def printName(name: Name) {
    println(name)
  }

  val name = new Name("Snowy")
  println(name.length)
  printName(name)
}
```

The class Name has an immutable field named value, a method to return the length of the name, and one to get a string representation. The printName() method receives an instance of Name, as we'd expect. The name variable is of type Name. Let's compile this code and look at relevant parts of the bytecode:

```
      5: ldc            #76                // String Snowy
      7: invokespecial #79                // Method
Name."<init>":(Ljava/lang/String;)V
     10: putfield       #71                // Field name:LName;
     13: getstatic      #64                // Field
scala/Predef$.MODULE$:Lscala/Predef$;
     16: aload_0
     17: invokevirtual #81                // Method name:()LName;
     20: invokevirtual #85                // Method Name.length:()I
     23: invokestatic  #91                // Method
scala/runtime/BoxesRunTime.boxToInteger:(I)Ljava/lang/Integer;
     26: invokevirtual #68                // Method
scala/Predef$.println:(Ljava/lang/Object;)V
     29: aload_0
     30: aload_0
```

```
31: invokevirtual #81              // Method name:()LName;
34: invokevirtual #93              // Method printName:(LName;)V
37: return
```

There are no surprises here—the compiler creates an instance of Name, invokes the length() method on that instance, and passes the instance to printName(). Name is a full-blown class. Value classes give us all the benefits of abstraction, but the underlying representation is preserved as a primitive like String, int, and so forth.

By rewriting the Name class as a value class—since it merely wraps a string—we can reap all the benefits of abstraction and preserve it as primitive at the bytecode level. Here's the change to the Name class.

```scala
class Name(val value: String) extends AnyVal {
```

Now let's compile and take a peek at the relevant bytecode again:

```
1: ldc           #78              // String Snowy
3: putfield      #75              // Field
name:Ljava/lang/String;
6: getstatic     #64              // Field
scala/Predef$.MODULE$:Lscala/Predef$;
9: getstatic     #83              // Field Name$.MODULE$:LName$;
12: aload_0
13: invokevirtual #85             // Method
name:()Ljava/lang/String;
16: invokevirtual #89             // Method
Name$.length$extension:(Ljava/lang/String;)I
19: invokestatic  #95             // Method
scala/runtime/BoxesRunTime.boxToInteger:(I)Ljava/lang/Integer;
22: invokevirtual #72             // Method
scala/Predef$.println:(Ljava/lang/Object;)V
25: aload_0
26: aload_0
27: invokevirtual #85             // Method
name:()Ljava/lang/String;
30: invokevirtual #97             // Method
printName:(Ljava/lang/String;)V
33: return
```

A small change to the source code, but it's a lot more efficient at the bytecode level. At the source code level printName() is still receiving an instance of Name, but at the bytecode level it is taking an instance of String. Likewise the call to the length() method changed from a call on an instance to a call of an extension method. Also, the variable name is of type String instead of Name.

Once again, a value class helped eliminate instantiation, but at the same time, it helped create a better abstraction in code.

That was pretty neat, but don't assume that value classes always avoid instance creation. Scala bends over backward to optimize code and eliminate instantiation; however, there are times when it does create instances for value classes.

Scala will create an instance of value classes if you assign the value to another type or treat it as if it were another type. For example, try adding the following code to the previous example.

```
val any : Any = name
```

If you compile and examine the bytecode, you'll notice an instance of Name is created. In order to treat the value as Any, or anything else other than the inherent type of the underlying primitive—String in this example—Scala will create an instance of the value classes. Likewise, if you assign values to an array or make decisions based on its runtime type information, Scala will create instances of the value classes.

Since Scala does not guarantee that objects are not created, it appears as though it will be quite challenging to know for sure if there's a overhead or not. You may wonder whether you should be peeking at the bytecode each time—but don't sweat it. Scala creates instances only under these situations and for the most part it will optimize the code. If performance of the code is quite adequate, don't worry if a particular optimization was done or not. If performance of the code needs improvement, based on real usage and not beliefs, then dig into the bytecode to ensure the optimizations happen where you expect.

Using Implicit Conversions

Let's create a practical example of implicit conversions using string interpolators. Scala has some nice built-in string interpolators—see *String Interpolation*, on page 34—but you can also create your own custom interpolators quite easily by using the concepts we've seen in this chapter. We'll create a custom interpolator that will mask out select values from the processed string. To show that the interpolation can return something other than String—just about any object—we'll return a StringBuilder as the result of processing the string. But first let's revisit string interpolation to explore some concepts we need for the implementation.

When Scala sees the form

```
interpolatorName"text1 $expr1 text2 $expr2"
```

the compiler turns that into a function call on a special class named StringContext after separating the texts and the expressions. In effect, it translates the example form to

```
new StringContext("text1", "text2", "").interpolatorName(expr1, expr2)
```

The separated-out texts are sent as arguments to the constructor of StringContext and are available through its parts property. The expressions, on the other hand, are passed as arguments to the StringContext's method with the name of the interpolator. In the arguments sent to the constructor, each argument is a piece of text before an expression, with the last argument representing text that follows the last expression. In this example, it's empty ("") since there's no text after the last expression.

As we saw earlier, the three functions that StringContext already provides are s(), f(), and raw(). We'll create a new interpolator named mask() that will only partially display select expressions in the processed string. Let's first use the interpolator as if it were a built-in function. Once we get a grasp of the intent from an example use, we'll then create the interpolator.

MakingUseOfTypes/mask.scala
```scala
object UseInterpolator extends App {
  import MyInterpolator._

  val ssn = "123-45-6789"
  val account = "0246781263"
  val balance = 20145.23

  println(mask"""Account: $account
    |Social Security Number: $ssn
    |Balance: $$^${balance}
    |Thanks for your business.""".stripMargin)
}
```

The call to println() receives a string with the yet-to-be-written mask interpolation. The string attached to mask is a heredoc (see *Strings and Multiline Raw Strings*, on page 33) with texts and expressions. Our mask() interpolator will return a StringBuilder with each expression's string representation converted, where all but the last four characters are replaced with "...," unless the expression is preceded with a caret (^). In the example, we're asking the mask() function to keep the value of balance intact by placing a caret in front of it, but the display of the other two expressions, account and ssn, will be altered.

To process this string Scala will transform the code with mask() to

```
new StringContext("Account:", "Social...", ...).mask(account, ssn, balance)
```

However, there is no mask() method in StringContext. That should not deter us; there's no days() function in integer but we made the code 2 days ago work. We'll apply the same trick of implicit conversion here.

Since the compiler is looking to call a method on the StringContext, our implicit value class should take an instance of StringContext as its constructor parameter and implement the mask() method—it's that simple. Let's get to the code.

```
MakingUseOfTypes/MyInterpolator.scala
object MyInterpolator {
  implicit class Interpolator(val context: StringContext) extends AnyVal {
    def mask(args: Any*) = {
      val processed = context.parts.zip(args).map { item =>
        val (text, expression) = item
        if(text.endsWith("^"))
          s"${text.split('^')(0)}$expression"
        else
          s"$text...${expression.toString takeRight 4}"
      }.mkString

      new StringBuilder(processed).append(context.parts.last)
    }
  }
}
```

The implicit value class Interpolator is housed in the singleton MyInterpolator. It takes an instance of StringContext as the constructor parameter, and extends AnyVal.

As its core behavior, the mask() method combines the expressions given as parameters and the texts available in the StringContext's parts. We can easily combine these two collections into one, much like the way we can combine the two sides of a winter jacket—using the zip() function. This function works with two arrays—the texts and the expressions in this example—and produces one array of tuples. Each element in the tuple has one text and the expression that follows the text. One excess text that follows the last expression is discarded by the zip() function—we'll take care of this in the last step. We use the map() method that we saw in Chapter 1, *Exploring Scala*, on page 3 to transform from this array of tuples to an array of combined strings. As we iterate through each text-expression pair, if a text ends with a caret, we leave the expression intact. Otherwise, we replace it with the ellipsis and last four characters using the takeRight() method. Finally we combine the array of strings with the mkString() method and append the final text that follows the last expression to the result StringBuilder.

Let's compile and run the code using the following commands:

```
scalac MyInterpolator.scala mask.scala
scala UseInterpolator
```

The output of our interpolator, in full glory, is shown next:

```
Account: ...1263
Social Security Number: ...6789
Balance: $20145.23
Thanks for your business.
```

This is a little example, but it brought together a number of nice little concepts. We used singletons, implicit value classes, the map() function with functional style to iterate and process the elements, a custom string interpolator, and more.

Take some time to play with the code, evolve it, introduce some more formatting, and implement it, while keeping the implementation close to the functional style.

Wrapping Up

In this chapter, we discussed the static typing in Scala and its type inference capabilities. You learned about some important types in Scala and also how to take advantage of implicit conversions. These features make code concise and expressive, in addition to facilitating good type verification. With the understanding of typing, type inference, and the idiomatic style of writing methods, you're all set to learn and enjoy concepts that lead to more conciseness in the next chapter.

Part II

Diving Into Scala

It's time to dive deeper into Scala. You'll learn:
- *to create and use function values*
- *to program with traits*
- *to make use of different collections*
- *the power of pattern matching*
- *about tail call optimization*

CHAPTER 6

Function Values and Closures

Functions are first-class citizens in functional programming. You can pass functions to functions as parameters, return them from functions, and even nest functions within functions. These higher-order functions are called *function values* in Scala. Closures are special forms of function values that close over or bind to variables defined in another scope or context.

In addition to object decomposition, you can structure applications around function values as building blocks, since Scala supports both the OO and functional styles of programming. This can lead to concise, reusable code. In this chapter, you'll learn to use function values and closures in Scala.

Limitations of Normal Functions

At the core of functional programming are functions or so-called higher-order functions. To get a feel for what these are, let's start with a familiar function.

To find the sum of values in a given range 1 to number we'd probably write code like this:

```
def sum(number: Int) = {
  var result = 0
  for(i <- 1 to number) {
    result += i
  }
  result
}
```

That's familiar code—we've all written code like this a million times over in different languages. That's called imperative style—you tell not only what to do, but also how to do it. That's dictating a low level of details. In Scala, you can write imperative code like this where it make sense, but you're not restricted to that.

While this code got the work done, it's not extensible. Now, if in addition, we need to count the number of even numbers and the number of odd numbers in the given range, that code will fall flat; we'd be tempted to use the infamous reuse by copy-paste-and-change pattern. Cringe! That's the best we can do with normal functions, but that'd lead to code duplication with poor reuse.

Let's take another shot at the simple problem on hand. Instead of the imperative style, we can program the same problem in functional style. We can pass an anonymous function to the function that iterates over the range. In other words, we make use of a level of indirection. The functions we pass can hold different logic to achieve different tasks over the iteration. Let's rewrite the previous code in functional style.

Extensibility with Higher-Order Functions

Functions that can take other functions as parameters are called *higher-order functions*. They reduce code duplication, increase reuse, and make code concise as well. We can create functions within functions, assign them to references, and pass them around to other functions. Scala internally deals with these so-called function values by creating them as instances of special classes. In Scala, function values are really objects.

Let's rewrite the previous example using function values. With this new version, we can perform different operations, such as summing numbers or counting the number of even numbers on a range of values.

We'll start by first extracting the common code into a method named totalResultOverRange(), by looping over the range of values:

```
def totalResultOverRange(number: Int, codeBlock: Int => Int) = {
  var result = 0
  for (i <- 1 to number) {
    result += codeBlock(i)
  }
  result
}
```

We've defined two parameters for the method totalResultOverRange(). The first one is an Int for the range of values to iterate over. The second one is special; it's a function value. The name of the parameter is codeBlock, and its type is a function that accepts an Int and returns an Int. The result of the method totalResultOverRange() is itself an Int.

The symbol => specifies and separates the function's expected input to the left and the expected return type to the right. The syntax form input => output is intended to help us think of a function as transforming input to output without having any side effects.

In the body of the totalResultOverRange() method we iterate over the range of values, and for each element we invoke the given function, referenced by the variable codeBlock. The given function is expected to receive an Int, representing an element in the range, and return an Int as a result of computation on that element. The computation or operation itself is left to be defined by the caller of the method totalResultOverRange(). We total the results of calls to the given function value and return that total.

The code in totalResultOverRange() removed the duplication from the example in *Limitations of Normal Functions*, on page 101. Here is how we'd call that method to get the sum of values in the range:

```
println(totalResultOverRange(11, i => i))
```

We passed two arguments to the method. The first argument is the upper limit (11) of the range we want to iterate over. The second argument is actually an anonymous just-in-time function—that is, a function with no name but only parameter(s) and an implementation. The implementation, in this example, simply returns the given parameter. The symbol =>, in this case, separates the parameter list on the left from the implementation on the right. Scala was able to infer that the type of the parameter, i, is an Int from the parameter list of totalResultOverRange(). Scala will give us an error if the parameter's type or the result type does not match with what's expected.

For a simple totaling of the values, it may appear that the call to totalResultOverRange() with a number and a function as arguments was rather cumbersome, compared to the call to the normal function sum() we wrote earlier. However, the new version is extensible and we can call it in a similar way for other operations. For example, instead of finding the sum, if we'd like to total the even numbers in the range, we'd call the function like this:

```
println(totalResultOverRange(11, i => if (i % 2 == 0) i else 0))
```

The function value we pass as argument in this case returns the input parameter if it is even; otherwise it returns a 0. Thus, the function totalResultOverRange() will only total even values in the given range.

If we'd like to total the odd numbers, we can call the function as follows:

```
println(totalResultOverRange(11, i => if (i % 2 != 0) i else 0))
```

Unlike the sum() function, we saw how the totalResultOverRange() function can be extended to perform a total for a different selection of values in the range.

This is a direct benefit of the indirection we achieved using higher-order functions.

Any number of parameters of a function or a method can be function values, and they can be any parameter, not just the trailing parameter.

It was quite easy to make the code DRY (see *The Pragmatic Programmer: From Journeyman to Master [HT00]* by Andy Hunt and David Thomas for details about the Don't Repeat Yourself [DRY] principle) using function values. We gathered up the common code into a function, and the differences were rolled into arguments of method calls. Functions and methods that accept function values are commonplace in the Scala library, as we'll see in Chapter 8, *Collections*, on page 129. Scala makes it easy to pass multiple parameters to function values, and define the types of arguments as well, if you desire.

Function Values with Multiple Parameters

In the previous example, the function values received one parameter. Function values can receive zero or more parameters. Let's take a look at a few examples to learn how to define function values with different numbers of parameters.

In its simplest form, a function value may not even receive any parameter, but may return a result. Such a function value is like a factory—it constructs and returns an object. Let's take a look at an example of defining and using a zero parameter function value:

```
def printValue(generator: () => Int) = {
  println(s"Generated value is ${generator()}")
}

printValue(() => 42)
```

For the method printValue() function, we've defined the parameter generator as a function value that takes no parameters, indicated by an empty set of parentheses, and returns an Int. Within the function, we call the function value like we call any function, like so: generator(). In the call to the printValue() function, we've created a function value that takes no parameters and returns a fixed value, 42. Instead of returning a fixed value, the function value may return a random value, a new value, or a pre-cached value.

You know how to pass zero or one arguments. To pass more than one argument you need to provide a comma-separated list of parameter types in the definition. Let's look at an example of a function inject() that passes the result of the operation on one element in an array of Int to the operation on the next element. It's a way to cascade or accumulate results from operations on each element.

```
def inject(arr: Array[Int], initial: Int, operation: (Int, Int) => Int) = {
  var carryOver = initial
  arr.foreach(element => carryOver = operation(carryOver, element) )
  carryOver
}
```

The inject() method takes three parameters: an array of Int, an initial Int value to inject into the operation, and the operation itself as a function value. In the method we set a variable carryOver to the initial value. We loop through the elements of the given array using the foreach() method. This method accepts a function value as a parameter, which it invokes with each element in the array as an argument. In the function that we send as an argument to foreach(), we're invoking the given operation with two arguments: the carryOver value and the context element. We assign the result of the operation call to the variable carryOver so it can be passed as an argument in the subsequent call to the operation. When we're done calling the operation for each element in the array, we return the final value of carryOver.

Let's look at a couple of examples of using the inject() method. Here's how we would total the elements in the array:

```
val array = Array(2, 3, 5, 1, 6, 4)
val sum = inject(array, 0, (carry, elem) => carry + elem)
println(s"Sum of elements in array is $sum")
```

The first argument to the method inject() is an array whose elements we'd like to sum. The second argument is an initial value 0 for the sum. The third argument is the function that carries out the operation of totaling the elements, one at a time. If instead of totaling the elements we'd like to find the maximum value, we can use the same inject() method:

```
val max =
  inject(array, Integer.MIN_VALUE, (carry, elem) => Math.max(carry, elem))
println(s"Max of elements in array is  $max")
```

The function value passed as an argument to the inject() function in the second call returns the maximum of the two parameters passed to it.

Here's the output of executing the previous two calls to the inject() method:

```
Sum of elements in array is 21
Max of elements in array is  6
```

The previous example helped us see how to pass multiple parameters. However, to navigate over elements in a collection and perform operations, we don't have to really roll out our own inject() method. The Scala library already has this method built in. It is the foldLeft() method. Here's an example of using the built-in foldLeft() method to get the sum and max of elements in an array:

```
val array = Array(2, 3, 5, 1, 6, 4)

val sum = array.foldLeft(0) { (sum, elem) => sum + elem }
val max = array.foldLeft(Integer.MIN_VALUE) { (large, elem) =>
  Math.max(large, elem) }

println(s"Sum of elements in array is $sum")
println(s"Max of elements in array is $max")
```

In an effort to make the code more concise, Scala defines some shortcut names and notations for select methods. The foldLeft() method has an equivalent operator /:. We can use foldLeft() or the equivalent /: to perform the previous actions. Methods that end with a colon (:) are treated special in Scala, as you'll learn in *Method Name Convention*, on page 137. Let's quickly take a look at using the equivalent operators instead of foldLeft():

```
val sum = (0 /: array) { (sum, elem) => sum + elem }
val max =
  (Integer.MIN_VALUE /: array) { (large, elem) => Math.max(large, elem) }
```

As an observant reader, you probably noticed the function value was placed inside curly braces instead of being sent as an argument to the foldLeft() method. That looks a lot better than sending those functions as arguments within parentheses. However, if we attempt the following on the inject() method, we will get an error:

FunctionValuesAndClosures/Inject3.scala
```
val sum = inject(array, 0) {(carryOver, elem) => carryOver + elem}
```

The previous code will result in the following error:

```
Inject3.scala:9: error: not enough arguments for method inject: (arr:
Array[Int], initial: Int, operation: (Int, Int) => Int)Int.
Unspecified value parameter operation.
val sum = inject(array, 0) {(carryOver, elem) => carryOver + elem}
                 ^

one error found
```

That was not quite what we'd like to see. Before you can get the same benefit of using the curly braces that the library method enjoyed, you have to learn one more concept—currying.

Currying

Currying in Scala transforms a function that takes more than one parameter into a function that takes multiple parameter lists. If you're calling a function multiple times with the same set of arguments, you can reduce the noise and spice up the code by using currying.

Let's see how Scala provides support for currying. Instead of writing a method that takes one parameter list with multiple parameters, write it with multiple parameter lists with one parameter each; you may have more than one parameter in each list as well. That is, instead of def foo(a: Int, b: Int, c: Int) = {}, write it as def foo(a: Int)(b: Int)(c: Int) {}. You can then call it as, for example, foo(1)(2)(3), foo(1){2}{3}, or even foo{1}{2}{3}.

Let's examine what goes on when we define a method with multiple parameter lists. Take a look at the following interactive REPL session:

```
scala> def foo(a: Int)(b: Int)(c:Int) = {}
foo: (a: Int)(b: Int)(c: Int)Unit

scala> foo _
res0: Int => (Int => (Int => Unit)) = <function1>

scala> :quit
```

We first defined the function foo() we discussed previously. Then we called foo _ to create a partially applied function—that is, a function with one or more parameters unbound. Partially applied functions are quite useful to create reusable convenience functions from other functions—we'll explore that in more detail in *Partially Applied Functions*, on page 112. We could've assigned the created partially applied function to a variable but did not care to in this example. We're focused on the message from the REPL. It shows a series of three transformations. Each function in the chain takes one Int and returns a partially applied function. The last one, however, results in a Unit.

The creation of partially applied functions when we curry is Scala's internal business. From a practical point of view, *currying* helps us to pass function values with syntactic sugar. Let's use currying to rewrite the inject() method from the previous section:

FunctionValuesAndClosures/Inject4.scala
```
def inject(arr: Array[Int], initial: Int)(operation: (Int, Int) => Int) = {
  var carryOver = initial
  arr.foreach(element => carryOver = operation(carryOver, element))
  carryOver
}
```

The multiple parameter lists are the only difference between the two versions of the inject() method. The first parameter list takes two parameters, and the second one takes only the function value.

Now we don't have to send the function values as comma-separated parameters within parentheses anymore. We can use the much nicer curly bracket to call this method:

FunctionValuesAndClosures/Inject4.scala
```
val sum = inject(array, 0) { (carryOver, elem) => carryOver + elem }
```

We managed to move the function value out of the parentheses by using currying. Nice syntax sugar, but we can go further—the function value itself can be made more concise in cases where the parameters are used once, as you'll see next.

Positional Notation for Parameters

Scala provides the notation _, the underscore, to represent parameters of a function value. While at first the underscore may appear cryptic, once you get used to it, you'll see that it makes the code concise and easy to work with. You can use this symbol to represent a parameter, but only if you plan to refer to the parameter just once in the function value. You can use the underscore multiple times in a function value, but each use represents a subsequent parameter. Let's look at an example to learn about this feature. In the following code we have a function value with two parameters:

FunctionValuesAndClosures/Underscore.scala
```
val arr = Array(1, 2, 3, 4, 5)

val total =  (0 /: arr) { (sum, elem) => sum + elem }
```

The /: method is used in this example to compute the sum of elements in the array represented by the variable arr. Within the function value, we're using each of the parameters, sum and elem, only once. Instead of naming these two parameters explicitly, we can replace these two names with an underscore:

FunctionValuesAndClosures/Underscore.scala
```
val total = (0 /: arr) { _ + _ }
```

The first occurrence of _ represents the first parameter, sum—the value carried over in the invocation of the function. The second occurrence represents the second parameter, elem—an element in the array.

Let that sink in—it's perfectly normal if that appears cryptic; once you get a good grasp of what's going on, it becomes easy to read and will soon become habitual when coding in Scala.

When you define parameters explicitly, in addition to providing the names you can define their types. When you use an underscore, both the name and the types are implied. If Scala can't determine the type, it will complain. If that happens, either provide the type for _ or step back to using parameter names with type.

Some may argue that code with underscores is terse and hard to read—the names sum and elem after all are quite helpful to have. That is a valid point. At the same time, especially for a single occurrence variable, the mere naming and immediate use of the parameter may not be all that helpful. In that case, you may want to use the _ instead. Use _ in places where the code is concise without any loss of readability, like in the following example:

FunctionValuesAndClosures/Underscore.scala
```
val negativeNumberExists1 = arr.exists { elem => elem < 0 }
val negativeNumberExists2 = arr.exists { _ < 0 }
```

The underscore replaced the explicit parameter elem and along the way reduced the noise in the function value. We can take this another step forward and reduce the noise further; let's see how.

Parameter Routing

Where it makes sense, you can make function values more concise than you've seen so far. Let's first create an example to find the maximum of an array of values, using the Math.max method to compare two values:

```
val largest =
  (Integer.MIN_VALUE /: arr) { (carry, elem) => Math.max(carry, elem)}
```

In the function value, we're sending the parameters carry and elem as arguments to the method max() to determine which of those two is larger. We use the result of that computation to eventually determine the largest element in the array. As you learned in the previous section, we can use _ to make the function value concise and eliminate the explicit parameters, like so:

```
val largest = (Integer.MIN_VALUE /: arr) { Math.max(_, _)}
```

The _ can represent not only a single parameter; it can represent the entire parameter list as well. We can modify the call to max() as follows:

```
val largest = (Integer.MIN_VALUE /: arr) { Math.max _ }
```

In the previous code, the _ represents the entire parameter list, that is, (parameter1, parameter2). To merely pass the received parameters to the underlying method in the same order as received, we don't even need the ceremony of the _. We can further simplify the previous code:

```
val largest = (Integer.MIN_VALUE /: arr) { Math.max }
```

The Scala compiler is doing quite a bit of work to verify that this code is syntactically correct. It first looks up the signature of the method /: to determine that it takes two parameter lists—the first parameter list expects an object and the second expects a function value. The compiler further determines that the function value should take two parameters. Once the compiler knows the signature of the expected function value, it decides the function value we provided takes two parameters since it's missing the parameter list—there's no => symbol; we only provided an implementation. The compiler also knows that the method max() takes two arguments but we specified none. It puts two and two together and performs the direct routing.

During the compilation check, if the inference in any of these steps fail, the compiler will report an error. For instance, suppose in the function value we called a method that took more than two parameters but we didn't specify any of the arguments. In this case the compiler will complain that it does not have enough arguments on hand, from the implicit parameters, to pass to that method.

Adjust the conciseness dial of Scala to the extent you're comfortable. While making use of the conciseness, ensure that the code doesn't become cryptic —strike that gentle balance.

You learned the different options to define function values. Function values are concise, but repeating the same function value in different calls will result in duplication. Let's look at ways to remove that duplication.

Reusing Function Values

Function values help create more reusable code and eliminate code duplication. But, embedding a piece of code as an argument to a method doesn't encourage reuse of that code. It's easy to avoid that duplication—you can create references to function values and therefore reuse them as well. Let's look at an example.

Let's create a class Equipment that expects a calculation routine for its simulation. We can send in the calculation as a function value to the constructor:

FunctionValuesAndClosures/Equipment.scala
```
class Equipment(val routine : Int => Int) {
  def simulate(input: Int) = {
    print("Running simulation...")
    routine(input)
  }
}
```

When we create instances of Equipment, we can pass in a function value as a parameter to the constructor, like so:

FunctionValuesAndClosures/EquipmentUseNotDry.scala

```
object EquipmentUseNotDry extends App {
  val equipment1 = new Equipment(
    {input => println(s"calc with $input"); input })
  val equipment2 = new Equipment(
    {input => println(s"calc with $input"); input })

  equipment1.simulate(4)
  equipment2.simulate(6)
}
```

Here's the output:

```
Running simulation...calc with 4
Running simulation...calc with 6
```

In the code, we want to use the same calculation code for both the Equipment instances. Unfortunately, that code is duplicated. The code is not DRY, and if we decide to change the calculation, we'd have to change both. It would be good to create the calculation once and reuse it. We can assign the function value to a val and reuse it like this:

FunctionValuesAndClosures/EquipmentUseDry.scala

```
object EquipmentUseDry extends App {
  val calculator = { input : Int => println(s"calc with $input"); input }

  val equipment1 = new Equipment(calculator)
  val equipment2 = new Equipment(calculator)

  equipment1.simulate(4)
  equipment2.simulate(6)
}
```

The output is shown here:

```
Running simulation...calc with 4
Running simulation...calc with 6
```

We stored the function value into a reference named calculator. Scala needed a little help with the type information when we defined this function value. In the earlier example, Scala inferred the parameter input as Int based on the context of the call. However, since we're defining this function value as standalone, we had to tell Scala the type of the parameter. We then passed the name of the reference as an argument to the constructor in the two instances we created.

In the previous example, we created a reference calculator to a function value. This may feel more natural since we're used to defining references/variables within functions or methods. However, in Scala, we can define full functions within other functions. Thus, there's a more idiomatic way of achieving the goal of reuse. Scala makes it easy to do the right thing. We can pass in a normal function where a function value is expected.

FunctionValuesAndClosures/EquipmentUseDry2.scala
```scala
object EquipmentUseDry2 extends App {
  def calculator(input: Int) = { println(s"calc with $input"); input }

  val equipment1 = new Equipment(calculator)
  val equipment2 = new Equipment(calculator)

  equipment1.simulate(4)
  equipment2.simulate(6)
}
```

We created our calculation as a function and passed in the name of the function as an argument to the constructor when we created those two instances. Scala comfortably treated that as a reference to a function value within the Equipment.

We don't have to compromise on good design principles and code quality when programming in Scala. On the contrary, it promotes good practices, and we should strive to make use of that when coding in Scala.

Saving away function values in variables and the ability to pass functions are not the only ways to reuse function values, as you'll see in the next section.

Partially Applied Functions

When you invoke a function, you're said to be *applying* the function to the arguments. If you pass all the expected arguments, you've fully applied the function and you get the result of the application or call. However, if you pass fewer than all the required parameters, you get back another function. This function is called a partially applied function. This gives the convenience of binding some arguments and leaving the rest to be filled in later. Here's an example:

FunctionValuesAndClosures/Log.scala
```scala
import java.util.Date

def log(date: Date, message: String) = {
 //...
 println(s"$date ---- $message")
}
```

```
val date = new Date(1420095600000L)
log(date, "message1")
log(date, "message2")
log(date, "message3")
```

In this code, the log() method takes two parameters: date and message. We want to invoke the method multiple times, with the same value for date but different values for message. We can eliminate the noise of passing the date to each call by partially applying that argument to the log() method.

In the next code sample, we first bind a value to the date parameter. We use the _ to leave the second parameter unbound. The result is a partially applied function that we've stored in the reference logWithDateBound. We can now invoke this new method with only the unbound argument message:

FunctionValuesAndClosures/Log.scala
```
val date = new Date(1420095600000L)
val logWithDateBound = log(date, _ : String)
logWithDateBound("message1")
logWithDateBound("message2")
logWithDateBound("message3")
```

Let's invite the Scala REPL to our party to help us better understand the partially applied function created from the log() function:

```
scala> import java.util.Date
import java.util.Date

scala> def log(date: Date, message: String) =  println(s"$date ----
$message")
log: (date: java.util.Date, message: String)Unit

scala> val logWithDateBound = log(new Date, _ : String)
logWithDateBound: String => Unit = <function1>

scala> :quit
```

From the details displayed by the REPL we can tell that the variable logWith-DateBound is a reference to a function that takes a String as a parameter and returns a Unit as result.

When you create a partially applied function, Scala internally creates a new class with a special apply() method. When you invoke the partially applied function, you're actually invoking that apply() method—see *Common Scala Collections*, on page 129 for more details on the apply() method. Scala makes extensive use of partially applied functions when pattern-matching messages that are received from an actor, as you'll see in Chapter 13, *Programming with Actors*, on page 195.

Next we'll dig into the scope in function values.

Closures

In the examples you've seen so far in this chapter, the variables and values used in the function values or code blocks were bound. You clearly knew what they were bound to, local variables or parameters. In addition, you can create code blocks with variables that are not bound. You'll have to bind them before you can invoke the function; however, they could bind to, or *close over*, variables outside of their local scope and parameter list. That's why they're called *closures*.

Let's look at a variation of the totalResultOverRange() method you saw earlier in this chapter. The method loopThrough() in this example iterates over the elements from 1 to a given number:

FunctionValuesAndClosures/Closure.scala
```scala
def loopThrough(number: Int)(closure: Int => Unit) {
  for (i <- 1 to number) { closure(i) }
}
```

The loopThrough() method takes a code block as the second parameter, and for each element in the range of 1 through its first parameter, it calls the given code block. Let's define a code block to pass to this method:

FunctionValuesAndClosures/Closure.scala
```scala
var result = 0
val addIt = { value:Int => result += value }
```

Here, we have defined a code block and assigned it to the variable named addIt. Within the code block, the variable value is bound to the parameter. However, the variable result is not defined within the block or its parameter list. This is actually bound to the variable result outside the code block. The code block stretches its hands and binds to a variable outside. Here's how we can use the code block in calls to the method loopThrough():

FunctionValuesAndClosures/Closure.scala
```scala
loopThrough(10) { elem => addIt(elem) }
println(s"Total of values from 1 to 10 is $result")

result = 0
loopThrough(5) { addIt }
println(s"Total of values from 1 to 5 is $result")
```

When we pass the closure to the method loopThrough(), the parameter value is bound to the parameter passed by loopThrough(), while result is bound to the variable in the context of the caller of loopThrough().

The binding did not get a copy of the variable's current value; it's actually bound to the variable itself. When we reset the value of result to 0, the closure sees this change as well. Furthermore, when the closure sets result, we see it in the main code. Here's another example of a closure bound to yet another variable product:

FunctionValuesAndClosures/Closure.scala

```
var product = 1
loopThrough(5) { product *= _ }
println(s"Product of values from 1 to 5 is $product")
```

In this case, the _ refers to the parameter passed in by loopThrough(), and product is bound to the variable with that name in the caller of loopThrough(). Here's the output from the three calls to loopThrough():

```
Total of values from 1 to 10 is 55
Total of values from 1 to 5 is 15
Product of values from 1 to 5 is 120
```

You've come a long way in this chapter; you learned about function values and how to use them. Let's now put function values to a practical use with the help of a design pattern.

Execute Around Method Pattern

Java programmers are familiar with the synchronized block. When we enter a synchronized block, it obtains a monitor (lock) on the given object. That monitor is automatically released when we leave the block. The release happens even if the code within the block throws an unhandled exception. That kind of deterministic behavior is nice to have in a number of other situations far beyond that specific example.

Thanks to function values, you can implement those constructs in Scala quite easily. Let's look at an example.

We have a class named Resource that needs to start some transaction automatically and end the transaction deterministically as soon as we're done using the object. We can rely on the constructor to correctly start the transaction. It's the ending part that poses the challenge. This falls right into the Execute Around Method pattern (see Kent Beck's *Smalltalk Best Practice Patterns* *[Bec96]*). We want to execute a pair of operations in tandem around an arbitrary set of operations on an object.

We can use function values to implement this pattern in Scala. Here is the code for the Resource class along with its companion object—see *Stand-alone and Companion Objects*, on page 62 for details on companion objects:

FunctionValuesAndClosures/Resource.scala
```scala
class Resource private() {
  println("Starting transaction...")
  private def cleanUp() { println("Ending transaction...") }
  def op1() = println("Operation 1")
  def op2() = println("Operation 2")
  def op3() = println("Operation 3")
}

object Resource {
  def use(codeBlock: Resource => Unit) {
    val resource = new Resource
    try {
      codeBlock(resource)
    }
    finally {
      resource.cleanUp()
    }
  }
}
```

We've marked the constructor of the Resource class private. Thus, we can't create an instance of this class outside the class and its companion object. This design forces us to use the object in a certain way, thus guaranteeing automatic and deterministic behavior. The cleanUp() method is declared private as well. The print statements are used as placeholders for real transaction operations. The transaction starts when the constructor is called and ends when cleanUp() is implicitly called. The usable instance methods of the Resource class are methods like op1(), op2(), and so on.

In the companion object, we have a method named use() that accepts a function value as a parameter. In the use() method we create an instance of Resource, and within the safeguard of the try and finally blocks, we send the instance to the given function value. In the finally block, we call the private instance method cleanUp() of the Resource. Pretty simple, eh? That's all it took to provide a deterministic call to necessary operations.

Now let's take a look at how we can use the Resource class. Here's some example code:

FunctionValuesAndClosures/Resource.scala
```scala
Resource.use { resource =>
  resource.op1()
  resource.op2()
```

Execute Around Method Pattern • 117

```
  resource.op3()
  resource.op1()
}
```

Here's the output:

```
Starting transaction...
Operation 1
Operation 2
Operation 3
Operation 1
Ending transaction...
```

We invoke the use() method of the Resource companion object and provide it with a code block. It sends an instance of Resource to us. By the time we get access to resource, the transaction has been started. We invoke the methods we desire—like op1() and op2()—on the instance of Resource. When we're done, at the time we leave the code block, the cleanUp() method of the Resource is automatically called by the use() method.

A variation of the previous pattern is described as the Loan pattern (see Appendix 2, *Web Resources*, on page 253). Use it if your intent is to deterministically dispose of non-memory resources. The resource-intensive object is considered to be on loan, and we're expected to return it promptly.

Here's an example of how to use this pattern:

FunctionValuesAndClosures/WriteToFile.scala
```
import java.io._

def writeToFile(fileName: String)(codeBlock : PrintWriter => Unit) = {
  val writer = new PrintWriter(new File(fileName))
  try { codeBlock(writer) } finally { writer.close() }
}
```

Now we can use the function writeToFile() to write some content to a file:

FunctionValuesAndClosures/WriteToFile.scala
```
writeToFile("output/output.txt") { writer =>
  writer write "hello from Scala"
}
```

When we run the code, the contents of the file output.txt are as follows:

```
hello from Scala
```

As a user of the method writeToFile(), we don't have to worry about closing the file. The file is on loan to us for use within the code block. We can write to the PrintWriter instance given to us, and upon return from the block, the file is automatically closed by the method.

Wrapping Up

In this chapter, we explored the concepts related to function values; functions are first-class citizens in Scala. You can use code blocks to enhance the functionality of another function. You can use them to specify a predicate, a query, or a constraint to the logic being implemented in a method. You can use them to alter the control flow of a method—for example, when iterating over a collection of values. You also learned about the Execute Around Method pattern, a valuable feature that you'll use quite frequently in Scala, both in your own code and most commonly when using the Scala library. In the next chapter, we'll walk through another interesting Scala idiom: traits.

CHAPTER 7

Traits

Java permits only single implementation inheritance, but that forces a model of linear hierarchy. The real world, however, is full of crosscutting concerns —concepts that cut across and affect abstractions that do not fall under a single class hierarchy. Security, logging, validation, transactions, and resource management are all examples of such crosscutting concerns in a typical enterprise application. Since we're limited to single class hierarchy, implementing these crosscutting concerns gets quite hard—it often requires duplication of code or use of heavyweight tools. Scala solves the problem using traits.

Traits are like interfaces with a partial implementation. Traits provide a middle ground between single and multiple inheritance because you can mix them in or include them in other classes. With this facility you can enhance a class or an instance with crosscutting features. With Scala's traits you can apply crosscutting concerns to arbitrary classes without the pain that arises from multiple implementation inheritance, as you'll learn in this chapter.

Understanding Traits

A *trait* is a behavior that can be mixed into or assimilated into a class hierarchy. For example, to model a *friend* abstraction, we can mix a Friend trait into any class—Man, Woman, Dog, and so on—without having to inherit all those classes from a common base class.

To understand the benefits of traits, let's design an example first without them. We'll start with a class Human and make it friendly. In the simplest form, a friend is someone who listens. To support this abstraction, here is the listen method that we'd add to the Human class:

```
class Human(val name: String) {
  def listen() = println(s"Your friend $name is listening")
}

class Man(override val name: String) extends Human(name)
class Woman(override val name: String) extends Human(name)
```

One disadvantage in this code is the friendly quality does not quite stand out and is merged into the Human class. Furthermore, a few weeks into development, we realize we forgot man's best friend. Dogs are great friends—they listen to us quietly when we have a lot to unload. But, it's hard to make a Dog a friend in the current design. We can't inherit a Dog from a Human for that purpose.

This is where Scala's traits come in. A *trait* is like an interface with a partial implementation. The vals and vars we define and initialize in a trait get internally implemented in the classes that mix the trait in. Any vals and vars defined but not initialized are considered abstract, and the classes that mix in these traits are required to implement them. We can reimplement the Friend concept as a trait:

UsingTraits/Friend.scala
```
trait Friend {
  val name: String
  def listen() = println(s"Your friend $name is listening")
}
```

Here we have defined Friend as a trait. It has a val named name that is treated as abstract. We also have the implementation of a listen() method. The actual definition or the implementation of name will be provided by the class that mixes in this trait. Let's look at ways to mix in the trait:

UsingTraits/Human.scala
```
class Human(val name: String) extends Friend

class Woman(override val name: String) extends Human(name)
class Man(override val name: String) extends Human(name)
```

The class Human mixes in the Friend trait. If a class does not extend from any other class, then use the extends keyword to mix in the trait. The class Human and its derived classes Man and Woman simply use the implementation of the listen() method provided in the trait. We can override this implementation if we like, as you'll see soon.

We can mix in any number of traits. To mix in additional traits, use the keyword with. We'll also use the keyword with to mix in the first trait if a class already extends from another class like the Dog in this next example. In addition to mixing in the trait, we have overridden its listen() method in Dog.

UsingTraits/Dog.scala

```scala
class Dog(val name: String) extends Animal with Friend {
  //optionally override method here.
  override def listen() = println(s"$name's listening quietly")
}
```

The base class of Dog is Animal, defined separately here:

UsingTraits/Animal.scala

```scala
class Animal
```

We can call the methods of a trait on the instances of classes that mix it in, and also treat a reference to such classes as a reference of the trait:

UsingTraits/UseFriend.scala

```scala
object UseFriend extends App {
  val john = new Man("John")
  val sara = new Woman("Sara")
  val comet = new Dog("Comet")

  john.listen
  sara.listen
  comet.listen

  val mansBestFriend : Friend = comet
  mansBestFriend.listen

  def helpAsFriend(friend: Friend) = friend.listen

  helpAsFriend(sara)
  helpAsFriend(comet)
}
```

Here's the output from the previous code:

```
Your friend John is listening
Your friend Sara is listening
Comet's listening quietly
Comet's listening quietly
Your friend Sara is listening
Comet's listening quietly
```

Traits look similar to classes but have some significant differences. First, they require the mixed-in class to implement the uninitialized (abstract) variables and values declared in them. Second, their constructors cannot take any parameters. Traits are compiled into Java interfaces with corresponding implementation classes that hold any methods implemented in the traits.

Traits do not suffer from the method collision problem that generally arises from multiple inheritance. They avoid it by late binding with the method of the class that mixes them in. A call to super within a trait resolves to a method on another trait or the class that mixes it in, as you'll soon see.

Mixing traits is not limited to classes. We can mix them into instances as well, as you'll learn next.

Selective Mixins

In the previous example, we mixed the trait Friend into the Dog class. Thus, *any* instance of the Dog class can now be treated as a Friend; that is, all Dogs are Friends.

That may be too sweeping in some cases. If we desire, we could mix traits selectively at an instance level. In that case, we can treat a specific instance of a class as a trait. Let's look at an example:

UsingTraits/Cat.scala
```
class Cat(val name: String) extends Animal
```

Cat does not mix in the Friend trait, so we can't treat an instance of Cat as a Friend. Any attempts to do so, as we can see here, will result in compilation errors:

UsingTraits/UseCat.scala
```
object UseCat extends App {
  def useFriend(friend: Friend) = friend.listen

  val alf = new Cat("Alf")
  val friend : Friend = alf // ERROR

  useFriend(alf) // ERROR
}
```

Here we can see the errors:

```
UseCat.scala:5: error: type mismatch;
 found    : Cat
 required: Friend
  val friend : Friend = alf // ERROR
                        ^
UseCat.scala:7: error: type mismatch;
 found    : Cat
 required: Friend
  useFriend(alf) // ERROR
            ^
two errors found
```

Scala, however, does offer help for cat lovers, and we can exclusively treat our special pet, *Angel*, as a Friend. When creating an instance, simply mark it using the with keyword:

```
UsingTraits/TreatCatAsFriend.scala
def useFriend(friend: Friend) = friend.listen

val angel = new Cat("Angel") with Friend
val friend : Friend = angel
angel.listen

useFriend(angel)
```

Here's the output:

```
Your friend Angel is listening
Your friend Angel is listening
```

Scala gives you the flexibility to treat all the instances of a class as a trait or to select only the instances you want. The latter is especially useful if you want to apply traits to preexisting classes, third-party classes, and even Java classes.

Next you'll see how traits can be used to implement a popular design pattern.

Decorating with Traits

You can use traits to decorate objects with capabilities—see the Decorator pattern in Gamma et al.'s *Design Patterns: Elements of Reusable Object-Oriented Software [GHJV95]*. This pattern can help keep the inheritance hierarchy relatively flat while providing reasonable extensibility. We'll explore this pattern, and how traits play a vital role, with an example.

Suppose we want to run different checks on an applicant—credit, criminal records, employment, and so on. We're not interested in all the checks all the time. An applicant for an apartment may need to be checked for credit history and a criminal record. On the other hand, an applicant for employment may need to be checked for a criminal record and previous employment. If we resort to creating specific classes for these groups of checks, we'll end up creating several classes for each permutation of checks we needed. Furthermore, if we decide to run additional checks, the class handling that group of checks would have to change. No, we want to avoid such class proliferation. We can be productive and mix in only specific checks required for each situation. Let's see how.

We'll introduce an abstract class Check that runs a general check on the application details:

```
UsingTraits/Decorator.scala
abstract class Check {
  def check : String = "Checked Application Details..."
}
```

For different types of checks like credit, criminal record, and employment, we create traits like these:

```
UsingTraits/Decorator.scala
trait CreditCheck extends Check {
  override def check : String = s"Checked Credit... ${super.check}"
}

trait EmploymentCheck extends Check {
  override def check : String = s"Checked Employment...${super.check}"
}

trait CriminalRecordCheck extends Check {
  override def check : String = s"Check Criminal Records...${super.check}"
}
```

We've extended these traits from the class Check since we intend to mix them into only those classes that extend from Check. In Scala, traits may be stand-alone or may be extended from a class. Extending adds two capabilities to traits: these traits can be mixed in only with classes that extend the base, and we can use the methods of the base within these traits.

We're interested in enhancing or decorating the implementation of the method check(), so we have to mark it as override. In our implementation of check(), we invoke super.check(). Within a trait, calls to a method using super go through late binding. This is not a call on the base class. Instead the call is forwarded to the class into which the trait is mixed in. If multiple traits are mixed in, the call is forwarded to the next trait in the chain, closer to the class the traits are mixed in to. We'll see this behavior when we complete this example.

We have one abstract class and three traits in the example so far. We don't have any concrete classes—we don't need any. If we want to run checks for an apartment application, we can put together an instance from the previous traits and the abstract class:

```
UsingTraits/Decorator.scala
val apartmentApplication =
  new Check with CreditCheck with CriminalRecordCheck

println(apartmentApplication.check)
```

On the other hand, we could run checks for employment like this:

UsingTraits/Decorator.scala

```
val employmentApplication =
  new Check with CriminalRecordCheck with EmploymentCheck

println(employmentApplication.check)
```

To run a different combination of checks, we simply have to mix in the traits the way we like. Let's look at the output of calling check() on the apartmentApplication and the employmentApplication instances:

```
Check Criminal Records...Checked Credit... Checked Application Details...
Checked Employment...Check Criminal Records...Checked Application
Details...
```

In both the calls, the rightmost traits serve as the first handlers and picked up the call to check(). They then, upon the call to super.check(), passed the call over to the trait on their left. Finally, the leftmost traits invoked the check() on the actual instances.

Traits are a powerful tool in Scala that help mix in crosscutting concerns, and we can use them to create highly extensible code with low ceremony. Rather than creating a hierarchy of classes and interfaces, we can cut down to the essential minimal code to achieve the design.

You know how to mix multiple traits, and you got a glimpse of method chaining. Scala handles method chaining quite effectively, in a way that enhances the already powerful mixin capability, as you'll see next.

Method Late Binding in Traits

In the previous example, the method check() of the Check class was concrete. Our traits extended from this class to override that method. We saw how the call to super.check() within the traits were bound to either the trait on the left or the class that mixes in. Things get a bit more complicated if the method(s) in the base class are abstract—the method binding has to be postponed until a concrete method is known. Let's explore this further here.

Let's write an abstract class Writer with one abstract method, writeMessage():

UsingTraits/MethodBinding.scala

```
abstract class Writer {
  def writeMessage(message: String)
}
```

Any class extending from this class is required to implement the writeMessage() method. If we extend a trait from this abstract class and call the abstract method using super, Scala will demand that we declare the method as abstract override. The combination of these two keywords is rather odd but conveys a dual intent. By using the keyword override, we're expressing our intention to provide an implementation of a known method from the base class. At the same time, we convey that the actual final "terminal" implementation for this method will be provided by the class that mixes in the trait. So, here's an example of traits that extend the previous class:

UsingTraits/MethodBinding.scala
```scala
trait UpperCaseWriter extends Writer {
  abstract override def writeMessage(message: String) =
    super.writeMessage(message.toUpperCase)
}

trait ProfanityFilteredWriter extends Writer {
  abstract override def writeMessage(message: String) =
    super.writeMessage(message.replace("stupid", "s-----"))
}
```

Scala does two things on the call to super.writeMessage() in this code. First, it performs late binding of that call. Second, it will insist that the class that mixes these traits provides an implementation of the method.

The UpperCaseWriter trait converts the given string to uppercase and passes it down the chain. The ProfanityFilteredWriter removes mildly rude words only—and only if they appeared in lowercase. This is with the intent to illustrate the ordering of the mixin.

Now, let's make use of these traits. First, let's write a class StringWriterDelegate that extends from the abstract class Writer and delegates writing the message to an instance of StringWriter:

UsingTraits/MethodBinding.scala
```scala
class StringWriterDelegate extends Writer {
  val writer = new java.io.StringWriter

  def writeMessage(message: String) = writer.write(message)
  override def toString : String = writer.toString
}
```

We could have mixed in one or more traits in the previous definition of String-WriterDelegate. Instead, let's mix in the traits at the time of creating an instance:

UsingTraits/MethodBinding.scala
```scala
val myWriterProfanityFirst =
  new StringWriterDelegate with UpperCaseWriter with ProfanityFilteredWriter

val myWriterProfanityLast =
  new StringWriterDelegate with ProfanityFilteredWriter with UpperCaseWriter
```

```
myWriterProfanityFirst writeMessage "There is no sin except stupidity"
myWriterProfanityLast writeMessage "There is no sin except stupidity"

println(myWriterProfanityFirst)
println(myWriterProfanityLast)
```

Since the ProfanityFilteredWriter is the rightmost trait in the first statement, it takes effect first. However, it takes effect second in the example in the second statement. Take the time to study the code. The method execution sequence for the two instances is shown in the following figure.

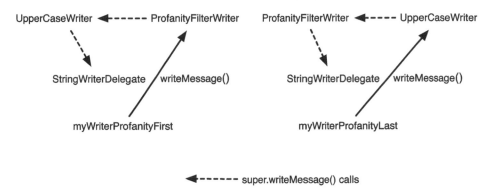

Here's the output from running the code:

```
THERE IS NO SIN EXCEPT S-----ITY
THERE IS NO SIN EXCEPT STUPIDITY
```

Scala nicely avoided method collision issues and chained the calls in the order of right to left—the last trait that is mixed has the highest priority to intercept method calls.

Wrapping Up

In this chapter, we explored an interesting and powerful Scala feature that promotes extensibility. Traits are a great design tool to create extensible code with dynamic behavior beyond what's provided by one single class. They nicely avoid method collisions when multiple implementations are brought together. You saw how powerful patterns like the Decorator pattern can be elegantly implemented with traits.

In the next chapter, we'll take a look at Scala's support for collections of objects.

CHAPTER 8

Collections

The Scala library contains a rich set of collections classes along with powerful operations to compose, iterate over, and extract elements. Working with these collections is commonplace when creating Scala applications. Learning these collections thoroughly is essential if you want to be productive in Scala.

In this chapter, you'll learn how to create instances of common Scala collections and how to iterate through them. You can still use the collections from the JDK such as ArrayList, HashSet, and simple arrays, but in this chapter we'll focus on the Scala-specific collections and how to work with them.

Common Scala Collections

Scala has three main types of collections:

- List—as you'd expect, an ordered collection of objects
- Set—an unordered collection
- Map—a dictionary of key-value pairs

Scala favors immutable collections, even though mutable versions are also available. If you want to modify a collection and if all the operations on the collection are all within a single thread, you can choose a mutable collection. However, if you plan to use the collection across threads or actors, the immutable collections are better. Immutable collections are thread safe, free from side effects, and help with program correctness. You can choose between these versions by selecting a class in one of these two packages: scala.collection.mutable or scala.collection.immutable.

If you don't mention a package name, then, by default, Scala brings on board immutable collections. Here's an example of using a Set—the immutable version, of course:

```
UsingCollections/UsingSet.scala
val colors1 = Set("Blue", "Green", "Red")
println(s"colors1: $colors1")

val colors2 = colors1 + "Black"
println(s"colors2: $colors2")
println(s"colors1: $colors1")
```

We started with a Set of three colors. When we added the color black, we did not modify the original set. Instead, we got a new set with four elements, as we see here:

```
colors1: Set(Blue, Green, Red)
colors2: Set(Blue, Green, Red, Black)
colors1: Set(Blue, Green, Red)
```

By default you get the immutable set. This is because the object Predef (included by default) provides aliases for Set and Map to point to the immutable implementations. Set and Map are traits in the scala.collection package that are refined by corresponding mutable versions in the package scala.collection.mutable and by immutable versions in scala.collection.immutable.

In the previous example, we created an instance of Set without using new. Internally, Scala created an instance of an inner class Set3, as we see from the following REPL interaction:

```
scala>  val colors = Set("Blue", "Green", "Red")
colors: scala.collection.immutable.Set[String] = Set(Blue, Green, Red)

scala> colors.getClass
res0: Class[_ <: scala.collection.immutable.Set[String]] = class
scala.collection.immutable.Set$Set3

scala> :quit
```

Set3 is a class that represents an implementation of a set with three elements. Since Set is immutable and the values must be provided at construction time, Scala optimizes the implementation of Set for smaller values, and creates an implementation of HashSet for values higher than 4.

Based on the parameters we provided, Scala figured out that we need a Set[String]. Similarly, if we write Set(1, 2, 3), we'll get a Set[Int]. This ability to create an object without new is possible because of a special apply() method, also called a *factory method*. A statement like X(...), where X is a class name or an instance reference, is treated as X.apply(...). Scala automatically calls an apply() method on the companion object of the class, if present. This ability to use the hidden apply() method is available on Map and List as well.

Using a Set

Suppose we're writing an RSS feed reader and we want to frequently update the feeds, but we don't care about the order. We can store the feed URLs in a Set. Assume we have the following feeds stored in two Sets:

```
val feeds1 = Set("blog.toolshed.com", "pragdave.me", "blog.agiledeveloper.com")
val feeds2 = Set("blog.toolshed.com", "martinfowler.com/bliki")
```

If we want to update only select feeds from feeds1, say the ones that have the word "blog," we can get those feeds using the filter() method:

```
val blogFeeds = feeds1 filter ( _ contains "blog" )
println(s"blog feeds: ${blogFeeds.mkString(", ")}")
```

We'll get this output:

```
blog feeds: blog.toolshed.com, blog.agiledeveloper.com
```

The mkString() method creates a string representation of each element of a Set and concatenates the results with the argument string, a comma in this example.

To merge two Sets of feeds to create a new Set, we can use the ++() method:

```
val mergedFeeds = feeds1 ++ feeds2
println(s"# of merged feeds: ${mergedFeeds.size}")
```

Set will hold an element at most once, so, as we can see in the output, the common feeds in the two sets will be stored only once in the merged set:

```
# of merged feeds: 4
```

To determine what feeds we have in common with a friend's, we can import our friend's feeds and perform the intersect operation (&()):

```
val commonFeeds = feeds1 & feeds2
println(s"common feeds: ${commonFeeds.mkString(", ")}")
```

Here's the effect of the intersect operation on the two previous feeds:

```
common feeds: blog.toolshed.com
```

To prefix each feed with the string "http://," use the map() method. This applies the given function value to each element, collects the result into a Set, and finally returns that set:

```
val urls = feeds1 map ( "http://" + _ )
println(s"One url: ${urls.head}")
```

We should see this:

```
One url: http://blog.toolshed.com
```

Finally, when we're ready to iterate over the feeds and refresh them one at a time, we can use the built-in iterator foreach() like this:

```
println("Refresh Feeds:")
feeds1 foreach { feed => println(s"  Refreshing $feed...") }
```

Here's the result:

```
Refresh Feeds:
  Refreshing blog.toolshed.com...
  Refreshing pragdave.me...
  Refreshing blog.agiledeveloper.com...
```

So that's the unordered collection of elements. Next let's explore the associative map.

Associative Maps

Suppose we want to attach the feed author's name to feeds; we can store it as a key-value pair in a Map:

```
val feeds = Map("Andy Hunt"    -> "blog.toolshed.com",
                "Dave Thomas" -> "pragdave.me",
                "NFJS"         -> "nofluffjuststuff.com/blog")
```

If we want to get a Map of feeds for folks whose name starts with "D," we can use the filterKeys() method:

```
val filterNameStartWithD = feeds filterKeys( _ startsWith "D" )
println(s"# of Filtered: ${filterNameStartWithD.size}")
```

Here's the result:

```
# of Filtered: 1
```

On the other hand, if we want to filter on the values, in addition to or instead of the keys, we can use the filter() method. The function value we provide to filter() receives a (key, value) tuple, and we can use it as in this example:

```
val filterNameStartWithDAndPragprogInFeed = feeds filter { element =>
  val (key, value) = element
  (key startsWith "D") && (value contains "pragprog")
}
print("# of feeds with auth name D* and pragprog in URL: ")
println(filterNameStartWithDAndPragprogInFeed.size)
```

Here's the output:

```
# of feeds with auth name D* and pragprog in URL: 1
```

To get a feed for a person, simply use the get() method. Since there may not be a value for the given key, the return type of get() is Option[T]—see *Option*

Type, on page 78. The actual result of the method may be either a Some[T] or a None, where T is the type of values in the Map:

```
println(s"Get Andy's Feed: ${feeds.get("Andy Hunt")}")
println(s"Get Bill's Feed: ${feeds.get("Bill Who")}")
```

The output from the previous code is shown here:

```
Get Andy's Feed: Some(blog.toolshed.com)
Get Bill's Feed: None
```

Alternately, we can use the apply() method to get the values for a key—remember, this is the method Scala calls when we use parentheses on a class or an instance. The apply() method, however, instead of returning Option[T], returns the value. Unlike get(), if there's no value for a given key, it throws an exception. Use caution—make sure to place the code within a try-catch block:

```
try {
  println(s"Get Andy's Feed Using apply(): ${feeds("Andy Hunt")}")
  print("Get Bill's Feed: ")
  println(feeds("Bill Who"))
}
catch {
  case ex : java.util.NoSuchElementException => println("Not found")
}
```

Here's the output from the use of apply():

```
Get Andy's Feed Using apply(): blog.toolshed.com
Get Bill's Feed: Not found
```

To add a feed, use the updated() method. Since we're working with an immutable collection, updated() does not affect the original Map. Instead, it returns a new *updated* Map, as the method name alludes to, with the additional element:

```
val newFeeds1 = feeds.updated("Venkat Subramaniam", "blog.agiledeveloper.com")
println("Venkat's blog in original feeds: " + feeds.get("Venkat Subramaniam"))
println("Venkat's blog in new feed: " + newFeeds1("Venkat Subramaniam"))
```

Let's see the effect of the updated() method:

```
Venkat's blog in original feeds: None
Venkat's blog in new feed: blog.agiledeveloper.com
```

Instead of calling updated() explicitly, you can take advantage of another Scala trick. If you use the parentheses on a class or instance on the left side of an assignment, Scala automatically calls a special method named update(). So, X() = b is equivalent to X.update(b). If update() takes more than one parameter, you can place all but the trailing parameter within the parentheses. So, X(a) = b is equivalent to X.update(a, b).

We can use the implicit call on immutable collections, like this: val newFeed = feeds("author") = "blog". However, it loses the syntactic elegance because of multiple assignments, one for the update() and the other to save the newly created Map. If we were returning the newly created map from a method, the implicit update() is elegant to use. However, if our intent is to update the map in place, it makes more sense to use the implicit call on mutable collections.

```
val mutableFeeds = scala.collection.mutable.Map(
    "Scala Book Forum" -> "forums.pragprog.com/forums/87")
mutableFeeds("Groovy Book Forum") = "forums.pragprog.com/forums/246"
println(s"Number of forums: ${mutableFeeds.size}")
```

We get the following result:

```
Number of forums: 2
```

Now that you've seen Sets and Maps, we can no longer ignore the most common collection of all—List.

Immutable Lists

Scala makes it easier and faster to access the first element of a list using the head method. Everything except the first element can be accessed using the tail method. Accessing the last element of the list requires traversing the list and so is more expensive than accessing the head and the tail. So, most operations on the list are structured around operations on the head and tail.

Let's continue with the feeds example to learn about List. We can maintain an ordered collection of the feeds using a List:

```
val feeds = List("blog.toolshed.com", "pragdave.me", "blog.agiledeveloper.com")
```

This creates an instance of List[String]. We can access the elements of the List using an index from 0 to list.length - 1. When we invoke feeds(1), we're using List's apply() method. Thus, feeds(0) is a short form for feeds.apply(0). To access the first element, we can use either feeds(0) or the head() method:

```
println(s"First feed: ${feeds.head}")
println(s"Second feed: ${feeds(1)}")
```

The output from the code is shown here:

```
First feed: blog.toolshed.com
Second feed: pragdave.me
```

If we want to prefix an element—that is, place it in the front of the list—we can use the special method ::(). Read a :: list as "prefix a to the list." This method is an operation on the list, even though the list follows the operator; see *Method Name Convention*, on page 137 for details on how this works.

```scala
val prefixedList = "forums.pragprog.com/forums/87" :: feeds
println(s"First Feed In Prefixed: ${prefixedList.head}")
```

The output from the previous code is shown here:

```
First Feed In Prefixed: forums.pragprog.com/forums/87
```

Suppose we want to append a list, say listA, to another, say list. We would achieve that by actually prefixing list to the listA using the :::() method. So, the code would be list ::: listA and would read "prefix list to listA." Since lists are immutable, we did not affect either one of the previous lists. We simply created a new one with elements from both. Here's an example of appending:

```scala
val feedsWithForums =
  feeds ::: List("forums.pragprog.com/forums/87",
    "forums.pragprog.com/forums/246")
println(s"First feed in feeds with forum: ${feedsWithForums.head}")
println(s"Last feed in feeds with forum: ${feedsWithForums.last}")
```

And here's the output:

```
First feed in feeds with forum: blog.toolshed.com
Last feed in feeds with forum: forums.pragprog.com/forums/246
```

Again, the method :::() is called on the list that follows the operator.

To append an element to our list, we can use the same :::() method. We place the element we'd like to append into a list and prefix the original list to it:

```scala
val appendedList = feeds ::: List("agilelearner.com")
println(s"Last Feed In Appended: ${appendedList.last}")
```

We should see this output:

```
Last Feed In Appended: agilelearner.com
```

Notice that to append an element or a list to another list, we actually used the prefix operator on the latter. The reason for this is that it's much faster to access the head element of a list than to traverse to its last element. So, the same result is achieved but with better performance.

To select only feeds that satisfy some condition, use the filter() method. If we want to check whether all feeds meet a certain condition, we can use forall(). If, on the other hand, we want to know whether any feed meets a certain condition, exists() will help us.

```scala
println(s"Feeds with blog: ${feeds.filter( _ contains "blog" ).mkString(", ")}")
println(s"All feeds have com: ${feeds.forall( _ contains "com" )}")
```

```
println(s"All feeds have dave: ${feeds.forall( _ contains "dave" )}")
println(s"Any feed has dave: ${feeds.exists( _ contains "dave" )}")
println(s"Any feed has bill: ${feeds.exists( _ contains "bill" )}")
```

We'll get this:

```
Feeds with blog: blog.toolshed.com, blog.agiledeveloper.com
All feeds have com: true
All feeds have dave: false
Any feed has dave: true
Any feed has bill: false
```

Suppose we want to know the number of characters we need to display each feed name. We can use the map() method to work on each element to get a list of the result, as shown here:

```
println(s"Feed url lengths: ${feeds.map( _.length ).mkString(", ")}")
```

Here's the output:

```
Feed url lengths: 17, 21, 23
```

If we're interested in the total number of characters of all feeds put together, we can use the foldLeft() method like this:

```
val total = feeds.foldLeft(0) { (total, feed) => total + feed.length }
println(s"Total length of feed urls: $total")
```

The output from the previous code is shown here:

```
Total length of feed urls: 61
```

Notice that although the previous method is performing the summation, it did not deal with any mutable state. It's pure functional style. A new updated value was accumulated as the method progressed through the elements in the list without changing anything, however.

The foldLeft() method will invoke the given function value (code block) for each element in the list, starting from the left. It passes two parameters to the function value. The first parameter is a partial result from the execution of the function value for the previous element, which is why it's called *folding*—it's as if the list is folded into the result of these computations. The second parameter is an element in the list. The initial value for the partial result is provided as the parameter to the method (Zero in this example). The foldLeft() method forms a chain of elements and carries the partial result of computation in the function value from one element to the next, starting from the left. Similarly, foldRight() will do the same, starting at the right.

Scala provides alternate methods to make the previous methods concise. The method /:() is equivalent to foldLeft() and \:() to foldRight(). Here's the previous example written using /::

```
val total2 = (0 /: feeds) { (total, feed) => total + feed.length }
println(s"Total length of feed urls: $total2")
```

The output from the previous code is shown here:

```
Total length of feed urls: 61
```

Programmers either love this conciseness, like I do, or hate it; I don't think there will be anything in between.

We can reach out to Scala conventions here and make the code even more concise as follows:

```
val total3 = (0 /: feeds) { _ + _.length }
println(s"Total length of feed urls: $total3")
```

Here's the output:

```
Total length of feed urls: 61
```

You saw some interesting methods of List in this section. There are several other methods in List that provide additional capabilities. For a complete documentation, refer to "The Scala Language API" in Appendix 2, *Web Resources*, on page 253.

The colons in these method names have great significance in Scala and it's quite important to grok that; let's explore that next.

Method Name Convention

The feature you're going to look at in this section is pretty cool (I really think so), but it's also something that can be a bit hard to grasp. If an oxygen mask appears in front of you as you read these pages, secure your mask first before assisting your fellow programmers.

In *Operator Overloading*, on page 38, you saw how Scala supports operator overloading even though it doesn't have operators. Operators are methods with a crafty method naming convention. You saw that the first character of a method decides the precedence. Here we see that the last character of their names also has an effect—it determines the target of the method call.

The convention of : may be surprising at first, but as you get used to it (or as you "develop a Scala eye," to put it aptly), you'll see it improves fluency. For example, if you want to prefix a value to a list, you can write it as value :: list.

Although it reads "value is prefixed to the list," the target of the method is actually the list with the value as the argument—that is, list.::(value).

Some programmers ask if they could attach a colon to existing methods during call. No, Scala doesn't provide facilities to decorate existing method names; the convention is only for method names that happen to end with this special symbol.

If a method name ends with a colon (:), then the target of the call is the instance that follows the operator. Scala doesn't permit an operator to succeed a method name with alphanumeric characters, unless you prefix that operator with an underscore. So, a method named jumpOver:() is rejected, but jumpOver_:() is accepted.

In this next example, ^() is a method defined on the class Cow, while ^:() is an independent method defined on the class Moon:

UsingCollections/Colon.scala
```scala
class Cow {
  def ^(moon: Moon) = println("Cow jumped over the moon")
}
class Moon {
  def ^:(cow: Cow) = println("This cow jumped over the moon too")
}
```

Here's an example of using these two methods:

UsingCollections/Colon.scala
```scala
val cow = new Cow
val moon = new Moon

cow ^ moon
cow ^: moon
```

The calls to the two methods look almost identical, the cow to the left and the moon to the right of the operators. However, the first call is on cow, whereas the second call is on moon; the difference is so subtle. It can be frustrating for someone new to Scala, but this convention is quite common in list operations, so we'd better get used to it. The output from the previous code looks like this:

```
Cow jumped over the moon
This cow jumped over the moon too
```

The last call in the previous example is equivalent to this code as well:

```scala
moon.^:(cow)
```

In addition to operators that end with :, there are a set of operators that also are targeted at the instance that follow them. These are the unary operators +, -, !, and ~. The unary + maps over to a call to unary_+(), the unary - to unary_-(), and so on.

Here's an example of defining unary operators on a Sample class:

UsingCollections/Unary.scala
```
class Sample {
  def unary_+() = println("Called unary +")
  def unary_-() = println("called unary -")
  def unary_!() = println("called unary !")
  def unary_~() = println("called unary ~")
}

val sample = new Sample
+sample
-sample
!sample
~sample
```

The output from the previous code is shown here:

```
Called unary +
called unary -
called unary !
called unary ~
```

As you get comfortable with Scala, you'll develop a Scala eye—soon the mental processing of these notations and conventions will become second nature.

The for Expression

The foreach() method provides internal iterators on collections—you don't control the looping. You simply provide code to execute in the context of each iteration. However, if you'd like to control the looping or work with multiple collections at the same time, you can use an external iterator, the for() expression. Let's look at a simple loop:

UsingCollections/PowerOfFor.scala
```
for (i <- 1 to 3) { print("ho ") }
```

The code prints "ho ho ho." It's a short form of the general syntax of the following expression:

```
for([pattern <- generator; definition*]+; filter*)
  [yield] expression
```

The for expression takes as a parameter one or more generators, with zero or more definitions and zero or more filters. These are separated from each other by semicolons. The yield keyword is optional and, if present, tells the expression to return a list of values instead of a Unit. That was a boatload of details, but don't worry, because we'll take a look at it with examples, so you'll get quite comfortable with it in no time.

Let's start with the yield first. Suppose we want to take values in a range and multiply each value by 2. Here's a code example to do that:

UsingCollections/PowerOfFor.scala
```
val result = for (i <- 1 to 10)
  yield i * 2
```

The previous code returns a collection of values where each value is a double of the values in the given range 1 to 10.

We could've also performed the previous logic using the map() method like this:

UsingCollections/PowerOfFor.scala
```
val result2 = (1 to 10).map(_ * 2)
```

Behind the scenes, Scala translates the for expression into an expression that uses a combination of methods like map() and filter() depending on the complexity of the expression.

Now suppose we want to double only even numbers in the range. We can use a filter:

UsingCollections/PowerOfFor.scala
```
val doubleEven = for (i <- 1 to 10; if i % 2 == 0)
  yield i * 2
```

Read the previous for expression as "Return a collection of i * 2 where i is a member of the given range and i is even." So, the previous expression is really like a SQL query on a collection of values—this is called *list comprehension* in functional programming.

If you find the semicolons in the previous code too noisy, drop them and use curly braces instead of parentheses like this:

```
for {
  i <- 1 to 10
  if i % 2 == 0
}
 yield i * 2
```

You can place a definition along with a generator. Scala defines a new val with that name through each iteration.

Here's an example of iterating over a collection of Person and printing their last names:

UsingCollections/Friends.scala
```
class Person(val firstName: String, val lastName: String)
object Person {
  def apply(firstName: String, lastName: String) : Person =
    new Person(firstName, lastName)
}
val friends = List(Person("Brian", "Sletten"), Person("Neal", "Ford"),
  Person("Scott", "Davis"), Person("Stuart", "Halloway"))

val lastNames =
  for (friend <- friends; lastName = friend.lastName) yield lastName

println(lastNames.mkString(", "))
```

The output from the code is shown here:

```
Sletten, Ford, Davis, Halloway
```

The previous code is also an example of the Scala syntax sugar where the apply() method is working under the covers—the code is concise and readable, but we've created a new list of Persons.

If you provide more than one generator in the for expression, each generator forms an inner loop, with the rightmost generator controlling the innermost loop. Here's an example of using two generators:

UsingCollections/MultipleLoop.scala
```
for (i <- 1 to 3; j <- 4 to 6) {
  print(s"[$i,$j] ")
}
```

The output from the previous code is shown here:

```
[1,4] [1,5] [1,6] [2,4] [2,5] [2,6] [3,4] [3,5] [3,6]
```

With multiple generators you can easily combine the values to create powerful combinations, for example.

Wrapping Up

In this chapter, you learned how to use the three major types of collections provided in Scala. You also saw the power of the for() expression and list comprehension. Next you'll learn about pattern matching, one of the most powerful features in Scala.

CHAPTER 9

Pattern Matching and Regular Expressions

Pattern matching is the second most widely used feature of Scala, after function values and closures. Scala's superb support for pattern matching means you'll use it extensively when you receive messages from actors in concurrent programming. In this chapter, you'll learn about Scala's mechanism for pattern matching, the case classes, and the extractors, as well as how to create and use regular expressions.

Comprehensive Matching

Scala's pattern matching is quite versatile—you can match literals, constants, and arbitrary values with wildcards, tuples, and lists; you can even match based on types and guards. Let's explore all that, one at a time.

Matching Literals and Constants

Messages passed between actors are normally String literals, numbers, or tuples. If your message is a literal, you don't have to do much to match it. Simply type the literal you'd like to match, and you're done. Suppose we need to determine activities for different days of the week. Assume we get the day as a String and we respond with our activity for that day. Here's an example of how we can pattern-match the days:

PatternMatching/MatchLiterals.scala
```
def activity(day: String) {
  day match {
    case "Sunday" => print("Eat, sleep, repeat... ")
    case "Saturday" => print("Hang out with friends... ")
    case "Monday" => print("...code for fun...")
    case "Friday" => print("...read a good book...")
  }
}
List("Monday", "Sunday", "Saturday").foreach { activity }
```

The match is an expression that acts on Any. In this example, we're using it on a String. It performs pattern matching on the target and invokes the appropriate case expression with the matching pattern value. The output from the code is shown here:

```
...code for fun...Eat, sleep, repeat... Hang out with friends...
```

You can directly match against literals and constants. The literals can be different types; the match does not care. However, the type of the target object to the left of match may restrict the type. In this example, since this was of type String, the match could be any string.

Matching a Wildcard

In the previous example, we did not handle all possible values of day. If there is a value that is not matched by one of the case expressions, we'll get a MatchError exception. We can control the values day can take by making the parameter an enum instead of a String. Even then we may not want to handle each day of the week. We can avoid the exception by using a wildcard:

```
PatternMatching/Wildcard.scala
object DayOfWeek extends Enumeration {
  val SUNDAY = Value("Sunday")
  val MONDAY = Value("Monday")
  val TUESDAY = Value("Tuesday")
  val WEDNESDAY = Value("Wednesday")
  val THURSDAY = Value("Thursday")
  val FRIDAY = Value("Friday")
  val SATURDAY = Value("Saturday")
}

def activity(day: DayOfWeek.Value) {
  day match {
    case DayOfWeek.SUNDAY => println("Eat, sleep, repeat...")
    case DayOfWeek.SATURDAY => println("Hang out with friends")
    case _ => println("...code for fun...")
  }
}

activity(DayOfWeek.SATURDAY)
activity(DayOfWeek.MONDAY)
```

We've defined an enumeration for the days of the week. In our activity() method, we matched SUNDAY and SATURDAY and let the wildcard, represented by an underscore (_), handle the rest of the days.

If we run the code, we'll get the match for SATURDAY followed by MONDAY being matched by the wildcard:

```
Hang out with friends
...code for fun...
```

Matching Tuples and Lists

Matching literals and enumerations is simple. But messages are often not a single literal—they're often a sequence of values in the form of either tuples or lists. You can use the case expression to match against tuples and lists also. Suppose we are writing a service that needs to receive and process geographic coordinates. The coordinates can be represented as a tuple that we can match like this:

PatternMatching/MatchTuples.scala
```scala
def processCoordinates(input: Any) {
  input match {
    case (lat, long) => printf("Processing (%d, %d)...", lat, long)
    case "done" => println("done")
    case _ => println("invalid input")
  }
}

processCoordinates((39, -104))
processCoordinates("done")
```

This matches any tuple with two values in it, plus the literal "done". Run the code to see the output:

```
Processing (39, -104)...done
```

If the argument we send is not a tuple with two elements or doesn't match "done" then the wildcard will handle it. The printf() statement used to print the coordinates has a hidden assumption that the values in the tuple are integers. If they're not, our code will unfortunately fail at runtime. We can avoid that by providing type information for matches, as you'll see in the next section.

You can match Lists the same way you matched tuples. Simply provide the elements you care about, and you can leave out the rest using the array explosion symbol (_*):

PatternMatching/MatchList.scala
```scala
def processItems(items: List[String]) {
  items match {
    case List("apple", "ibm") => println("Apples and IBMs")
    case List("red", "blue", "white") => println("Stars and Stripes...")
    case List("red", "blue", _*) => println("colors red, blue,... ")
    case List("apple", "orange", otherFruits @ _*) =>
      println("apples, oranges, and " + otherFruits)
  }
}
```

```
processItems(List("apple", "ibm"))
processItems(List("red", "blue", "green"))
processItems(List("red", "blue", "white"))
processItems(List("apple", "orange", "grapes", "dates"))
```

In the first and second case, we expected two and three specific items in the List, respectively. In the remaining two cases, we expect two or more items, but the first two items must be as specified. If we need to reference the remaining matching elements, we can place a variable name (like otherFruits) before a special @ symbol as in the last case. The output from the code is shown here:

```
Apples and IBMs
colors red, blue,...
Stars and Stripes...
apples, oranges, and List(grapes, dates)
```

Matching with Types and Guards

Sometimes you may want to match based on the type of values. For example, you may want to handle a sequence of, say, Ints differently from how you handle a sequence of Doubles. Scala lets you ask the case statement to match against types, like in this example:

PatternMatching/MatchTypes.scala
```
Line 1  def process(input: Any) {
   -      input match {
   -        case (a: Int, b: Int) => print("Processing (int, int)... ")
   -        case (a: Double, b: Double) => print("Processing (double, double)... ")
   5        case msg : Int if (msg > 1000000) => println("Processing int > 1000000")
   -        case msg : Int => print("Processing int... ")
   -        case msg: String => println("Processing string... ")
   -        case _ => printf(s"Can't handle $input... ")
   -      }
   10 }
   -
   -   process((34.2, -159.3))
   -   process(0)
   -   process(1000001)
   15 process(2.2)
```

You see how to specify types for single values and elements of a tuple in the case. Also, you can use guards to constrain the match even more. In addition to matching the pattern, the guard provided by the if clause must be satisfied for the expression following => to evaluate. The output from the code is shown here:

```
Processing (double, double)... Processing int... Processing int > 1000000
Can't handle 2.2...
```

When writing multiple case expressions, their order matters. Scala will evaluate the case expressions from the top down. So, for example, we shouldn't swap line numbers 5 and 6 in the code—it'll result in a warning and a different result since the case with the guard will never be executed.

Pattern Variables and Constants in case Expressions

You already saw how to define placeholder vals for what you're matching, like lat and long when matching tuples. These are pattern variables. However, you have to be careful when defining them. By convention, Scala expects the pattern variables to start with a lowercase letter and constants to be capitalized.

If you use a capitalized name, it will look for a constant in the scope; however, if you use a noncapitalized name, it will merely assume it's a pattern variable —any variable or constant with the same noncapitalized name in the scope will be ignored. In the next code, we're defining a pattern variable with the same name as a field, but the code will not give us the desired result—the pattern variable hides the field.

```
PatternMatching/MatchWithField.scala
class Sample {
  val max = 100

  def process(input: Int) {
    input match {
      case max => println(s"You matched max $max")
    }
  }
}

val sample = new Sample
try {
  sample.process(0)
} catch {
  case ex: Throwable => println(ex)
}
sample.process(100)
```

The output shows that the variable max was inferred by Scala as a pattern variable and not as a constant value defined in the field:

```
You matched max 0
You matched max 100
```

You can refer to the hidden fields from the case expression with explicit scoping (like ObjectName.fieldName if ObjectName is a singleton or companion object or obj.fieldName if obj is a reference), like so:

```
case this.max => println(s"You matched max $max")
```

In this version, Scala knows we're referring to a field:

```
scala.MatchError: 0 (of class java.lang.Integer)
You matched max 100
```

Instead of using the dot notation to resolve the scope, you can also give a hint to Scala by wrapping the variable name in a pair of tick symbols:

```
case `max` => println(s"You matched max $max")
```

Again, in this modified version, Scala resolves the variable appropriately in the current scope:

```
scala.MatchError: 0 (of class java.lang.Integer)
You matched max 100
```

You can use either of the alternatives to instruct Scala to treat a noncapitalized name as a predefined value in the scope instead of as a pattern variable. However, it's better to avoid that—use uppercase names for true constants, like in the next example:

PatternMatching/MatchWithValsOK.scala

```
class Sample {
  val MAX = 100

  def process(input: Int) {
    input match {
      case MAX => println("You matched max")
    }
  }
}

val sample = new Sample
try {
  sample.process(0)
} catch {
  case ex: Throwable => println(ex)
}
sample.process(100)
```

With this change, Scala and you are seeing eye-to-eye and the result is exactly what you'd expect.

```
scala.MatchError: 0 (of class java.lang.Integer)
You matched max
```

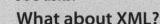

Joe asks:
What about XML?

You can pattern-match XML fragments as well. You don't have to embed XML into strings. You can directly place the XML fragments as parameters to the case statement. The capability is quite powerful; however, because we need to first discuss XML handling in Scala, let's defer this topic to Chapter 15, *Creating an Application with Scala*, on page 227.

In a realistic application, you will soon outgrow matching simple literals, lists, tuples, and objects. You'll want to match against more complicated patterns. Two options are available in Scala: case classes and *extractors*. Let's take a look at each of these in turn.

Matching Using case Classes

case classes are special classes that can be used in pattern matching with case expressions. A case class is concise and easy to create, and it exposes each of its constructor parameters as values. You can use case classes to create lightweight value objects or data holders with meaningful names for the class and its properties.

Suppose we want to receive and process stock-trading transactions. The messages for selling and buying might be accompanied by information such as the name of a stock and a quantity. It's convenient to store this information in objects, but how would we pattern-match them? This is the purpose of case classes. These are classes that the pattern matcher readily recognizes and matches. Here's an example of a few case classes:

```
PatternMatching/TradeStock.scala
trait Trade
case class Sell(stockSymbol: String, quantity: Int) extends Trade
case class Buy(stockSymbol: String, quantity: Int) extends Trade
case class Hedge(stockSymbol: String, quantity: Int) extends Trade
```

We've defined Trade as a trait since we don't expect any direct instances of it, much like the way we'd define an interface in Java. We've extended the case classes Sell, Buy, and Hedge from it. These three take a stock symbol and quantity as their constructor parameters.

Now we can readily use these in case statements:

PatternMatching/TradeStock.scala

```scala
object TradeProcessor {
  def processTransaction(request : Trade) {
    request match {
      case Sell(stock, 1000) => println(s"Selling 1000-units of $stock")
      case Sell(stock, quantity) =>
            println(s"Selling $quantity units of $stock")
      case Buy(stock, quantity) if (quantity > 2000) =>
        println(s"Buying $quantity (large) units of $stock")
      case Buy(stock, quantity) =>
            println(s"Buying $quantity units of $stock")
    }
  }
}
```

We match the request against Sell and Buy. The stock symbol and quantity we receive are matched and stored in the pattern variables stock and quantity, respectively. We can specify constant values, like 1000 for quantity, or even use a guarded match, like checking if quantity > 2000. Here's an example of using the TradeProcessor singleton:

PatternMatching/TradeStock.scala

```scala
TradeProcessor.processTransaction(Sell("GOOG", 500))
TradeProcessor.processTransaction(Buy("GOOG", 700))
TradeProcessor.processTransaction(Sell("GOOG", 1000))
TradeProcessor.processTransaction(Buy("GOOG", 3000))
```

The output from the code is shown here:

```
Selling 500 units of GOOG
Buying 700 units of GOOG
Selling 1000-units of GOOG
Buying 3000 (large) units of GOOG
```

In the example, all the concrete case classes took parameters. If you have a case class that takes no parameter, then place empty parentheses after the class name to indicate an empty parameter list—otherwise the Scala compiler will generate a warning.

There's one other complication when dealing with case classes that take no parameters—use caution when passing them as messages. In this example, we have case classes that don't take any parameters:

PatternMatching/ThingsAcceptor.scala

```scala
case class Apple()
case class Orange()
case class Book ()

object ThingsAcceptor {
  def acceptStuff(thing: Any) {
```

```
    thing match {
      case Apple() => println("Thanks for the Apple")
      case Orange() => println("Thanks for the Orange")
      case Book() => println("Thanks for the Book")
      case _ => println(s"Excuse me, why did you send me $thing")
    }
  }
}
```

In the following code, we forgot to place parentheses next to Apple in the last call:

PatternMatching/ThingsAcceptor.scala
```
ThingsAcceptor.acceptStuff(Apple())
ThingsAcceptor.acceptStuff(Book())
ThingsAcceptor.acceptStuff(Apple)
```

The result of the calls is shown here:

```
Thanks for the Apple
Thanks for the Book
Excuse me, why did you send me Apple
```

When we forgot the parentheses, instead of sending an instance of the case class, we are sending its companion object. The companion object mixes in the scala.Function0 trait, meaning it can be treated as a function. So, we end up sending a function instead of an instance of the case class. If the acceptStuff() method received an instance of a case class named Thing, this would not be a problem. Let's give that idea a try.

```
abstract class Thing
case class Apple() extends Thing

object ThingsAcceptor {
  def acceptStuff(thing: Thing) {
    thing match {
      //...
      case _ =>
    }
  }
}

ThingsAcceptor.acceptStuff(Apple) //error: type mismatch;
```

Receiving an instance of the case class is much safer than receiving Any. However, sometimes you don't have control over this. For example, when passing messages to actors, you can't control what is received in a type-safe manner at compile time. So, use caution when passing around case classes.

Although the Scala compiler may evolve to fix the previous problem, these kinds of edge cases can still arise. This emphasizes the need for good testing even in a statically typed language (see Chapter 16, *Unit Testing*, on page 241).

Extractors and Regular Expressions

Scala's powerful pattern matching does not stop with built-in matching facilities. You can create custom matching using extractors and, there too, Scala gives us a few different alternatives.

Matching Using Extractors

You can take pattern matching to the next level by matching arbitrary patterns using Scala extractors. As the name indicates, an extractor will extract matching parts from the input. Suppose we're writing a service that will process stock-related input. The first task on hand is for us to receive a stock symbol and return the price for that stock. Here's an example of calls we can expect:

```
StockService process "GOOG"
StockService process "IBM"
StockService process "ERR"
```

The process() method needs to validate the given symbol and, if it is valid, return the price for it. Here's the code for that:

```
object StockService {
  def process(input : String) {
    input match {
      case Symbol() => println(s"Look up price for valid symbol $input")
      case _ => println(s"Invalid input $input")
    }
  }
}
```

The process() method performs pattern matching using the yet-to-be-defined extractor Symbol. If the extractor determines the symbol is valid, it returns true; otherwise, it returns false. If it returns true, the expression associated with the case is executed—in this example we merely print a message to illustrate that the match succeeded. Otherwise, the pattern match continues to the next case. Now, let's take a look at the missing piece, the extractor:

```
object Symbol {
  def unapply(symbol : String) : Boolean = {
    // you'd look up a database... here only GOOG and IBM are recognized
    symbol == "GOOG" || symbol == "IBM"
  }
}
```

The extractor has one method named unapply() that accepts the value we'd like to match. The match expression automatically sends the input as a parameter to the unapply() method when case Symbol() => ... is executed. When we execute the previous three pieces of code (remember to put the sample calls to the service toward the bottom of your file), we'll get the following output:

```
Look up price for valid symbol GOOG
Look up price for valid symbol IBM
Invalid input ERR
```

unapply() may strike you as an odd name for a method. You may expect a method like evaluate() for the extractor. The reason for this method name is that the extractor can take an optional apply() method. These two methods, apply() and unapply(), perform the opposite actions. unapply() breaks down the object into pieces that match a pattern, whereas apply() is intended to optionally put it back together.

Let's move further with this example. Now that we're able to ask for a stock quote, as a next task, for our service, let's ask for the price of a stock. Assume that the message for this arrives in the format "SYMBOL:PRICE." We need to pattern-match this format and take action. Here's the modified process() method to handle this additional task:

PatternMatching/Extractor.scala
```
object StockService {
  def process(input : String) {
    input match {
      case Symbol() => println(s"Look up price for valid symbol $input")
      case ReceiveStockPrice(symbol, price) =>
        println(s"Received price $$$price for symbol $symbol")
      case _ => println(s"Invalid input $input")
    }
  }
}
```

We've added a new case with a yet-to-be-written extractor ReceiveStockPrice. This extractor will be different from the Symbol extractor we wrote earlier—it simply returned a Boolean result. ReceiveStockPrice, however, needs to parse the input and return to us two values: symbol and price. These are specified as arguments to ReceiveStockPrice in the case statement; however, they aren't passed in arguments. These are arguments that are passed out from the extractor. So, we're not sending the values for symbol and price. Instead, we are receiving them.

Let's take a look at the ReceiveStockPrice extractor. As you'd expect, it should have an unapply() that will split input over the : character and return a tuple of symbol and price. However, there is one catch; the input may not conform to the format "SYMBOL:PRICE." To handle this possibility, the return type of this method should be Option[(String, Double)], and at runtime we'll receive either Some(String, Double) or None (the types you learned about in *Option Type*, on page 78). Here's the code for the extractor ReceiveStockPrice:

PatternMatching/Extractor.scala

```scala
object ReceiveStockPrice {
  def unapply(input: String) : Option[(String, Double)] = {
    try {
      if (input contains ":") {
        val splitQuote = input split ":"
        Some(splitQuote(0), splitQuote(1).toDouble)
      }
      else {
        None
      }
    }
    catch {
      case _ : NumberFormatException => None
    }
  }
}
```

Here's how we might use the updated service:

PatternMatching/Extractor.scala

```scala
StockService process "GOOG"
StockService process "GOOG:310.84"
StockService process "GOOG:BUY"
StockService process "ERR:12.21"
```

The output from the code is shown here:

```
Look up price for valid symbol GOOG
Received price $310.84 for symbol GOOG
Invalid input GOOG:BUY
Received price $12.21 for symbol ERR
```

The code handled the first three requests well. It accepted what's valid and rejected what was not. The last request, however, did not go well. Even though the input was in a valid format, it should reject the request due to the invalid symbol ERR. There are two ways we can handle that. One is to check whether the symbol is valid within ReceiveStockPrice. However, this will result in a duplication of effort. Alternately, we can apply multiple pattern matches in one case statement. Let's modify the process() method to do this:

```scala
case ReceiveStockPrice(symbol @ Symbol(), price) =>
  println(s"Received price $$$price for symbol $symbol")
```

We first apply the ReceiveStockPrice extractor, which returns a pair of results if successful. On the first result (symbol), we further apply the Symbol extractor to validate the symbol. We can intercept this symbol on its way from one extractor to another using a pattern variable followed by the @ sign, as shown in the code.

Now if we rerun the sample calls on this modified service, we'll get the following output:

```
Look up price for valid symbol GOOG
Received price $310.84 for symbol GOOG
Invalid input GOOG:BUY
Invalid input ERR:12.21
```

You see how powerful extractors are. They allow you to match arbitrary patterns. You can pretty much take control of the matching in the unapply() method and return as many matching parts as you desire.

You can greatly benefit from the power of extractors if the format of the input is complex. However, if the format is fairly simple, like something that can be expressed easily using a regular expression, you wouldn't want to go to the extent of defining a custom extractor. You'd want something that takes a lot less work. Regular expressions can be used as extractors, but before we explore that option, let's see how to create regular expressions in Scala.

Regular Expressions

Scala supports regular expressions through classes in the scala.util.matching package—for a detailed discussion on regular expressions, refer to Jeffrey E. F. Friedl's *Mastering Regular Expressions [Fri97]*. When you create a regular expression, you're working with an instance of the Regex class in that package. Let's create a regular expression to check whether a given String contains either the word *Scala* or the word *scala*:

PatternMatching/RegularExpr.scala
```
val pattern = "(S|s)cala".r
val str = "Scala is scalable and cool"
println(pattern findFirstIn str)
```

We create a String and call the r() method on it. Scala implicitly converts the String to a RichString and invokes that method to get an instance of Regex. Of course, if our regular expression needs escape characters, we're better off using raw strings instead of strings. It's easier to write and read """\d2:\d2:\d4""" than "\\d2:\\d2:\\d4".

To find a first match of the regular expression, simply call the findFirstIn() method. In the example, this will find the word Scala in the text.

If instead of finding only the first occurrence we'd like to find all occurrences of the matching word, we can use the findAllIn() method:

PatternMatching/RegularExpr.scala
```
println((pattern findAllIn str).mkString(", "))
```

This will return a collection of all matching words. In this example, that would be (Scala, scala). We finally concatenated the resulting list of elements using the mkString() method.

If we'd like to replace matching text, we can use replaceFirstIn() to replace the first match (as in the following example) or replaceAllIn() to replace all occurrences:

PatternMatching/RegularExpr.scala
```
println("cool".r replaceFirstIn(str, "awesome"))
```

The output from executing all three of the regular expression methods is shown here:

```
Some(Scala)
Scala, scala
Scala is scalable and awesome
```

If you're already familiar with regular expressions, using them in Scala is straightforward.

Regular Expressions as Extractors

Scala regular expressions offer a buy-one-get-one-free option. You create a regular expression, and you get an extractor for free. Scala regular expressions *are* extractors, so you can readily use them in case expressions. Scala rolls each match you place within parentheses into a pattern variable. So, for example, "(S|s)cala".r will hold an unapply() method that returns an Option[String]. On the other hand, "(S|s)(cala)".r's unapply() will return Option[String, String]. Let's explore this with an example. Here's a way to pattern-match "GOOG:price" and extract the price, using regular expressions:

PatternMatching/MatchUsingRegex.scala
```
def process(input : String) {
  val GoogStock = """^GOOG:(\d*\.\d+)""".r
  input match {
    case GoogStock(price) => println(s"Price of GOOG is $$$price")
    case _ => println(s"not processing $input")
  }
}
```

```
process("GOOG:310.84")
process("GOOG:310")
process("IBM:84.01")
```

We created a regular expression to match a string that starts with "GOOG:" followed by a positive decimal number. We stored that in a val named GoogStock. Behind the scenes, Scala created an unapply() method for this extractor. It will return the value that matches the pattern within the parentheses—price:

```
Price of GOOG is $310.84
not processing GOOG:310
not processing IBM:84.01
```

The extractor we just created is not really reusable. It looks for the symbol "GOOG," but if we want to look for other symbols, that's not very useful. With hardly any effort, we can make it reusable:

```
def process(input : String) {
  val MatchStock = """^(.+):(\d*\.\d+)""".r
  input match {
    case MatchStock("GOOG", price) => println(s"We got GOOG at $$$price")
    case MatchStock("IBM", price) => println(s"IBM's trading at $$$price")
    case MatchStock(symbol, price) => println(s"Price of $symbol is $$$price")
    case _ => println(s"not processing $input")
  }
}
process("GOOG:310.84")
process("IBM:84.01")
process("GE:15.96")
```

In the example, our regular expression matches a string that starts with any character or digit, followed by a colon and then a positive decimal number. The part before the : and the part after it are returned as two separate pattern variables by the generated unapply() method. We can match for specific stocks like "GOOG" and "IBM" or we can simply receive whatever symbol that's given to us, as shown in the case expressions. The output from the code is shown here:

```
We got GOOG at $310.84
IBM's trading at $84.01
Price of GE is $15.96
```

As you can see, Scala takes a no-sweat approach to using regular expressions in pattern matching.

The Omnipresent Underscore Character

That little character _ (underscore) seems to be everywhere in Scala—you've seen it a few times in this book so far; it's probably the most widely used symbol in Scala. Knowing the different places where it's used can alleviate surprises when you encounter it the next time. Here's a list of various uses of the symbol.

The _ symbol may be used:

- *as a wildcard in imports* For example, import java.util._ is the Scala equivalent of import java.util.* in Java.

- *as a prefix to index a tuple* Given an tuple val names = ("Tom", "Jerry") you can access the two values using the syntax names._1 and names._2, respectively.

- *as implied arguments to a function value* The code list.map { _ * 2 } is equivalent to list.map { e => e * 2 }. Likewise, the code list.reduce { _ + _ } is equivalent to list.reduce { (a, b) => a + b }.

- *to initialize variables with default values* For example, var min : Int = _ initializes min to 0 while var msg : String = _ initializes the variable msg to null.

- *to mix operators in function names* As you'll recall, in Scala operators are defined as methods; for example, the :: method that's used to prefix an element to a list. Scala does not permit directly mixing operators with alphanumeric characters; for example, foo: is not allowed. However, you may use an underscore to get around that restriction, like so: foo_:.

- *as a wildcard in pattern matching* case _ will match any value given whereas case _: Int will match any integer value. Furthermore, case <people>{_*}</people> will match an XML element named people with zero or more children.

- *with case in the catch block, when handling exceptions.*

- *as part of the explosion operation, for example, max(arg: _*) to transform an array or list argument to discrete values before passing to a function that expects a varargs.*

- *for partially applying a function* For example, in the code val square = Math.pow(_: Int, 2) we've partially applied the pow() method to create a square() function.

The _ symbol is intended to make the code concise and expressive. Use your judgement when deciding when to make use of that symbol. Use it only when the code truly appears concise—that is,the code is transparent and easy to understand and maintain. Avoid it if you feel the code is getting to be terse, hard to understand, or cryptic.

Wrapping Up

In this chapter, you saw one of the most powerful features of Scala. Right off the shelf, you can match simple literals, types, tuples, lists, and so on. If you want a bit more control on the matching, you can use the case class or the all-too-charming extractors. You also saw how regular expressions manifest as extractors. If you want to match simple literals, the match is quite adequate. If you want to match arbitrary patterns, Scala extractors are your friend. You'll see pattern matching shine in concurrent programming later in this book.

CHAPTER 10

Handling Exceptions

Java's checked exceptions force you to catch errors, including those you don't care to handle, so programmers often place empty catch blocks, thus suppressing exceptions instead of naturally propagating them to be handled at the right place. Scala doesn't do that. It lets you handle only exceptions you care about and leave out the rest. Those you don't handle are propagated automatically. In this chapter, you'll learn how to handle exceptions in Scala.

Exceptions in Scala

Scala supports the Java semantics for exception handling, but the syntax for try-catch is quite different. Also, Scala does not distinguish between checked and unchecked exceptions—it treats all exceptions as if they're unchecked.

In Scala you throw exceptions just like in Java; for example:

```
throw new IllegalArgumentException
```

Remember, you can leave out the empty parentheses after the class name when creating an instance and semicolons are optional.

Also, you can use a try block just like in Java. Scala, however, doesn't force you to catch exceptions that you don't care about—not even checked exceptions. This prevents you from adding unnecessary catch blocks—you simply let the exceptions you don't care to catch propagate up the chain. For example, if we want to call the Thread's sleep(), then instead of this:

```
// Java code
try {
  Thread.sleep(1000);
}
catch(InterruptedException ex) {
  // Losing sleep over what to do here?
}
```

we can simply write this:

```
Thread.sleep(1000)
```

Scala did not insist that we write an unnecessary try-catch block.

Of course, you certainly should handle exceptions you can do something about—that's what catch is for. The syntax of catch is quite different in Scala; you use pattern matching for handling the exceptions. Let's look at an example of try-catch. First, here's the code that may throw different exceptions:

ExceptionHandling/Tax.scala
```
object Tax {
  def taxFor(amount: Double) = {
    if (amount < 0)
      throw new IllegalArgumentException("Amount must be greater than zero")

    if (amount < 0.01)
      throw new RuntimeException("Amount too small to be taxed")

    if (amount > 1000000) throw new Exception("Amount too large...")

    amount * 0.08
  }
}
```

Let's call the taxFor() method and handle some of the exceptions.

ExceptionHandling/ExceptionHandling.scala
```
for (amount <- List(100.0, 0.009, -2.0, 1000001.0)) {
  try {
    print(s"Amount: $$$amount ")
    println(s"Tax: $$${Tax.taxFor(amount)}")
  }
  catch {
    case ex: IllegalArgumentException => println(ex.getMessage)
    case ex: RuntimeException => {
      // if you need a block of code to handle exception
      println(s"Don't bother reporting...${ex.getMessage}")
    }
  }
}
```

Here's the output from the code, with a partial stack trace:

```
Amount: $100.0 Tax: $8.0
Amount: $0.009 Don't bother reporting...Amount too small to be taxed
Amount: $-2.0 Amount must be greater than zero
Amount: $1000001.0 java.lang.Exception: Amount too large...
        at Tax$.taxFor(Tax.scala:9)
...
```

The taxFor() method may throw three different exceptions depending on the input. The catch block has case statements for handling two of these exceptions. The output shows how these blocks handled these two exceptions. The third unhandled exception results in termination of the program with details of the stack trace being printed. The order of the case statements is important, as we discuss in the next section.

In the previous example, we saw how to catch specific exceptions. If we want to catch just about anything thrown, we can catch Throwable and also use an _ (underscore) for the variable name if we don't care to know the exception details, as shown in the following example:

ExceptionHandling/CatchAll.scala
```
for (amount <- List(100.0, 0.009, -2.0, 1000001.0)) {
  try {
    print(s"Amount: $$$amount ")
    println(s"Tax: $$${Tax.taxFor(amount)}")
  }
  catch {
    case ex : IllegalArgumentException => println(ex.getMessage)
    case _ : Throwable => println("Something went wrong")
  }
}
```

The catchall case caught all but the IllegalArgumentException, which had its own special catch block, as we see in the output:

```
Amount: $100.0 Tax: $8.0
Amount: $0.009 Something went wrong
Amount: $-2.0 Amount must be greater than zero
Amount: $1000001.0 Something went wrong
```

Scala also supports the finally block—just as in Java, it's executed irrespective of whether the code in the try block threw an exception.

Just as catching checked exceptions is optional in Scala, so too is declaring checked exceptions optional. Scala doesn't require us to declare what exceptions we intend to throw. See *Extending Classes*, on page 223 for issues related to intermixing the code with Java.

Mind the Catch Order

Unlike Java, we have to be mindful of the order in which we place the catch blocks. The Java compiler is more vigilant than Scala in this area. When attempting to handle exceptions, Java watches over the order in which we place multiple catch blocks. The following example will give us a compilation error:

ExceptionHandling/JavaCatchOrder.java

```java
//Java code—will not compile due to incorrect catch order

public class JavaCatchOrder {
  public void catchOrderExample() {
    try {
      String str = "hello";
      System.out.println(str.charAt(31));
    }
    catch(Exception ex) { System.out.println("Exception caught"); }
    catch(StringIndexOutOfBoundsException ex) { //ERROR
      System.out.println("Invalid Index"); }
  }
}
```

If we compile this code, we'll get the following error:

```
JavaCatchOrder.java:10: error: exception StringIndexOutOfBoundsException
has already been caught
    catch(StringIndexOutOfBoundsException ex) { //ERROR
    ^

1 error
```

The pattern matching style that Scala uses for its catch blocks takes effect in the order in which you present. Sadly, Scala doesn't warn you if a former statement handles exceptions that you intend to handle in later statements. We can see this in the following example:

ExceptionHandling/CatchOrder.scala

```scala
val amount = -2
try {
  print(s"Amount: $$$amount ")
  println(s"Tax: $$${Tax.taxFor(amount)}")
}
catch {
  case ex : Exception => println("Something went wrong")
  case ex : IllegalArgumentException => println(ex.getMessage)
}
```

Here's the output from the previous code:

```
Amount: $-2 Something went wrong
```

The first case matches Exception and all of its subclasses. As a result, unfortunately, the second case became redundant without warning or error. When using multiple catch blocks, you must ensure that exceptions are being handled properly by the catch blocks, the way you intended.

Wrapping Up

In this short chapter, you learned about Scala's concise and elegant way of handling exceptions. Scala also doesn't require you to catch exceptions that you don't care to handle. This allows for the exception to be propagated unaltered to higher levels in the code for proper handling. In addition to the different syntax, you learned about the caveats related to proper ordering of the catch blocks.

CHAPTER 11

Programming Recursions

The idea of recursion—solving a problem using solutions to its subproblems—is alluring. Many algorithms and problems are recursive in nature. Once we get the hang of it, designing solutions using recursion becomes highly expressive and intuitive.

In general, the biggest catch with recursions is stack overflow for large input values. But, thankfully that's not so in Scala for specially structured recursions. In this chapter we explore the powerful tail call optimization techniques and the support classes baked into Scala and its library, respectively. Using these easy-to-access facilities, you can implement highly recursive algorithms and reap their benefits for really large input values without blowing out the stack.

A Simple Recursion

Recursion is used quite extensively in a number of algorithms, like quick sort, dynamic programming, stack-based operations...and the list goes on. Recursion is highly expressive and intuitive. Sometimes we also use recursion to avoid mutation. Let's look at a use of recursion here. We'll keep the problem simple so we can focus on the issues with recursion instead of dealing with problem or domain complexities.

ProgrammingRecursions/factorial.scala

```scala
def factorial(number: Int) : BigInt = {
  if(number == 0)
    1
  else
    number * factorial(number - 1)
}
```

The factorial() function receives a parameter and returns a value of 1 if the parameter is zero. Otherwise, it recursively calls itself to return a product of that number times the factorial of the number minus one.

Writing a recursive function in Scala is much like writing any function, except the return-type inference takes a vacation—Scala insists on seeing the return-type explicitly for recursive functions. The reason for this is, since the function calls itself in at least one path of execution, Scala doesn't want to take the burden of figuring out the return type.

Let's run the factorial() function for a relatively small input value:

```
println(factorial(5))
```

The call will run quickly and produce the desired result, showing that Scala handled the recursive call quite well:

```
120
```

Take a close look at the code on line 5 in the factorial() function; the last operation is the multiplication (*). In each call through the function, the value of the number parameter will be held in a level of stack, while waiting for the result from the subsequent call to arrive. If the input parameter is 5, the call will get six levels deep before the recursion terminates.

The stack is a limited resource and can't grow boundlessly. For a large input value, simple recursion will run into trouble rather quickly. For example, try calling the factorial() function with a large value, like so:

```
println(factorial(10000))
```

Here's the fate of that call:

```
java.lang.StackOverflowError
```

It's quite sad that such a powerful and elegant concept meets such a terrible fate, incapable of taking on some real demand.

Most languages that support recursion have limitations on the use of recursion. Thankfully, some languages, like Scala, have some nice support to avoid these issues, as you'll see next.

Tail Call Optimization (TCO)

Although many languages support recursion, some compilers go a step further to optimize recursive calls. As a general rule, they convert recursions into iterations as a way to avoid the stack overflow issue.

Iterations don't face the stack overflow issue that recursions are prone to, but iterations aren't as expressive. With the optimization, we can write highly expressive and intuitive recursive code and let the compiler transform recursions into safer iterations before runtime—see *Structure and Interpretation of Computer Programs [AS96]* by Abelson and Sussman. Not all recursions, however, can be transformed into iterations. Only recursions that have a special structure—*tail recursions*—enjoy this privilege. Let's explore this further.

In the factorial() function, the final call on line 5 is multiplication. In a *tail* recursion, the final call will be to the function itself. In that case, the function call is said to be in the tail position. We'll rework the factorial() function to use tail recursion, but first let's explore the benefit of doing so using another example.

No Optimization for Regular Recursions

Scala performs optimizations for tail recursion but doesn't provide any optimization for regular recursions. Let's see the difference with an example.

In the next example, the mad() function throws an exception when it meets a parameter value of 0. Note that the last operation in the recursion is multiplication.

ProgrammingRecursions/mad.scala
```
def mad(parameter: Int) : Int = {
  if(parameter == 0)
    throw new RuntimeException("Error")
  else
    1 * mad(parameter - 1)
}
```

```
mad(5)
```

Here's an excerpt from the output of running the code:

```
java.lang.RuntimeException: Error
        at Main$$anon$1.mad(mad.scala:3)
        at Main$$anon$1.mad(mad.scala:5)
        at Main$$anon$1.mad(mad.scala:5)
        at Main$$anon$1.mad(mad.scala:5)
        at Main$$anon$1.mad(mad.scala:5)
        at Main$$anon$1.mad(mad.scala:5)
        at Main$$anon$1.<init>(mad.scala:8)
```

The exception stack trace shows that we're six levels deep in the call to the mad() function before it blew up. This is regular recursion at work, just the way we'd expect.

TCO to the Rescue

Not all languages that support recursion support TCO; for example, Java doesn't have support for TCO and all recursion, at the tail position or not, will face the same fate of stack overflow for large input. Scala readily supports TCO.

Let's change the mad() function to remove the redundant product of 1. That'd make the call tail recursive—the call to the function is the last, or in the tail position.

```
def mad(parameter: Int) : Int = {
  if(parameter == 0)
    throw new RuntimeException("Error")
  else
    mad(parameter - 1)
}

mad(5)
```

Let's look at the output from this modified version:

```
java.lang.RuntimeException: Error
        at Main$$anon$1.mad(mad2.scala:3)
        at Main$$anon$1.<init>(mad2.scala:8)
```

The number of recursive calls to the mad() function is the same in both the versions. However, the stack trace for the modified version shows we're only one level deep, instead of six levels, when the exception was thrown. That's due to the handy work of Scala's tail call optimization.

You can see this optimization firsthand by running the scala command with the -save option, like so: scala -save mad.scala. This will save the bytecode in a file named mad.jar. Then run jar xf mad.jar followed by javap -c -private Main\$\$anon\$1.class. This will reveal the bytecode generated by the Scala compiler.

Let's first look at the bytecode for the mad() function written as a regular recursion:

```
  private int mad(int);
    Code:
       0: iload_1
       1: iconst_0
       2: if_icmpne     15
       5: new           #14                  // class
java/lang/RuntimeException
       8: dup
       9: ldc           #16                  // String Error
      11: invokespecial #20                  // Method
```

```
java/lang/RuntimeException."<init>":(Ljava/lang/String;)V
      14: athrow
      15: iconst_1
      16: aload_0
      17: iload_1
      18: iconst_1
      19: isub
      20: invokespecial #22                // Method mad:(I)I
      23: imul
      24: ireturn
```

Toward the end of the mad() method, the invokeSpecial bytecode, marked as line 20, shows the call is recursive. Now, modify the code to make it tail recursive and then take a peek at the generated bytecode using the earlier steps.

```
  private int mad(int);
    Code:
       0: iload_1
       1: iconst_0
       2: if_icmpne     15
       5: new           #14                // class
java/lang/RuntimeException
       8: dup
       9: ldc           #16                // String Error
      11: invokespecial #20                // Method
java/lang/RuntimeException."<init>":(Ljava/lang/String;)V
      14: athrow
      15: iload_1
      16: iconst_1
      17: isub
      18: istore_1
      19: goto          0
```

Instead of the invokeSpecial we see a goto, which is a simple jump, indicating a simple iteration instead of a recursive method call—that's smart optimization without much effort on our part.

Ensuring TCO

The compiler automatically transformed the tail recursion into an iteration. This quiet optimization is nice, but a bit unsettling—there's no immediate visible feedback to tell. To infer, we'd have to either examine the bytecode or check if the code fails for large inputs. Neither of those is appealing.

Thankfully, Scala has a nice little annotation to help program tail recursions with intention. You can mark any function with the annotation tailrec and Scala will verify at compile time that the function is tail recursive. If by mistake the function is not tail recursive, and hence can't be optimized, the compiler will give a stern error.

To see this annotation at work, place it on the factorial() function, like so:

```
@scala.annotation.tailrec
def factorial(number: Int) : BigInt = {
  if(number == 0)
    1
  else
    number * factorial(number - 1)
}

println(factorial(10000))
```

Since this version of the factorial() function is a regular recursion and not a tail recursion, the compiler will report an appropriate error:

```
error: could not optimize @tailrec annotated method factorial: it contains
a recursive call not in tail position
    number * factorial(number - 1)
            ^
error found
```

Turning the regular recursion into tail recursion is not hard. Instead of performing the multiplication operation upon return from the recursive call to the method, we can pre-compute it and push the partial result as a parameter. Let's refactor the code for that:

```
@scala.annotation.tailrec
def factorial(fact: BigInt, number: Int) : BigInt = {
  if(number == 0)
    fact
  else
    factorial(fact * number, number - 1)
}

println(factorial(1, 10000))
```

The factorial() function in this modified version takes two parameters, with fact —the partial result computed so far—as the first parameter. The recursive call to the factorial() function is in the tail position. which complies with the annotation at the top of the function. With this change, Scala won't complain; instead it will apply the optimization for the call.

Run this version of the function to see the output:

```
284625968091705451890641321211986889014805140170279923079417999427441134000
...
```

The TCO in Scala kicks in automatically for any tail recursive functions. The annotation is optional and, when used, makes the intention clear and expressive. It is a good idea to use the annotation. It ensures that the tail recursion stays that way through refactorings and also conveys the intent to fellow programmers who may come to refactor the code at a later time.

Trampoline Calls

Even though the TCO support in Scala is quite powerful, it's limited. The compiler only detects direct recursions—that is, a function calling itself. If two functions call each other, known as a trampoline call, Scala doesn't detect such recursion and performs no optimization.

Though the Scala compiler provides no support for trampoline calls, we can use the TailRec class to avoid stack overflow issues.

Let's first take a look at an example with trampoline calls that will run into the stack overflow error for large input values.

ProgrammingRecursions/words.scala
```
import scala.io.Source._

def explore(count: Int, words: List[String]) : Int =
  if(words.size == 0)
    count
  else
    countPalindrome(count, words)

def countPalindrome(count: Int, words: List[String]) : Int  = {
  val firstWord = words.head

  if(firstWord.reverse == firstWord)
    explore(count + 1, words.tail)
  else
    explore(count, words.tail)
}

def callExplore(text: String) = println(explore(0, text.split(" ").toList))

callExplore("dad mom and racecar")

try {
  val text =
    fromURL("https://en.wikipedia.org/wiki/Gettysburg_Address").mkString
  callExplore(text)
} catch {
  case ex : Throwable => println(ex)
}
```

The explore() function takes a partial result count and a list of words as its parameters. If the list is empty, the function immediately returns the given count; otherwise, it calls the countPalindrome() method. That method in turn checks if the first word in the list is a palindrome or not. If it is, it calls the explore() method with an increased value of count. Otherwise, it calls the explore() method with the value of count unaltered. In either case, it passes forward, to the explore() function, the list with the first word removed.

The callExplore() function takes a string of text, splits it into words separated by spaces, converts that array to a list, and forwards it to the explore() function. It finally reports the result.

We call callExplore() twice, first with a small string and then with a large piece of text we obtain from the web. Let's take a look at the response from the execution of the code:

```
3
java.lang.StackOverflowError
```

For the short string, the code correctly identified the number of palindromes. However, for the longer text it ran into trouble.

Marking any of the functions in this example with @scala.annotation.tailrec won't help—you'll get an error that none of these functions are recursive. The Scala compiler doesn't recognize recursion that spans across methods.

In cases like this where the recursion involves functions calling each other, we can use the TailRec class and the functions available in the scala.util.control.Tail-Calls package.

An instance of TailRec simply holds a function value (see Chapter 6, *Function Values and Closures*, on page 101). The function result() of TailRec is a simple iterator or a loop. It gets the inner function held in the TailRec and checks if it's actually an instance of a subclass Call or Done. If an instance of Call is received, it signals continuation of the calls and the iteration continues to execute the inner function for further processing. If an instance of Done is received, it signals the termination of the iteration and the result held in the inner function is returned.

If you'd like to continue the recursion, use the tailcall() function. To terminate the recursion, use the done() function, which will in turn create an instance of Done. Let's apply these ideas to the previous code example by refactoring it to use TailRec.

ProgrammingRecursions/wordsTrampoline.scala
```scala
import scala.io.Source._
```

```scala
import scala.util.control.TailCalls._

def explore(count: Int, words: List[String]) : TailRec[Int] =
  if(words.size == 0)
    done(count)
  else
    tailcall(countPalindrome(count, words))

def countPalindrome(count: Int, words: List[String]) : TailRec[Int]  = {
  val firstWord = words.head

  if(firstWord.reverse == firstWord)
    tailcall(explore(count + 1, words.tail))
  else
    tailcall(explore(count, words.tail))
}

def callExplore(text: String) =
  println(explore(0, text.split(" ").toList).result)

callExplore("dad mom and racecar")

try {
  val text =
    fromURL("https://en.wikipedia.org/wiki/Gettysburg_Address").mkString
  callExplore(text)
} catch {
  case ex : Throwable => println(ex)
}
```

The explore() method returns a TailRec instead of an Int. If the list is empty, it returns the result of a call to done() with the desired result. To continue the recursion, it calls tailcall(). Likewise, the countPalindrome() continues the recursion by calling tailcall() with the appropriate values.

The key idea to remember here is that both done() or tailcall() simply wrap their parameters into a function for later evaluation or lazy evaluation, and return immediately from the function. The actual decision to continue execution or to terminate is made within the result() function, which is called on the result of the explore() function. This critical step is carried out in the callExplore() function.

Run this modified version and you can see that the code doesn't suffer the stack overflow problem:

3
352

Although Scala does automatic optimization for calls that are tail recursive, it doesn't provide direct compiler support for trampoline calls. But as you saw, we can easily avoid running into the stack overflow issue by using the facility provided in the Scala library.

Wrapping Up

Recursions provide a nice, intuitive, and expressive solution to many problems. However, programmers often either avoid recursions or are rather reluctant to use them because of the issue with stack overflow for large input values. The Scala compiler has built-in support to optimize recursions that are at the tail position into iterations, so you can avoid this problem. This optimization allows us to more liberally use recursions where it makes sense, without the worry of blowing out stacks. You also saw the Scala library support for working easily with trampoline recursions. Between these two solutions, solving critical algorithms and problems becomes a matter of writing just a few lines of code with fewer concerns to worry about.

Talking about critical algorithms and problems, we will look next at how Scala's support for concurrency can make code execution faster and more responsive.

Part III

Concurrency in Scala

Concurrency is one of those accidental complexities.
Scala provides some elegant solutions to deal with
this complex topic. You'll learn:

- *the benefits of lazy evaluations*
- *the difference between strict and lazy collec-*
  tions
- *to use parallel collections*
- *to avoid shared mutability*
- *to program with actors*

CHAPTER 12

Lazy Evaluations and Parallel Collections

Responsiveness—that's one thing that can make or break just about any application. Other factors like business value, ease of use, availability, cost, and resilience, are also important. But responsiveness is at the top—we humans take about 250 milliseconds to cognitively perceive any action; after five seconds any delay begins to feel like eternity. Any effort to lower the response time will directly impact our ability to make customers happy and, in turn, earn their loyalty.

You can make applications responsive in one of two ways. You could run computations faster by using multiple threads—that is, instead of running tasks one after another, run them in parallel. Alternatively, instead of running faster, run wisely. Postpone execution of tasks until the last possible moment.

Postponing, or evaluating lazily, can help in two ways. First, you can run tasks that are relevant now and get to those other tasks later. Second, if the results of the postponed tasks are not needed for the job on hand, you saved the time and resources that would otherwise go into running those tasks. This is often called lazy evaluation, and it's a great way to gain efficiency and responsiveness.

In this chapter you'll learn how to make use of both of these techniques—to apply lazy evaluations and to exploit parallelism using collections.

Let's Get Lazy

If you're new to lazy evaluation, you probably have used it without really calling it that. Many languages support short-circuit evaluation for conditions. If the evaluation of an argument in a condition with multiple && or || is enough to determine the truth, then the remaining arguments in that expression are not evaluated. Here's an example of a simple short-circuit evaluation.

Parallel/shortCircuit.scala

```
def expensiveComputation() = {
  println("...assume slow operation...")
  false
}

def evaluate(input: Int) = {
  println(s"evaluate called with $input")
  if(input >= 10 && expensiveComputation())
    println("doing work...")
  else
    println("skipping")
}

evaluate(0)
evaluate(100)
```

The expensiveComputation() function will not be executed from within the evaluate() function if the value of the parameter is less than 10, as we see in the output:

```
evaluate called with 0
skipping
evaluate called with 100
...assume slow operation...
skipping
```

We can say that the program was pretty lazy in evaluating the expensiveComputation() method. The function is evaluated only if input is 10 or greater. The program is not utterly lazy, however. To see this let's change that code just a bit.

```
val perform = expensiveComputation()
if(input >= 10 && perform)
```

We first invoked the expensiveComputation() function, stored the result in an immutable variable named perform, and then used that value in the condition. When we run this modified version, even if the value of perform is not needed or used, the program eagerly evaluates the function as we see from the output —how sad.

```
evaluate called with 0
...assume slow operation...
skipping
evaluate called with 100
...assume slow operation...
skipping
```

Scala didn't look ahead to see that the result of this computation may not really be needed, but we can tell it to be lazy, to postpone evaluating the value until it's really needed. And doing that takes almost no effort—after all, you don't want to work hard to be lazy.

Let's make one more change to the code that would enable lazy evaluation of the variable.

```
lazy val perform = expensiveComputation()
if(input >= 10 && perform)
```

We declared the immutable variable perform as lazy. This tells the Scala compiler to delay the binding of the variable to its value, until that value is used. If we never used that value, then the variable goes unbound, and thus, the function to yield the value is never evaluated. We can see this behavior from the output:

```
evaluate called with 0
skipping
evaluate called with 100
...assume slow operation...
skipping
```

You can mark any variable as lazy and the binding to its value will be postponed until the first use of that variable.

That seems nifty, why not mark all variables as lazy in that case? The reason is *side effects*. Suppose that the computations that will yield the values for lazy variables don't have any side effects—that is, they don't affect any external state nor are they affected by any external state. In that case, we should have no problem with the order in which they're evaluated. However, if the computations have side effects, then the order in which the variables are bound matters. To understand this better, let's look at an example with two lazy variables.

Parallel/lazyOrder.scala
```
import scala.io._

def read = StdIn.readInt()

lazy val first = read
lazy val second = read

if(Math.random() < 0.5)
  second

println(first - second)
```

The read() function reads an Int value from the console. We call that function twice but assign the result of the calls to two variables, first and second, respectively. Since the two variables are declared as lazy neither of them will be bound to their values at this time. Then, if the value of the call to random() is less than 0.5, the second variable is referenced in the body of the if statement, and this causes the variable second to be bound and evaluated before the first variable. When we run this code, about half the time the variable second will be referenced first and so it will be bound first. About the other half the time, however, the variable first will be bound before the variable second. As a result, the values read from the calls to the read() function will be bound to the two variables in a random order. The result in this case is that non-commutative computations will become unpredictable.

Let's run the code twice, each time with exactly the same input, 1 and 2 in that sequence, and take a look at the output:

```
> scala lazyOrder.scala
1
2
1
> scala lazyOrder.scala
1
2
-1
>
```

It takes no effort to declare variables lazy, but you do have to be quite careful what you make lazy.

Making Strict Collections Lazy

You learned how to make a single variable lazy. Why stop there? You can make an entire collection lazy.

All the collections you worked with in Chapter 8, *Collections*, on page 129 are called *strict* collections. Actions on them are strictly performed upon call. That's good at times, but there's a benefit to being lazy. Let's explore this with some examples.

In order to see the eager vs. lazy evaluation, we'll use print statements to show what calls are being made in the next example. We start with a list of tuples where each element contains a name and an age value. We're interested in selecting the first person from the list whose name starts with J and who is older than 17. Let's program that with a strict collection first.

Parallel/strictCollection.scala
```scala
val people = List(("Mark", 32), ("Bob", 22), ("Jane", 8), ("Jill", 21),
("Nick", 50), ("Nancy", 42), ("Mike", 19), ("Sara", 12), ("Paula", 42),
("John", 21))
```

```
def isOlderThan17(person: (String, Int)) = {
  println(s"isOlderThan17 called for $person")
  val (_, age) = person
  age > 17
}

def isNameStartsWithJ(person: (String, Int)) = {
  println(s"isNameStartsWithJ called for $person")
  val (name, _) = person
  name.startsWith("J")
}
```

```
println(people.filter {isOlderThan17}.filter {isNameStartsWithJ}.head)
```

We created a list with ten tuples and assigned it to the variable people. Each tuple holds a string and an integer, representing the name and age of a fictitious person. The isOlderThan17() function returns true if the second value in the tuple is greater than 17. Likewise, isNameStartsWithJ() returns true if the first value in the tuple starts with the letter J. We perform the main operation on the list in that concise argument to the println() method. We start with the list, filter out tuples based on age, then filter out based on the name, and finally only retain the first value of the resulting list.

Run this code to see the final result as well as the various operations that were performed along the way.

```
isOlderThan17 called for (Mark,32)
isOlderThan17 called for (Bob,22)
isOlderThan17 called for (Jane,8)
isOlderThan17 called for (Jill,21)
isOlderThan17 called for (Nick,50)
isOlderThan17 called for (Nancy,42)
isOlderThan17 called for (Mike,19)
isOlderThan17 called for (Sara,12)
isOlderThan17 called for (Paula,42)
isOlderThan17 called for (John,21)
isNameStartsWithJ called for (Mark,32)
isNameStartsWithJ called for (Bob,22)
isNameStartsWithJ called for (Jill,21)
isNameStartsWithJ called for (Nick,50)
isNameStartsWithJ called for (Nancy,42)
isNameStartsWithJ called for (Mike,19)
isNameStartsWithJ called for (Paula,42)
isNameStartsWithJ called for (John,21)
(Jill,21)
```

If you think that doesn't look very efficient, you're right on. The first filter() operation examined each and every one of the tuples in the original collection —it's strict. That resulted in a new collection with only tuples representing folks over 17 years. Then the second filter() examined each tuple in that second list to produce the final result of adults whose names start with the letter J. Finally the head operation picked the first one. That was a lot of work.

You can turn a strict collection into lazy using the view() method. While a strict collection will evaluate the operations immediately on call, the lazy collections postpone operations. The operations are executed if and only when a result that's represented by a non-lazy or non-view is requested. In other words, it stays lazy, and avoids doing work, until you ask for a strict or non-lazy result. Let's convert the strict collection in the previous example to a lazy collection before calling the first filter() operation on it.

```
println(people.view.filter {isOlderThan17}.filter {isNameStartsWithJ}.head)
```

We changed people to people.view in the last line of the code—that's the only change we made. Now let's run this modified version and take a look at the output:

```
isOlderThan17 called for (Mark,32)
isNameStartsWithJ called for (Mark,32)
isOlderThan17 called for (Bob,22)
isNameStartsWithJ called for (Bob,22)
isOlderThan17 called for (Jane,8)
isOlderThan17 called for (Jill,21)
isNameStartsWithJ called for (Jill,21)
(Jill,21)
```

This modified lazy collection version of code did less work to produce the same result compared to the strict collection version. When we called the filter() method, the operation of examining the elements wasn't done immediately this time, nor was it done in strict order.

It's the call to head() that triggered the execution. If you remove the call to the head() function from the code and run it, you'll notice that the two functions isOlderThan17() and isNameStartsWithJ() are not called. That's not the only difference.

During the strict evaluation, all the elements in the original list were first examined and then all elements in the transformed list were evaluated. In this modified version, right after the first filter operation passes on an element, the second filter operation is performed. If the second filter passes, then the head() function will be evaluated immediately. The next element in the list is examined only if either one of the filter operations failed. Once the operations yield the desired result, the processing of the remaining elements is totally skipped. Lazy is pretty efficient!

In the worst case, for example, if we desire the last element, then all the elements will be processed. The main benefit is it's possible that the result can be found without examining all the elements and that lazy evaluation makes that easy to write.

If lazy is so easy, why not make all collections lazy? Just like lazy binding of variables, we have to be careful making a collection lazy. Correctness should precede efficiency—both the strict and the lazy versions of any code should produce the same desired correct results. The only difference is that lazy is more efficient than strict.

Lazy is not the right option all the time. If we have to effectively perform all computations in order to compute the final result, then laziness may not give us any benefit at all over the strict solution. In fact, it may even be worse. For example, in the strict and lazy versions of the previous example, we saw 18 vs. 7 calls to those two functions passed to the filter() method. Try changing the last call from head() to last() and look at the output of both versions. You'll notice that the lazy version does a lot more work to produce the same result as the strict version.

Don't assume that lazy is always efficient—it's not. The nature of the problem or the algorithm has a significant impact on whether or not you get efficiency out of laziness. Take time to experiment and test laziness, to ensure that the result is correct and the execution is also efficient.

The Ultimately Lazy Streams

Placing a lazy view on a strict collection doesn't change the collection; it helps delay executing operations to the last possible moment. In other words, with a lazy view the values may all be in there; you simply won't process them urgently or eagerly. A Stream is lazy to the bone—it produces values only on demand.

That may sound odd at first and may raise a number of questions: how many values would it hold, when does it create it, how do we get the values? A stream may be finite or infinite—that's right, an infinite series. Wait a minute, if it is infinite in size, then how could we possibly store it on our machines, with the limited amount of memory we have? Well, now you know what this cloud computing is all about, with such abundant storage—just kidding. An infinite series generates values only when you ask it to, and produces only the values you ask for. In essence it says, "I'm infinite, but I dare you to ask for all the values."

We'll work through two examples so you can get the hang of streams and infinite series. Let's first create a number generator, much like the ones you'll find in offices that serve a large number of customers. With each pull a new number is generated, the one next in sequence. Here's the code that starts generating values, given a starting number.

```
Parallel/numberGenerator.scala
def generate(starting: Int) : Stream[Int] = {
  starting #:: generate(starting + 1)
}
```

```
println(generate(25))
```

The generate() function takes an integer starting as its parameter and returns a Stream of integers. Its implementation uses a special function #:: to concatenate the value in the variable starting and the result of a recursive call to the generate() function. In concept, the function #:: of Stream is much like the function :: of List; they both concatenate or prefix a value to the respective collection. However, the function on the Stream is lazy; it performs the concatenation only on demand, postponing the execution until the final result is requested.

Thus, unlike a regular recursion, the program won't eagerly pounce on that call. Instead, it lazily postpones calling that function. You must be curious to know the result of calling this function. We'll quench that thirst by calling the function and printing the result of that call.

```
Stream(25, ?)
```

The output tells us that we have a stream with the initial value 25 followed by a yet-to-be-computed value. That seems like the stream is throwing a challenge: "If you want the next one, come and get it." If you don't make any call on the stream, it won't do any real work or take up any space for elements.

There's only one way to make the stream generate values and do some work: you've got to *force* a result out of it. You could use a call to the force() method for that, but be careful not to call force() on a stream that is infinite—you'll end up running out of memory, even on the cloud! Alternately you can call a method that will force a result that is a non-stream or non-lazy, like a call to toList(), for example. Again, make sure to perform this on a finite stream.

That begs the question, how can we convert an infinite stream to a finite stream? The take() method can help us with that. This method also results in a stream, but unlike the original stream you call it on, the resulting stream is finite in size. Let's take a look at the code to get some data out of the stream we created.

Parallel/numberGenerator.scala
```
println(generate(25).take(10).force)
println(generate(25).take(10).toList)
```

The code shows examples of both force() and toList(). The first method will force the stream to generate values. The second method will do the same and, in addition, convert the result to a strict collection, a list. Let's take a look at the result in the output.

```
Stream(25, 26, 27, 28, 29, 30, 31, 32, 33, 34)
List(25, 26, 27, 28, 29, 30, 31, 32, 33, 34)
```

The force() method kept the result as a stream but finite in size as limited by the take() method. The toList() method helped transform that into a familiar list.

The take() method helped to constraint the stream to a finite number of elements. You may also ask the stream to keep generating—on force, of course —while a certain condition is not met. Let's ask the stream to generate values until it reaches a number, say 40.

Parallel/numberGenerator.scala
```
println(generate(25).takeWhile{ _ < 40 }.force)
```

We replaced the call to take() with takeWhile(), which takes a function value as a parameter. As long as the expression in this function value keeps returning true, the force() method will continue to generate values. Once the function value returns false the generation will terminate. We can see this from the output:

```
Stream(25, 26, 27, 28, 29, 30, 31, 32, 33, 34, 35, 36, 37, 38, 39)
```

We created an infinite series and then bound it. The series doesn't have to be continuous. Let's look at another example that shows how to create a series of prime numbers.

Parallel/primes.scala
```
def isDivisibleBy(number: Int, divisor: Int) = number % divisor == 0

def isPrime(number: Int) =
  number > 1 && !(2 to number - 1).exists { isDivisibleBy(number, _) }

def primes(starting: Int) : Stream[Int] = {
  println(s"computing for $starting")
  if(isPrime(starting))
    starting #:: primes(starting + 1)
  else
    primes(starting + 1)
}
```

The first two functions are self-explanatory. The interesting parts are in the primes() function. In this function we first print a message to display its call. If the given number is prime, we return that number with a request to lazily fetch all the primes that follow. If the given number isn't prime, we immediately proceed to search for the prime that follows this number.

This example is not much different from the number generator, except that the generation isn't contiguous. We'll use this example to learn about one other feature of streams: they memoize the values they generate. That's nothing but caching, but in our field we prefer to give weird names that no one understands. When the stream produces a new value on demand, it will cache it—I mean memoize it—before returning. Then if you ask for the same value again, it doesn't have to repeat the computations. Let's take a look at this by making two calls on the stream we create from the primes() function.

Parallel/primes.scala

```
val primesFrom100 = primes(100)

println(primesFrom100.take(3).toList)
println("Let's ask for more...")
println(primesFrom100.take(4).toList)
```

We store the stream returned by the call to primes() in the primesFrom100 variable. We use this variable twice: once to get the first three values and again to get the first four values. The first call to take(), with 3 as the argument, creates a finite stream that's backed by the original infinite stream. The call to toList() triggers the computations and places the result in a list. The second call to take() is back on the original infinite stream, but this time we ask for four values. It should give us the three values already generated and, in addition, produce a new value. That's because the values that the stream produced already are safely memoized and reused, as we see from the output—only the new value is generated:

```
computing for 100
computing for 101
computing for 102
computing for 103
computing for 104
computing for 105
computing for 106
computing for 107
List(101, 103, 107)
Let's ask for more...
computing for 108
computing for 109
List(101, 103, 107, 109)
```

Streams are one of the most charming features in the Scala library. They can come in quite handy to implement a variety of algorithms where we can conceptualize problems into a series that can be lazily generated and executed on demand. You already saw one such example, back in *Trampoline Calls*, on page 173. The tail recursion can be seen as an infinite series problem. The execution of a recursion may either produce another recursion, which can be lazily evaluated, or terminate a recursion, yielding a result. Now that you have the hang of infinite series, you'll soon be looking to see if streams are a fit for the problems you encounter.

Parallel Collections

If laziness is a road to efficiency, parallelism may be considered a flight to that destination. If two or more tasks can be executed in any sequence without any impact on the correctness of the result, then those tasks may very well be run in parallel. Scala provides a few different ways to achieve that. The easiest of those is parallel processing of elements in a collection.

We work with collections of data all the time. We may need to check the price of several products, update inventories based on the orders fulfilled, or tally up payments for recent transactions. When we have a collection of data to work with, we often use internal iterators like map(), filter(), and foldLeft() (we used a few of these in Chapter 8, *Collections*, on page 129) to perform the necessary operations and produce the desired results.

If the number of objects or items is large and/or the time to process each one of them is long, the overall response time to produce the result may become prohibitively high. Parallelizing these tasks to run on multiple threads and making use of multiple cores can tremendously improve the speed. But using low-level threading constructs and locks, unfortunately, can increase accidental complexity and the resulting concurrency-related errors, sucking the life out of programmers. Thankfully, you don't have to endure that in Scala. It's easy to parallelize operations on a collection of data.

Next we're going to implement an example to work with a collection of data sequentially, and then we'll parallelize that to improve speed.

Starting with a Sequential Collection

Let's take an example and implement it first sequentially and then refactor that to make it faster. We'll use an example to collect and display weather data—globetrotters keenly keep an eye on the weather in the cities they're heading to. Let's create a little program that will report the temperature and weather conditions in select cities.

We'll start with a list of city names, fetch the current weather condition, and report the details in sorted order by city. A request to the OpenWeatherMap's web service[1] will get us the data in different formats. We'll use the XML format since it's easy to parse that in Scala. We'll also report the time it takes to create this report.

We need a function to make a web service request and get the weather data for a given city. Let's write that first.

Parallel/weather.scala
```scala
import scala.io.Source
import scala.xml._

def getWeatherData(city: String) = {
  val url = "http://api.openweathermap.org/data/2.5/weather"

  val response = Source.fromURL(s"$url?q=$city&units=imperial&mode=xml")
  val xmlResponse = XML.loadString(response.mkString)
  val cityName = (xmlResponse \\ "city" \ "@name").text
  val temperature = (xmlResponse \\ "temperature" \ "@value").text
  val condition = (xmlResponse \\ "weather" \ "@value").text
  (cityName, temperature, condition)
}
```

The method getWeatherData() takes a city name as its parameter. In the method we first send a request to the appropriate URL for the OpenWeatherMap's web service. Since we opted to use the XML mode, the response from the service will be in that format. We then parse the XML response using the loadString() method of the XML class (we'll take a closer look at this class in Chapter 15, *Creating an Application with Scala*, on page 227). We finally use an XPath query to extract the data we desire from the XML response. The return value from this method is a tuple of three strings, with the city name, the current temperature, and the weather condition, in that order.

Next we'll create a helper function to print the weather data.

Parallel/weather.scala
```scala
def printWeatherData(weatherData: (String, String, String)) = {
  val (cityName, temperature, condition) = weatherData

  println(f"$cityName%-15s $temperature%-6s $condition")
}
```

---

1.   openweathermap.org

In the printWeatherData() method we receive a tuple with weather details and using the f string interpolator we format the data for printing on the console. We need one last step: a set of sample data and a way to measure the time. Let's create that function.

Parallel/weather.scala
```
def timeSample(getData: List[String] => List[(String, String, String)]) = {
  val cities = List("Houston,us", "Chicago,us", "Boston,us", "Minneapolis,us",
    "Oslo,norway", "Tromso,norway", "Sydney,australia", "Berlin,germany",
    "London,uk", "Krakow,poland", "Rome,italy", "Stockholm,sweden",
    "Bangalore,india", "Brussels,belgium", "Reykjavik,iceland")

  val start = System.nanoTime
  getData(cities) sortBy { _._1 } foreach printWeatherData
  val end = System.nanoTime
  println(s"Time taken: ${(end - start)/1.0e9} sec")
}
```

The timeSample() method takes a function value as its parameter. The idea is for the caller of timeSample() to send a function that will take in a list of cities and return a list of tuples with weather data. Within the timeSample() function we create a list of cities in different parts of the world. Then we measure the time it takes to get the weather data using the function value parameter, sort the result in the order of city names, and print the result for each city.

We're all set to use the function we've created. Let's make sequential calls to the web service to get the data.

Parallel/weather.scala
```
timeSample { cities => cities map getWeatherData }
```

We invoke the timeSample() function and pass a function value as a parameter. The function value receives a list of cities that's passed from within the time-Sample() function. It then calls the getWeatherData() function for each city in the list, one at a time. The result of the map() operation is a list of data returned by getWeatherData() calls—tuples of weather data.

Let's run this code and take a look at the output along with the execution time.

Parallel/output/weather.output
```
Bengaluru    84.2    few clouds
Berlin       45.63   broken clouds
Boston       52.23   scattered clouds
Brussels     50.83   Sky is Clear
Chicago      46.13   sky is clear
Cracow       40.39   moderate rain
Houston      54.01   light intensity drizzle
London       55.33   Sky is Clear
```

```
Minneapolis      42.82  sky is clear
Oslo             47.3   Sky is Clear
Reykjavik        31.17  proximity shower rain
Rome             58.42  few clouds
Stockholm        47.28  Sky is Clear
Sydney           68.9   Sky is Clear
Tromso           35.6   proximity shower rain
Time taken: 67.208944087 sec
```

The cities are listed in sorted order by their name along with temperature and weather conditions at the time of the request. It must have been a rare moment of execution for the report shows London with clear skies! The code took about 67 seconds to run—I was on a slow wireless network when I ran this code; the time you observe will vary depending on your network speed and congestion. Next we'll see how to make this faster with minimal change.

Speeding Up with a Parallel Collection

The previous example has two parts: the slow part, where we go across the wire and collect the data for each city, and the fast part, where we sort the data and display it. Quite conveniently, the slow part is wrapped into the function value that we pass as an argument to the timeSample() function. We only have to replace that part to improve speed; the rest of the code can stay intact.

The map() method, which is called on a list of cities in this example, calls the attached function getWeatherData() for each city, one at a time. This is the behavior of methods on sequential collections: they execute their operation sequentially on each element of their collection. However, the operation we pass to the map() function can be done in parallel; fetching the weather data for one city is independent of getting the data for another city. Thankfully, we don't have to work hard to tell the map() method to run the operation for each city in parallel. Simply convert the collection to a parallel version and we're done.

Scala has parallel versions for many of the sequential collections. For example, ParArray is the parallel counterpart of Array; likewise, ParHashMap, ParHashSet, and ParVector for HashMap, HashSet, and Vector, respectively. You can use the method pair par() and seq() to convert a sequential collection to a parallel version and vice versa, respectively.

Let's convert our list of cities to a parallel version using the par() method. Now the map() method will run its operations in parallel. When we're done, we'll use toList() to convert the resulting parallel collection to a sequential list, the result type of the function value. Let's rewrite the call to timeSample() using the parallel collection instead of the sequential collection.

Parallel/weather.scala

```
timeSample { cities => (cities.par map getWeatherData).toList }
```

The change was minimal and is entirely within the function value. The structure of the rest of the code is exactly the same between the sequential and the concurrent version. In fact, we're reusing the rest of the code as is between the two versions—sequential and parallel. Let's run this modified version and take a look at the output.

Parallel/output/weather.output

```
Bengaluru      84.2    few clouds
Berlin         45.63   broken clouds
Boston         52.23   scattered clouds
Brussels       50.83   Sky is Clear
Chicago        46.13   sky is clear
Cracow         40.39   moderate rain
Houston        54.01   light intensity drizzle
London         55.33   Sky is Clear
Minneapolis    42.82   sky is clear
Oslo           47.3    Sky is Clear
Reykjavik      31.17   proximity shower rain
Rome           58.42   few clouds
Stockholm      47.28   Sky is Clear
Sydney         68.9    Sky is Clear
Tromso         35.6    proximity shower rain
Time taken: 0.171599394 sec
```

The output shows exactly the same weather conditions, still an unusually bright day in London. The time it took for the code, however, is a lot different —for the better. We leveraged multiple threads to run the getWeatherData() function in parallel for different cities.

That was hardly any effort to convert from sequential to parallel. Given that, the logical question is why shouldn't we use parallel collections all the time? Short answer—context matters.

You wouldn't drive a car to get a bottle of milk from the kitchen refrigerator, but you most likely do to get it from the store, along with other groceries. Likewise, you wouldn't want to use parallel collections for already fast operations on small collections. The overhead of creating and scheduling threads should not be larger than the time it takes to run the tasks. For slow tasks or large collections, parallel collections may have benefits, but not for fast tasks on small collections.

There are a few other factors, in addition to speed of computation and size of the collection, that dictate whether or not we can use a parallel collection. If the operations invoked on the collection modify a global state, then the overall result of the computation is unpredictable—shared mutability is generally a bad idea. So don't use parallel collections if the operations have side effects. Furthermore, you shouldn't use parallel collections if the operations are nonassociative. The reason for this is the order of execution is nondeterministic in parallel collections. Operations like add do not care what order you total the values. However, an operation like subtraction is very much order dependent and is not suitable for parallelization.

Scala makes it almost trivial to use parallel collections; however, we have to make that critical decision whether parallelization is the right option and ensure that we're getting the right results with improved speed.

Wrapping Up

You learned a few techniques and features in Scala that can make code execution faster and more efficient. A lazy variable postpones the binding of the variable to the last possible moment it's first needed. You learned how to convert from a strict collection to its lazy view, how to use infinite and finite streams, and how to make use of parallel collections. You also picked up a few pointers on when to use them and when to avoid them.

We've merely scratched the surface of efficiency. In the next chapter we'll take on concurrent programming.

CHAPTER 13

Programming with Actors

We often use multithreading and concurrency when programming complex, time-consuming applications, to improve the response time or performance. Traditional concurrency solutions, sadly, lead to several issues, such as thread safety, race conditions, deadlocks, livelocks, and hard-to-read error prone code. Shared mutability is the number-one culprit.

Avoid shared mutability and you've removed so many issues. But how to avoid it? That's where actors come in. Actors help to turn shared mutability into isolated mutability. Actors are active objects that guarantee mutual exclusion of access. No two threads will ever work on an actor at the same time. Due to this natural self-imposed mutual exclusion, any data stored within actors is automatically thread-safe—no explicit synchronization is needed.

If you can meaningfully split a problem into subtasks—divide-and-conquer —then you can use actors to solve the problem with good design clarity and avoid the general concurrency issues.

In this chapter we'll take a problem that can benefit from concurrency, examine the issues, and then explore actors and use them to solve the problem.

A Sequential Time-Consuming Problem

Several applications can benefit from multi-cores and multiple threads: fetching a large volume of data from multiple web services, looking up stock prices, analyzing geological data, and so forth. Instead of getting lost in the details of a complex domain and lengthy code, let's take a relatively small problem that needs very little code. This will help us focus on key issues and explore possible solutions.

We'll work with a program that finds the number of files in the subdirectory hierarchy starting with a given directory as the root. Here's a sequential implementation of the code:

```
ProgrammingActors/countFilesSequential.scala
import java.io.File

def getChildren(file: File) = {
  val children = file.listFiles()
  if(children != null) children.toList else List()
}

val start = System.nanoTime
val exploreFrom = new File(args(0))

var count = 0L
var filesToVisit = List(exploreFrom)

while(filesToVisit.size > 0) {
  val head = filesToVisit.head
  filesToVisit = filesToVisit.tail

  val children = getChildren(head)
  count = count + children.count { !_.isDirectory }
  filesToVisit = filesToVisit ::: children.filter { _.isDirectory }
}

val end = System.nanoTime
println(s"Number of files found: $count")
println(s"Time taken: ${(end - start)/1.0e9} seconds")
```

The getChildren() function takes a File as its parameter and returns either an empty list if there are no children or a list of files and subdirectories under the given directory. The constant exploreFrom refers to an instance of File that points to a directory name entered as a command-line argument. We created two mutable variables—the first sign of trouble—named count and filesToVisit. These values are initially set to 0 and a list containing only the starting directory, respectively. The while loop will iterate as long as there are files to explore in the filesToVisit list. Within the loop, we pick one file at a time from the list of files to visit, get the children of that directory, and add to the mutable variable count the number of files found. We also add the directories among the children to the list of files to visit for further exploring.

Let's run the code and measure the time it takes using the command:

```
scala countFilesSequential.scala /Users/venkats/agility
```

Before running, replace the command-line argument with the full path of a valid directory on your system—the sample run shown here uses an agility directory on my system.

Let's run the code. It may take a while to run, depending on the number of files and the levels of nesting under the starting directory provided as the command-line argument:

```
Number of files found: 479758
Time taken: 66.524453436 seconds
```

The program reported the number of files it found; it took a little over 66 seconds to get that result. That's pretty darn slow; if this were a web or a mobile app, the users would've hit the refresh button a zillion times and be long gone. We have to make this faster—a lot faster.

The Treacherous Paths to Concurrency

A quick look at the Activity Monitor on my system shows that while one core is super busy running the code, the other cores are sitting around sipping iced tea. Since this program is I/O intensive, we can get better performance if we throw a few threads at the problem and make use of those other cores.

Put on your Java hat for a minute and think about ways to make the code faster. The mere thought of using the JDK concurrency library can be quite nerve-wracking. Starting threads is not really hard, only clumsy—you'd use the executors to create a pool for threads. You can schedule exploring different subdirectories to threads from the pool. But the problem stems from the two variables—the shared mutable variables. When multiple threads get the children directories, we have to update the count and the filesToVisit variables. Let's see why this would be a problem:

- To protect the count variable from concurrent change, we may use AtomicLong. This is problematic. We have to ensure that all changes to this variable have happened before the program sees there are no more files to visit and reports the count. In other words, although *atomic* guarantees thread safety for a single value, it doesn't guarantee atomicity across multiple values that may potentially change at the same time.

- We would have to use a thread-safe collection, a synchronous list or a concurrent list, to implement the filesToVisit list. This again will protect that one variable but does not address the issue of atomicity across two variables.

- We could wrap the two variables in a class and provide synchronized methods to update the two values in one shot. That will take care of ensuring the changes to the two variables are atomic. However, now we have to ensure that the synchronization is actually happening at the right place, for the right duration. If we forget to synchronize or synchronize at the wrong place, neither the Java compiler nor the runtime will give us any warnings.

In short, the change from sequential to concurrent often turns the code into a beast. The more mutable variables, the messier it gets and the harder it becomes to prove the correctness of the code. There's no point in writing code that runs really fast just to produce unpredictable errors.

The problem on hand is a great candidate to apply actors. We can decompose the problem into subtasks, using the divide-and-conquer approach. The mutable variables can be tucked away into an actor to prevent multiple threads from concurrently updating them. Change requests can be queued instead of threads blocking and waiting on each other. We'll implement the program using actors soon, but first let's work through a few examples to learn about actors and how to use them.

Creating Actors

You typically create objects and invoke methods on them. An actor is also an object, but you never call methods on it directly. Instead you send messages and each actor is backed by a message queue. If an actor is busy processing a message, then the messages that arrive are queued—the senders aren't blocked; they fire-and-forget. At most, one message is processed on an actor at any given time. Actors are born and built with thread safety.

Let's define an actor.

ProgrammingActors/HollywoodActor.scala

```
import akka.actor._

class HollywoodActor() extends Actor {
  def receive = {
    case message => println(s"playing the role of $message")
  }
}
```

Scala uses actors from Akka—a very powerful reactive library written in Scala. To create an actor, extend from the Actor trait and implement the receive() method. The body of the receive() method looks familiar; it's the pattern matching syntax minus the call to match(). The match is happening on an implicit message object. The body of the method is a partially applied function.

In this example, we simply print the message received; we'll soon bring more logic into the actor. Let's use the actor we just defined.

ProgrammingActors/CreateActors.scala

```
import akka.actor._

object CreateActors extends App {
  val system = ActorSystem("sample")

  val depp = system.actorOf(Props[HollywoodActor])

  depp ! "Wonka"

  system.shutdown()
}
```

Akka actors are hosted within an ActorSystem, which manages threads, message queues, and actor lifetime. Instead of using the traditional new to create an instance, we used a special actorOf() factory method to create the actor and assigned it to the reference named depp. Also, instead of the usual method call syntax, we pass a message to the actor "Wonka"—a mere string in this example—using the method named !. Instead of using the !() method, you could use a method named tell(), but that would require passing an additional parameter of sender. Also you wouldn't look as cool if you use a method name that's intuitive to the reader. Talking about being intuitive, they should've really called it action().

The actor system manages a pool of threads that stay active as long as the system is active. For the program to terminate when the main code completes, we have to tell the actor system to shutdown()—that is, exit its threads.

To compile the code, enter the following command:

```
scalac -d classes HollywoodActor.scala CreateActors.scala
```

The Scala installation has the Akka actors library bundled; we don't have to include anything in the classpath to compile the code. Likewise, we don't need to include any additional libraries to run. Here's the command:

```
scala -classpath classes CreateActors
```

Let's take a look at the output:

```
playing the role of Wonka
```

We didn't write a lot of code, but still, that's a boring output. So much went on in that code, but the details were totally lost in that output. Let's change the code to gain a better insight.

Let's modify the body of the receive() method:

```
case message => println(s"$message - ${Thread.currentThread}")
```

When a message is received, we print that along with the details of the executing thread. Let's change the calling code to send multiple messages to multiple actors:

```
val depp = system.actorOf(Props[HollywoodActor])
val hanks = system.actorOf(Props[HollywoodActor])

depp ! "Wonka"
hanks ! "Gump"

depp ! "Sparrow"
hanks ! "Phillips"
println(s"Calling from ${Thread.currentThread}")
```

This should give us some more interesting details to look at. Let's run and take a look at the output:

```
Wonka - Thread[sample-akka.actor.default-dispatcher-2,5,main]
Gump - Thread[sample-akka.actor.default-dispatcher-3,5,main]
Calling from Thread[main,5,main]
Phillips - Thread[sample-akka.actor.default-dispatcher-3,5,main]
Sparrow - Thread[sample-akka.actor.default-dispatcher-2,5,main]
```

We sent two messages to each of the actors: "Wonka" and "Sparrow" to the actor depp, and "Gump" and "Phillips" to the actor hanks. The output shows a number of interesting details:

- A pool of thread was made available to us without any fuss.

- The actors run in a different thread than the calling code's main thread.

- Each actor processes only one message at a time.

- The actors run concurrently, processing messages at the same time.

- The actors are asynchronous.

- The caller did not block—the main did not wait to run the println() until after the actors responded.

Even though we have a lot more ground to cover, you can already see the benefits of this approach. They come from what we did not do. We didn't explicitly create a pool of threads. Nor did we explicitly schedule tasks. Had we used the JDK concurrency library, we'd have used executors and calls to methods like submit()—we were saved from writing a lot of code. Instead we simply sent a message to the actor and the actor system took care of the rest. That's pretty cool, eh?

Actors and Threads

The previous example gave a good idea of what's going on with actors, but it also raises a question. In the previous output we see that the two messages sent to depp were both processed by the same thread whereas the two messages sent to hanks were both processed by one other thread. This may give an impression that actors hold on to their threads, but that's not true—in fact, on your machine you may even notice the actors switch threads.

Threads are to actors like service agents are to customers. When you call a customer service line, any available agent answers. If you drop the call and redial, the previous agent has moved on to another call and a totally random dude now answers. Only in an extreme coincidence would you speak to the same agent twice. Threads in the pool are much like that to actors. To see this, let's modify the calling code just a bit:

```
depp  !  "Wonka"
hanks  !  "Gump"

Thread.sleep(100)

depp  !  "Sparrow"
hanks  !  "Phillips"
```

Between the two sets of messages to the actors we added a small delay of 100 milliseconds. Let's take a look at the output of running this code:

```
Wonka - Thread[sample-akka.actor.default-dispatcher-3,5,main]
Gump - Thread[sample-akka.actor.default-dispatcher-4,5,main]
Sparrow - Thread[sample-akka.actor.default-dispatcher-4,5,main]
Phillips - Thread[sample-akka.actor.default-dispatcher-3,5,main]
Calling from Thread[main,5,main]
```

As soon as the two threads finished helping the actors process their first messages, they ran back to the water cooler to catch up with the daily gossip. But when the next set of messages arrive, the dutiful threads jump right back to their missions. They hold no affinity to the actors they once served. That's why the threads swapped the actors they serve after the delay. This is pure heuristics: each time you run the code, you may see a different pairing of threads to actors. In essence it shows that threads are not bound to actors— a pool of threads serves actors.

Akka provides a huge number of facilities to configure the thread pool size, the message queue size, and many other parameters, including interacting with remote actors.

Isolated Mutability

Before we can apply actors to our file exploring problem, we need to address one final issue—shared mutability. It's common for programmers to create shared mutable variables and beat around with synchronization primitives to provide thread safety. Largely this has been a disaster. It's hard to imagine getting concurrency right with the JDK library if the programmers haven't mastered Brian Goetz's *Java Concurrency in Practice [Goe06]*. But, once they master that book they soon realize that it's hard to get concurrency right with the JDK library, period.

This is not a dismissal of the JDK for concurrency. After all, Akka and other libraries that support different concurrency models like the Software Transactional Memory—see *Programming Concurrency on the JVM [Sub11]*—internally use the JDK concurrency library and the fork join API. However, these libraries raise the level of abstraction so we don't have to endure the low-level synchronization details and the resulting accidental complexities. In a way, you can see the JDK concurrency library as the assembly language of concurrent programming. Though some people code at such low levels as assembly —the rest of us can be thankful to them—others program at a higher level of abstraction. This helps the rest of us to deliver applications faster and avoid the pains people often endure at the lower levels of abstractions. Likewise, by using these higher levels of abstraction of the concurrency models, we can avoid the many perils of concurrency.

Let's see how actors remove the pain of shared mutability. Since an actor processes at most one message at a time, any field that's kept in an actor is automatically thread-safe. It's mutable, but not shared mutable. An actor's non-final fields are automatically isolated mutable.

Let's modify the HollywoodActor actor to keep track of the number of messages it receives. This would introduce state into the actor—actors can optionally store state.

```
import akka.actor._
import scala.collection.mutable._

case class Play(role: String)
case class ReportCount(role: String)

class HollywoodActor() extends Actor {
```

```
  val messagesCount : Map[String, Int] = Map()

  def receive = {
    case Play(role) =>
      val currentCount = messagesCount.getOrElse(role, 0)
      messagesCount.update(role, currentCount + 1)
      println(s"Playing $role")

    case ReportCount(role) =>
      sender ! messagesCount.getOrElse(role, 0)
  }
}
```

The new version of our actor will receive two types of message. The first message type is used to tell the actor to play a role. The second message type is used to query for the number of times the actor has played a role—that's the number of times it's received the same message. For the message types, we create two case classes—Play and ReportCount. case classes are ideal for this since they're concise, hold immutable data, and work nicely with Scala's pattern matching facility.

The modified version of the HollywoodActor actor class has a field named messagesCount, which refers to a mutable Map with the role names as keys and their counts as values—the reference itself is immutable, however.

In the receive() method, we match the message received against the two message types we defined. If the message is of type Play, we extract the string passed into the role pattern matching variable. Once we have the role in our hands, we look up that role name in the map and initialize the value of currentCount with that count; we've instructed the getOrElse() method to return a 0 if the role is not present as a key in the map. Finally we update the map with the incremented value of count. If the message type, on the other hand, is of type ReportCount, then we read the value for the given role as a key and send it as a message to the sender of the message.

The modified version of the actor is ready to keep count of how many times each message is received. Within the receive() method, without any worry, we read the current value of the count from the map and updated it. There's no synchronized or calls to Lock's methods like tryLock()—enough of those *trying* times.

Let's use the new stateful version of our HollywoodActor. We'll send a few messages to two actors and ask for the number of times each message was received by the actors. Sending the Play message is pretty straightforward; it's fire-and-forget—the caller doesn't have to do anything other than send. The ReportCount needs some extra work, however. The sender of this message would want to receive a response back from the actor. For this Akka provides an *ask* pattern. Since sending a message and waiting for a response could potentially lead to a livelock—the message may never arrive—this pattern forces the use of a timeout. Let's take a look at the code and then dig into the details further.

ProgrammingActors/UseActor.scala

```scala
import akka.actor._
import akka.pattern.ask
import akka.util.Timeout
import scala.concurrent.duration._
import scala.concurrent.Await

object UseActor extends App {
  val system = ActorSystem("sample")

  val depp = system.actorOf(Props[HollywoodActor])
  val hanks = system.actorOf(Props[HollywoodActor])

  depp ! Play("Wonka")
  hanks ! Play("Gump")

  depp ! Play("Wonka")
  depp ! Play("Sparrow")

  println("Sent roles to play")

  implicit val timeout = Timeout(2.seconds)
  val wonkaFuture = depp ? ReportCount("Wonka")
  val sparrowFuture = depp ? ReportCount("Sparrow")
  val gumpFuture = hanks ? ReportCount("Gump")

  val wonkaCount = Await.result(wonkaFuture, timeout.duration)
  val sparrowCount = Await.result(sparrowFuture, timeout.duration)
  val gumpCount = Await.result(gumpFuture, timeout.duration)

  println(s"Depp played Wonka $wonkaCount time(s)")
  println(s"Depp played Sparrow $sparrowCount time(s)")
  println(s"Hanks played Gump $gumpCount time(s)")

  system.shutdown()
}
```

There's nothing you haven't seen already in the code up to line 19—we initialized the actor system, created two actors, and sent a few messages of type Play to them. The messages sent so far were all fire-and-forget—that is, non-blocking.

On lines 22 to 24 we send three messages of type ReportCount. These messages need a response, so instead of using the !() method we use the method ?().

Remember !() stands for the more descriptive method named tell(). Likewise, the enigmatic method ?() stands for a more descriptively named method, ask(). To use this method we need the import akka.pattern.ask. To prevent livelocks, the ask() method requires a timeout, but that parameter is being passed in using the implicit variable defined on line 21—take a minute to review implicit variables in *Implicit Parameters*, on page 31.

Unlike the method !(), which returns nothing, the ?() method returns a Future. We store each of the Futures returned by the three calls in the variables wonkaFuture, sparrowFuture, and gumpFuture. Now that the messages have been sent, it's time to wait and receive the responses. We do that using the result() method of the Await class. This method takes the Future we're waiting on and the duration of time we're willing to wait patiently for the response to arrive. Finally, if the responses arrive before the timeout period, we print the results. Let's run the code and take a look at the output:

```
Sent roles to play
Playing Wonka
Playing Gump
Playing Wonka
Playing Sparrow
Depp played Wonka 2 time(s)
Depp played Sparrow 1 time(s)
Hanks played Gump 1 time(s)
```

The output shows that the actors processed their messages as they received them and, in addition, properly kept track of the number of times each message was received.

You saw earlier how easy it was to delegate tasks to different threads. In this section you learned how safely you can mutate variables without the threat of race conditions or the risks of thread-safety violations.

When we're programming using the lower-level threading and synchronization facilities in Java, it's our responsibility to ensure the threads coordinate access to variables—we have to endure the total pain of dealing with issues like *happens-before*, *happens-after*, and crossing the memory barrier—all the issues covered extensively in the seminal book *Java Concurrency in Practice [Goe06]*. When programming with actors we don't have to worry about these kinds of issues. Anytime a message is passed to an actor and anytime an actor picks a message for processing, the respective threads automatically cross the memory barrier. With the design clarity, less code, automatic thread switching, and thread safety provided by actors, you can enjoy peace of mind and gain productivity.

Concurrency with Actors

Let's rework the file exploration program we created in *A Sequential Time-Consuming Problem*, on page 195. The sequential run for the example agility directory took over 66 seconds to run. Let's implement that problem using actors and see how fast it can run.

The problem nicely fits under the divide-and-conquer approach. Given a starting directory, we want to count the number of files under that directory hierarchy. We can divide that problem into finding the number of files under each subdirectory of the given directory and then combining the result. That, in turn, tells us we have two major parts: one to explore the files and the other to combine the results.

Let's first work through a high-level design before diving into the code.

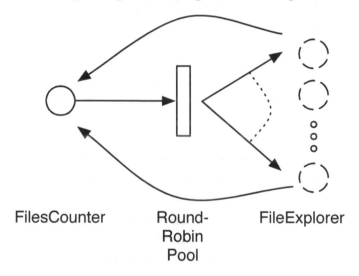

FilesCounter   Round-Robin Pool   FileExplorer

Finding a subdirectory under a given directory can be done concurrently for multiple directories. We only get a single computation out of a single actor at any given time. Since we need concurrent tasks running at the same time, we'd need multiple actors. In our design, FileExplorer is a stateless actor—we'll use several instances of this backed by an Akka-provided router called RoundRobinPool. As the name suggests, messages sent to this router will be routed evenly across all the actors backed by this router. We'll also use another actor, just a single instance of FilesCounter. This actor will be stateful —this is where the isolated mutable state will reside—and will keep track of the files count.

Let's first create the stateless FileExplorer actor:

ProgrammingActors/FileExplorer.scala

```scala
import akka.actor._
import java.io._

class FileExplorer extends Actor {
  def receive = {
    case dirName : String =>
        val file = new File(dirName)
        val children = file.listFiles()
        var filesCount = 0

        if(children != null) {
          children.filter { _.isDirectory }
                  .foreach { sender ! _.getAbsolutePath }
          filesCount = children.count { !_.isDirectory }
        }

        sender ! filesCount
  }
}
```

In the receive() method we look only for a String that holds the directory name. Upon receiving the message, we look for files and subdirectories under the given directory. We simply send each subdirectory to the sender of the message —a master—so it can get other actor instances of FileExplorer working to explore that subdirectory right away. Then we also send back to the sender a count of the number of files found under this directory.

Let's look at the stateful FilesCounter actor now:

ProgrammingActors/FilesCounter.scala

```scala
import akka.actor._
import akka.routing._
import java.io._

class FilesCounter extends Actor {
  val start = System.nanoTime
  var filesCount = 0L
  var pending = 0

  val fileExplorers =
    context.actorOf(RoundRobinPool(100).props(Props[FileExplorer]))

  def receive = {
    case dirName : String =>
      pending = pending + 1
      fileExplorers ! dirName
```

```
  case count : Int =>
    filesCount = filesCount + count
    pending = pending - 1

    if(pending == 0) {
      val end = System.nanoTime
      println(s"Files count: $filesCount")
      println(s"Time taken: ${(end - start)/1.0e9} seconds")
      context.system.shutdown()
    }
  }
}
```

This actor maintains a few fields. The start field notes the time when this actor is activated. filesCount and pending are mutable variables that hold a count of the number of files found and the number of outstanding file explorations currently in progress, respectively. The last field, fileExplorers, holds a reference to an instance of RoundRobinPool, the router, which itself is an actor that holds a pool of 100 FileExplorer actors.

We want the router that fileExplorers refers to, and the one hundred actors we created, to live in the same actor system and share the same pool of threads as the creating actor. For this we need to get access to the context actor system in which the FilesCounter actor is running—the context() method is useful for that. Also, we need to instruct the router to create instances of the FileExplorer actor. We use the Props class for this—consider this as equivalent to providing FileExplorer.class in Java.

We look for two types of messages in the receive() method: a String representing a directory name to be explored and an Int representing the count of files found so far. When a message with a directory name is received, we increment pending to indicate a file exploration is in progress and schedule the exploration of that directory to one of the FileExplorer actors using the router. When a count is received as a message, we add that count to the isolated mutable field file-sCount and decrement pending to indicate that a exploration of a subdirectory is over.

There's one last task in the receive() method. If the value of the variable pending falls to 0, that indicates that all subdirectories have been explored. In this case, we report the count and the time taken, and call on the actor system to shut down.

We have the two actors ready to do their work. We need bootstrapping code to create the actor system and the single instance of FilesCounter. Let's write that next:

ProgrammingActors/CountFiles.scala

```
import akka.actor._

object CountFiles extends App {
  val system = ActorSystem("sample")

  val filesCounter = system.actorOf(Props[FilesCounter])

  filesCounter ! args(0)
}
```

It's time to get this rolling. Compile the three files and run the CountFiles single-ton using the commands

```
scalac -d classes FilesCounter.scala FileExplorer.scala CountFiles.scala
scala -classpath classes CountFiles /Users/venkats/agility
```

Now take a look at the output:

```
Files count: 479758
Time taken: 5.609851764 seconds
```

The output shows a considerable speed improvement compared to the sequential version we started out with. We didn't need a lot of code to achieve this. Furthermore, there's no messy thread creation or synchronization code. The clarity that emerges from such code is quite reassuring. Unlike the JDK solution where we often don't know if the code is right, this code is easy to understand and easy to enhance as well.

Usage Recommendations

You learned to create actors, send messages to them, and also how to coordi-nate between multiple instances. You used a stateless actor and also a stateful actor. You used both one-way communication and two-way commu-nication. These options may seem a bit overwhelming. Let's explore some recommendations for good use.

- Rely more on stateless actors instead of stateful actors. Stateless actors don't have identity, they can provide more concurrency, they're easy to replicate, and they're easy to restart and reuse. State may not be avoidable, but keep the use of stateful actors to a minimum—use them sparingly.

- Keep the processing in the receive() method really fast, especially if the receiving actor is stateful. Long-running tasks that mutate state will lower concurrency—avoid them. It's less problematic if the tasks that don't manipulate state aren't super fast—we can replicate these actors quite easily to improve concurrency, like we did with FileExplorer.

- Ensure the messages passed between actors are immutable objects. In all the examples, we passed case class instances, String, or Int, all of which are immutable. Passing immutable objects guarantees that we don't inadvertently modify a shared state and end up with concurrency issues.

- As much as possible, avoid using ask(); two-way communication in general is not a good idea. The fire-and-forget model is much better due to the asynchronous nature and is also less error prone.

Wrapping Up

We made some nice progress in this chapter on such a complex topic as concurrency. You learned about actors, what problems they solve, and how to create and use them. You also learned about how a pool of threads works with actors, how to communicate between actors, and most important, how isolated mutability comes to the rescue. We also applied these concepts to implement a practical example that showed substantial speed improvement with only a small amount of code. In the next part, we'll look at applying various concepts of Scala we've explored throughout this book.

Part IV

Applying Scala

Now you know what Scala can do for you. Let's use Scala in the context of some practical applications. You'll learn to:

- *use Scala from Java*
- *parse and generate XML*
- *talk to a web service*
- *apply concurrency*
- *use ScalaTest to create unit tests*

CHAPTER 14

Intermixing with Java

A few powerful Scala libraries are out there and more are being developed. Not only can you use these libraries from Scala, you can use them from Java as well. But to do so you have to learn a few tricks.

In this chapter, you'll learn how to use Java classes from Scala and use Scala classes from Java. You can easily intermix Scala code with code written in Java and other languages on the JVM. Scala compiles into bytecode and you can package the generated class files into a JAR. Thus, you can use the generated bytecode from your Java and Scala applications. Make sure that the scala-library.jar file's in your classpath, and you're all set.

You'll learn how Scala idioms manifest on the Java side. Knowing this, you can write code in Scala with features like actors, pattern matching, and XML processing, and readily use them from within your Java applications. At the end of this chapter, you'll be equipped with what you need to take full advantage of Scala in your Java applications.

Using Scala Classes from Scala

Before diving into mixing Java and Scala, let's first look at using Scala classes from Scala. If you've created Scala classes in separate files, compile them to bytecode using the Scala compiler scalac. Then drop them into a JAR file using the jar tool. In the next example, we compile two classes, Person and Dog, and then create a JAR from the resulting class files. Let's take a look at the classes first:

Intermixing/Person.scala
```
class Person(val firstName: String, val lastName: String) {
  override def toString : String = firstName + " " + lastName
}
```

Intermixing/Dog.scala

```scala
class Dog(val name: String) {
  override def toString = name
}
```

Here are the commands to compile and create the JAR:

```
scalac Person.scala Dog.scala
jar cf /tmp/example.jar Person.class Dog.class
```

Running these commands will create a file named example.jar in the /tmp directory. Adjust the path to the tmp directory based on your operating system
before running those commands.

Let's now use these two classes from a Scala script:

Intermixing/usePerson.scala

```scala
val george = new Person("George", "Washington")

val georgesDogs = List(new Dog("Captain"), new Dog("Clode"),
  new Dog("Forester"), new Dog("Searcher"))

println(s"$george had several dogs ${georgesDogs.mkString(", ")}...")
```

To run the script, we need to provide the classpath with the location of the
JAR file containing the classes:

```
scala -classpath /tmp/example.jar usePerson.scala
```

Running the scala command with the classpath option and the script filename
will produce the result

```
George Washington had several dogs Captain, Clode, Forester, Searcher...
```

We successfully used the Scala classes we created from within a script. To
use the classes from other Scala classes or from singleton objects, instead of
from within a freestanding script, you need only one additional step: compile
the class or object that uses these other classes also using scalac.

Suppose we want to use the previous Person class in the following Scala code:

Intermixing/UsePersonClass.scala

```scala
object UsePersonClass extends App {
  val ben = new Person("Ben", "Franklin")
  println(s"$ben was a great inventor.")
}
```

If the Person class has already been compiled, we can simply compile the
UsePersonClass.scala file alone. If Person.class isn't located in the current directory,
use the classpath option to tell the compiler where to find it. Let's take a look

at the command to compile the file UsePersonClass.scala—the -d option specifies where to put the generated bytecode:

```
mkdir -p classes
scalac -d classes -classpath /tmp/example.jar UsePersonClass.scala
```

We can run the compiled bytecode either using the scala tool or using the traditional java tool. You can use the scala tool to run bytecode generated with any JVM language compiler, including scalac and javac. Here's an example of using the scala tool to run the UsePersonClass.class file:

```
scala -classpath classes:/tmp/example.jar UsePersonClass
```

On the other hand, if you want to run the compiled bytecode using the java tool, simply specify the scala-library.jar file in the classpath. Be sure to use the correct path to scala-library.jar on your machine—like so:

```
java -classpath $SCALA_HOME/lib/scala-library.jar:classes:/tmp/example.jar \
  UsePersonClass
```

You can see here that both of the previous approaches will yield the same result:

```
Ben Franklin was a great inventor.
```

Using Java Classes from Scala

Using Java classes from Scala is pretty straightforward. If the Java class you'd like to use is part of the standard JDK, then simply use it. You'll have to import the class if it's not part of the java.lang package. Let's use the java.util.Currency class from the JDK:

Intermixing/UseJDKClass.scala
```
import java.util.Currency

val currencies = Currency.getAvailableCurrencies
println(s"${currencies.size} currencies are available.")
```

No extra steps of compilation are needed. Scala scripts can directly use Java classes. To run this script, type the following:

```
scala UseJDKClass.scala
```

The output from running the script is

```
220 currencies are available.
```

If the Java class you'd like to use is not from the JDK but is your own or from a third party, make sure to specify to scala the classpath of where the bytecode is located. Suppose we have the following Java files:

```
Intermixing/java/InvestmentType.java
//Java code
package investments;

public enum InvestmentType {
  BOND,  STOCK, REAL_ESTATE,  COMMODITIES,  COLLECTIBLES, MUTUAL_FUNDS
}
```

```
Intermixing/java/Investment.java
//Java code
package investments;

public class Investment {
  private String investmentName;
  private InvestmentType investmentType;

  public Investment(String name, InvestmentType type) {
    investmentName = name;
    investmentType = type;
  }
  public int yield() { return 0; }
}
```

We can use these Java classes from Scala just like we use any Scala class. Here's an example of creating an instance of Investment in Scala:

```
Intermixing/UseInvestment.scala
import investments._

object UseInvestment extends App {
  val investment = new Investment("XYZ Corporation", InvestmentType.STOCK)
  println(investment.getClass)
}
```

Let's compile the Java code, place the bytecode in a directory named classes/investments, and then use that to compile the Scala code. Here are the commands to compile and run:

```
mkdir -p classes
javac -d classes java/InvestmentType.java java/Investment.java
scalac -classpath classes UseInvestment.scala
scala -classpath classes:. UseInvestment
```

Alternately, once we compile the source files, as a last step, instead of using the scala tool, we can also run it using the java tool:

```
java -classpath $SCALA_HOME/lib/scala-library.jar:classes:. UseInvestment
```

Make sure to set up the environment variable SCALA_HOME to point to the location where Scala is installed on your system. Also, if you're on Windows, replace the environment variable reference $SCALA_HOME with %SCALA_HOME%.

That worked seamlessly, but there's a catch. Use caution with the yield() method of the Investment class. If your Java code has methods or field names—like trait, yield, and so on—that conflict with Scala keywords, the Scala compiler will choke up when you call them. For example, the following code won't work:

```scala
val theYield1 = investment.yield    //ERROR
val theYield2 = investment.yield() //ERROR
```

Fortunately, Scala offers a solution to resolve keyword conflicts—you can place the affected variables/methods in a backtick. To get the previous two calls to work, modify the code as follows:

```scala
val investment = new Investment("XYZ Corporation", InvestmentType.STOCK)
val theYield1 = investment.`yield`
val theYield2 = investment.`yield`()
```

On seeing the backtick, Scala resolves the field or method as a member of the target instance instead of a keyword in the language.

Using Scala Methods from Java

Scala provides full round-trip interoperability with Java. Because Scala compiles to bytecode, you can use Scala classes from Java quite easily. Remember, Scala does not by default follow the JavaBean convention, and you'll have to use the @scala.reflect.BeanProperty annotation to generate getters and setters that conform to the JavaBean convention—see *Defining Fields, Methods, and Constructors*, on page 51. Let's look at how to use a method defined in Scala from Java.

Scala classes that follow standard Java constructs are pretty straightforward, and you can use them readily on the Java side. To illustrate intermixing from Java, let's write a Scala class:

Intermixing/Car.scala
```scala
package automobiles

class Car(val year: Int) {
  private[this] var miles : Int = 0

  def drive(distance: Int) { miles += distance }

  override def toString : String = s"year: $year miles: $miles"
}
```

Here's a sample Java class that uses the Scala class:

```
Intermixing/UseCar.java
//Java code
package automobiles.users;
import automobiles.Car;

public class UseCar {
  public static void main(String[] args) {
    Car car = new Car(2009);

    System.out.println(car);
    car.drive(10);
    System.out.println(car);
  }
}
```

We'll have to compile the Scala code using scalac and the Java code using javac:

```
mkdir -p classes
scalac -d classes Car.scala
javac -d classes -classpath $SCALA_HOME/lib/scala-library.jar:classes \
  UseCar.java
java -classpath $SCALA_HOME/lib/scala-library.jar:classes \
  automobiles.users.UseCar
```

We've placed the generated bytecode in the classes directory. It was pretty simple to use the Scala class from Java and invoke methods on an instance of that class.

The method we invoked from Java takes a simple parameter. What about functions that take function values as a parameter? Since Java 8 supports lambda expressions you'd think that it'd be easy to pass a Java 8 lambda to such functions. Although this is a reasonable thought, the function values in Scala are backed by Function traits and they aren't compatible with Java 8 functional interfaces. Future versions of Scala will address this issue and facilitate passing Java 8 lambdas to Scala functions.

Using Traits from Java

You'll run into a few idiosyncrasies when using traits from Java—nothing impossible, but there are some rough edges we have to work around, so let's walk through this section in smaller steps.

Scala traits with no method implementation are simple interfaces at the bytecode level. Scala doesn't support the interface keyword. If you want to create interfaces in Scala, you'd create traits with no implementation in them. Here's an example of a Scala trait, which in effect is simply an interface:

```
Intermixing/Writable.scala
trait Writable {
  def write(message: String) : Unit
}
```

The trait has one abstract method that should be implemented by any class that mixes in this trait. On the Java side, Writable is seen like any interface. Implementing that interface is straightforward:

```
Intermixing/AWritableJavaClass.java
//Java code
public class AWritableJavaClass implements Writable {
  public void write(String message) {
    //...code...
  }
}
```

When working with a trait with no implementation, think about it as a simple interface and implement it much like the way you'd implement interfaces in Java. Nothing to worry about—not yet.

If a trait has method implementations, then the Scala compiler creates two things: an interface with the abstract method declarations and, in addition, a corresponding abstract class that holds the implementations. If you merely want to implement that interface in Java, that's no problem. However, for a trait with implementations, you'd want to make use of the implementations from Java. That's the part that gets tricky, but only a bit.

Knowing what Scala really does is mandatory for intermixing with Java. Two things are very helpful when the going gets tough: a good dose of the caffeinated beverage of your choice and the javap tool. To understand this better, let's try out an example with a Printable trait that has one method with an implementation:

```
Intermixing/Printable.scala
trait Printable {
  def print() {
    println("running printable...")
  }
}
```

Let's see how to implement that trait in Java and also make use of the implementation that's in the trait.

Run the following commands to compile the trait:

```
mkdir -p classes
scalac -d classes Printable.scala
```

In the classes directory, the compiler creates two files: Printable.class and Printable$class.class (yep, that's really the name of the file—and people think my name's weird). Examine these two files with the following command:

```
javap classes/Printable.class classes/Printable\$class.class
```

The javap tool gives a clear view of what the Scala compiler has been up to:

```
Compiled from "Printable.scala"
public abstract class Printable$class {
  public static void print(Printable);
  public static void $init$(Printable);
}
Compiled from "Printable.scala"
public abstract class Printable$class {
  public static void print(Printable);
  public static void $init$(Printable);
}
```

The compiler took the trait we wrote and created an abstract class with the same name as the trait—Printable. For all practical purposes this is simply an interface. Furthermore, it created an abstract class with the name of the trait suffixed with a $class. This abstract class holds the implementations from the trait, but as static methods. With this insight we can swiftly move to implement the desired Java code that makes use of implementation in the Scala trait. Let's create a Java class that implements the trait and also makes use of the implementation in it—in essence we're mixing the Scala trait into our Java code.

Intermixing/APrintable.java
```java
public class APrintable implements Printable {
  public void print() {
    System.out.println("We can reuse the trait here if we like...");
    Printable$class.print(this);

  }

  public static void use(Printable printable) {
    printable.print();
  }

  public static void main(String[] args) {
    APrintable aPrintable = new APrintable();
    use(aPrintable);
  }
}
```

The APrintable Java class implements the interface part of the trait Printable. Within the print() method we're providing our own implementation, but we also turn around and make use of the implementation within the trait as well. To do this, on line 4 we call the static method in the abstract class that the Scala compiler generated.

To show that we can treat an instance of the Java class as an instance of the trait, the use() method receives an instance of Printable and we pass to it the instance aPrintable of the class APrintable. Within the use() method we invoke the print() method—this should use the implementation within the APrintable, which in turn uses the implementation within the Scala trait.

To run this code, let's first compile the Java code and then run the java command:

```
javac -d classes -classpath $SCALA_HOME/lib/scala-library.jar:classes \
  APrintable.java
java -classpath $SCALA_HOME/lib/scala-library.jar:classes APrintable
```

The steps to compile and run are pretty simple. We only need to ensure the classpath is set properly to include the Scala library and the classes related to our traits. Let's take a look at the output:

```
We can reuse the trait here if we like...
running printable...
```

The output shows that we successfully mixed the trait into our Java class and reused the implementation that's in the trait as well.

If you merely want to implement Scala traits in Java, then make your traits pure, with no implementation. Since traits are really interfaces, implementing them in Java is no big deal. On the other hand, if you want to mix a Scala trait into Java classes, then reach for that caffeinated beverage and the javap tool to get a grip on the lower-level details. Once you discover the actual class names that are generated, you can then move forward to use the trait from Java.

Using Singletons and Companion Objects from Java

Scala compiles singleton and companion objects into a "singleton class" with a special $ symbol at the end of its name. Scala, however, treats a singleton and a companion object differently, as you'll soon see.

When compiled, a Scala singleton turns into a Java class with static methods at the bytecode level. In addition, another regular class with methods that forward calls to the singleton class is created. So, for example, this code defines a singleton object Single, and Scala creates two classes, Single$ and the forward class Single:

Intermixing/Single.scala
```
object Single {
  def greet() { println("Hello from Single") }
}
```

We can use the singleton object from Java as we'd use any Java class with static methods, as shown here:

Intermixing/SingleUser.java
```
//Java code
public class SingleUser {
  public static void main(String[] args) {
    Single.greet();
  }
}
```

The output from the previous code is shown here:

```
Hello from Single
```

It gets a bit complicated if you're dealing with a companion object instead of a singleton. If your object is a companion object to a class with the same name, Scala creates two classes: one for the class and one for its companion. For example, Scala will compile the following Buddy class and its companion down to two files named Buddy and Buddy$, respectively.

Intermixing/Buddy.scala
```
class Buddy {
  def greet() { println("Hello from Buddy class") }
}

object Buddy {
  def greet() { println("Hello from Buddy object") }
}
```

In the example, there are two methods named greet(), one in the Buddy class and the other in its companion object. The equivalent of this is like having both an *instance* method and a *static* method with the same name in a Java class. Accessing the instance method is rather easy from Java, but reaching into the companion object takes some effort.

Accessing the companion class from Java is much like accessing it from Scala. In Scala we'd write, for example, new Buddy().greet(); the Java version is almost the same, except we'd have to add the obligatory semicolon to the end. On the other hand, the syntax for accessing the method in the companion object is quite different in the two languages. In Scala, we'd simply type Buddy.greet(), but from Java, well...take a look at line 5 in the following code:

Intermixing/BuddyUser.java

```
Line 1  //Java code
     2  public class BuddyUser {
     3    public static void main(String[] args) {
     4      new Buddy().greet();
     5      Buddy$.MODULE$.greet();
     6    }
     7  }
```

If that code hurts your head, please know it's not your fault. You had to jump through some hoops there, first getting to the companion object Buddy$ and then referring to its static MODULE$ property, which holds a reference to the instance. Finally you invoke the greet() method on that instance. Once again your buddy here is the javap tool, which you can use to dig into and reckon with the bytecode the compiler generated.

Let's compile and run the Java code to see the output:

```
Hello from Buddy class
Hello from Buddy object
```

At first, scanning through the code to access the methods on a companion object may induce a feeling of vertigo. If that happens, sit down and take your eyes off the code for a minute. Take some time to dig into the bytecode details presented by the javap tool and try to reason by walking through the object references. Once you get the hang of it, you'll have no problem mastering complex Scala APIs from Java code, if your project needs demands that.

Extending Classes

You can extend a Java class from a Scala class, and vice versa. For the most part, this should just work. As discussed earlier, if your methods accept function values as parameters, you'll have trouble overriding them. Exceptions are also a problem.

Scala doesn't have the throws clause. In Scala you can throw any exception from any method without having to explicitly declare that as part of the method signature. However, if you override such a method in Java, you'll run into trouble when you try to throw an exception. Let's look at an example. Suppose we have a Bird class defined in Scala:

```
abstract class Bird {
  def fly()
  //...
}
```

We also have another class, Ostrich:

Intermixing/Ostrich.scala
```scala
class Ostrich extends Bird {
  override def fly() {
    throw new NoFlyException
  }
  //...
}
```

where NoFlyException is defined like this:

Intermixing/NoFlyException.scala
```scala
class NoFlyException extends Exception {}
```

In the previous code, Ostrich's fly() method was able to throw the exception without any problem. However, if we implement a nonflying bird in Java, we'll run into trouble, as shown here:

Intermixing/Penguin.java
```java
//Java code
class Penguin extends Bird {
  public void fly() throws NoFlyException {
    throw new NoFlyException();
  }
  //...
}
```

First, if we simply throw the exception, Java will complain about an unreported exception being thrown. But if we declare the intention of throwing the exception with the throws clause, we'll get this:

```
Penguin.java:3: error: fly() in Penguin cannot override fly() in Bird
  public void fly() throws NoFlyException {
              ^
  overridden method does not throw NoFlyException
1 error
```

Even though Scala is flexible and doesn't insist that you specify what exceptions you throw, if you intend to extend from those methods in Java, you'll have to ask the Scala compiler to emit those details in the method signature. Scala provides a backdoor for that by defining the @throws annotation.

Even though Scala supports annotations, it doesn't provide any syntax to create an annotation. If you'd like to create your own annotations, you'll have to do that using Java. @throws is an annotation already provided for you to express the checked exceptions your methods throw. So, for us to implement the Penguin in Java, we have to modify the Bird class in Scala like this:

Intermixing/Bird.scala
```scala
abstract class Bird {
 @throws(classOf[NoFlyException]) def fly()
  //...
}
```

Now when we compile the class, the Scala compiler will place the necessary signature for the fly() method in the bytecode. The Penguin Java class will compile with no errors after this change.

Wrapping Up

Calling Java code from Scala is trivial. For most part, it's quite easy to call into Scala code from Java also. There are some rough edges related to working with companion objects and extending methods that throw exceptions. While at first this may look a bit intimidating, once you get the hang of it, using the help of tools like javap, you can quickly begin to intermix Java and Scala. In addition to opening the door for mixing the two languages in enterprise applications, this will greatly help you to use some powerful libraries written in Scala, right from your current Java applications. In the next chapter, you'll apply what you've learned in this book. We're going to create a small application and along the way pick up a few more techniques.

CHAPTER 15

Creating an Application with Scala

In this chapter, we'll bring together a lot of things you've learned so far in this book, and then some. We'll progressively build an application to find the net worth of investments in the stock market. You'll see several features shine in this exercise: conciseness and expressiveness, the power of pattern matching along with function values/closures, and concurrency. In addition, you'll learn about Scala's support for XML processing—a feature you'll greatly benefit from when building enterprise applications.

Getting Users' Input

We'll build an application that takes a list of stock ticker symbols along with the units of stock users hold and provides to them the total value of their investments as of the current date. This involves several things: getting users' input, reading files, parsing data, writing to files, fetching data from the web, and displaying information to users.

We're going to first develop the different parts of the application separately to get a good grasp of the parts individually. Then we'll put them together to create the application. Let's get started.

As a first step, we want to know the ticker symbols and units of each stock for which the application should find the values. Scala's StdIn class can help to get input from the command line.

The following code reads from the standard input:

UsingScala/ConsoleInput.scala
```scala
import scala.io._

print("Please enter a ticker symbol:")
val symbol = StdIn.readLine()
println(s"OK, got it, you own $symbol")
```

A sample execution of the code is shown here:

```
Please enter a ticker symbol:OK, got it, you own AAPL
```

If you ever have a need to create a console application in Scala, StdIn has you covered for reading different types of data from the console.

Reading and Writing Files

Now that you know how to get user input in Scala, it's time to see how to write data to a file. We can use the java.io.File object to achieve this. Here's an example of writing to a file:

UsingScala/WriteToFile.scala
```
import java.io._

val writer = new PrintWriter(new File("symbols.txt"))
writer write "AAPL"
writer.close()
```

This simple code writes the symbol "AAPL" to the file named symbols.txt.

Reading files is really simple as well. Scala's Source class and its companion object come in handy for this purpose. For illustration purposes, let's write a Scala script that reads itself:

UsingScala/ReadingFile.scala
```
import scala.io.Source

println("*** The content of the file you read is:")
Source.fromFile("ReadingFile.scala").foreach { print }
```

We read the file that contains this code and printed out its contents. As you know, reading a file is not such a simple task in Java, with all the try-catch code that gets in the way. The output from the code is shown here:

```
*** The content of the file you read is:
import scala.io.Source

println("*** The content of the file you read is:")
Source.fromFile("ReadingFile.scala").foreach { print }
```

The Source class is an Iterator over the input stream. The Source companion object has several convenience methods to read from a file, an input stream, a string, or even a URL, as you'll see soon. The foreach() method helps you get one character at a time—the input is buffered, so no worries about performance. If you're interested in reading a line at a time, you'd use the getLines() method instead.

Very soon we'll need to read information off the web. While discussing Source, let's take a look at its fromURL() method. This method is useful for reading the content of a website, a web service, or just about anything that you can point at using a URL. Here's an example that reads the content from the Apache web server running locally on my machine, the localhost:

```
UsingScala/ReadingURL.scala
import scala.io.Source
import java.net.URL

val source = Source.fromURL(new URL("http://localhost"))

println(s"What's Source?: ${source}")
println(s"Raw String: ${source.mkString}")
```

Here's the output from the program:

```
What's Source?: non-empty iterator
Raw String: <html><body><h1>It works!</h1></body></html>
```

We called fromURL() to obtain a Source instance from that URL. The Source is an iterator that can be used to traverse through the contents. We can use methods of Source, like getLines(), to process one line at a time. Alternately, we can concatenate all the lines into one String using the mkString() method.

Although the previous example may quench your thirst to read and write files and access a URL, we need to get back to the net asset application. We could store the ticker symbols and units as plain text. Reading the file is easy, but then parsing through the contents of the file to get various ticker symbols and units isn't going to be that easy. As much as we all hate XML for its verbosity, it does come in handy to organize this kind of information and parse it. Let's make use of XML for the net asset application.

XML as a First-Class Citizen

Scala treats XML as a first-class citizen. So, instead of embedding XML documents into strings, you can place them inline in your code like you'd place an int or a Double value. Let's take a look at an example:

```
UsingScala/UseXML.scala
val xmlFragment =
<symbols>
  <symbol ticker="AAPL"><units>200</units></symbol>
  <symbol ticker="IBM"><units>215</units></symbol>
</symbols>

println(xmlFragment)
println(xmlFragment.getClass)
```

We created a val named xmlFragment and directly assigned it to a sample XML content. Scala parsed the XML content and happily created an instance of scala.xml.Elem, as you see in the output:

```
<symbols>
  <symbol ticker="AAPL"><units>200</units></symbol>
  <symbol ticker="IBM"><units>215</units></symbol>
</symbols>
class scala.xml.Elem
```

The Scala package scala.xml provides a set of convenience classes to read, parse, create, and store XML documents. The ease of parsing XML documents in Scala is quite appealing, making XML quite bearable compared to using it in Java. Let's explore the facilities to parse XML.

You probably have played with XPath, which provides a very powerful way to query into XML documents. Scala provides an XPath-like query ability with one minor difference. Instead of using the familiar XPath forward slashes—/ and //—to query, Scala uses backward slashes—\ and \\—for methods that parse and extract contents. This difference was necessary since Scala follows the Java tradition of using the two forward slashes for comments and a single forward slash is the division operator. Let's parse this XML fragment we have on hand.

Here's a piece of code to get the symbol elements, using the XPath-like query:

UsingScala/UseXML.scala
```
var symbolNodes = xmlFragment \ "symbol"
symbolNodes foreach println
println(symbolNodes.getClass)
```

Let's look at the output generated by the code:

```
<symbol ticker="AAPL"><units>200</units></symbol>
<symbol ticker="IBM"><units>215</units></symbol>
class scala.xml.NodeSeq$$anon$1
```

We called the \() method on the XML element to look for all symbol elements. It retuned an instance of scala.xml.NodeSeq, which represents a collection of XML nodes.

The \() method looks only for elements that are direct descendants of the target element, the symbols element in this example. To search through all the elements in the hierarchy starting from the target element, use the \\() method. Also, use the text() method to get the text node within an element. Let's make use of those in an example:

```
UsingScala/UseXML.scala
var unitsNodes = xmlFragment \\ "units"
unitsNodes foreach println
println(unitsNodes.getClass)
println(unitsNodes.head.text)
```

Let's see what the code generated:

```
<units>200</units>
<units>215</units>
class scala.xml.NodeSeq$$anon$1
200
```

Even though the units elements are not direct children of the root element, the \\() method extracted those elements—the \() method won't do that. The text() method helped to further extract the text from one of the units elements. We can also use pattern matching to get the text value and other contents. If we want to navigate the structure of an XML document, the methods \() and \\() are useful. However, if we want to find matching content anywhere in the XML document at arbitrary locations, pattern matching will be more useful.

We saw the power of pattern matching in Chapter 9, *Pattern Matching and Regular Expressions*, on page 143. Scala extends that power to matching XML fragments as well. Let's see how:

```
UsingScala/UseXML.scala
unitsNodes.head match {
  case <units>{numberOfUnits}</units> => println(s"Units: $numberOfUnits")
}
```

The pattern matching extracted the following content for us:

```
Units: 200
```

We took the first units element and asked Scala to extract the text value. In the case statement we provided the match for the fragment we're interested in and a pattern matching variable, numberOfUnits, as a placeholder for the text content of that element.

That helped us get the units for one symbol. There are two problems, however. The previous approach works only if the content matches exactly with the expression in the case; that is, the units element contains only one content item or one child element. If it contains a mixture of child elements and text contents, the previous match will fail. Furthermore, we want to get the units for all symbols, not just the first one. We can ask Scala to grab all contents, elements and text, using the _* symbol, like so:

```
UsingScala/UseXML.scala
println("Ticker\tUnits")
xmlFragment match {
  case <symbols>{symbolNodes @ _* }</symbols> =>
    for(symbolNode @ <symbol>{_*}</symbol> <- symbolNodes) {
      println("%-7s %s".format(
        symbolNode \ "@ticker", (symbolNode \ "units").text))
    }
}
```

Let's take a look at the output before examining the code:

```
Ticker  Units
AAPL    200
IBM     215
```

Nice output, but the code to produce that is a bit dense. Let's take the time to understand it.

By using the wildcard symbol _*, we asked to read everything between the <symbols> and </symbols> into the placeholder variable symbolNodes. We saw an example using the @ symbol to place a variable name in *Matching Tuples and Lists*, on page 145. The good news: That call reads everything. The bad news: It reads everything, including the text nodes that represent the blank spaces in the XML fragment. You're quite used to this problem if you've used XML DOM parsers. To deal with this, when looping through the symbolNodes we iterate over only the symbol elements by pattern matching once more, this time in the parameter to the for() method.

Remember, the first parameter you provide for the for() method is a pattern (see *The for Expression*, on page 139). Finally, we perform an XPath query to get to the attribute ticker and the text value in the units elements; you'll recall from XPath that you use an @ prefix to indicate the attribute query.

Reading and Writing XML

Once we get an XML document in memory, we know how to parse it. The next step is to figure out a way to get an XML document loaded into the program and to save an in-memory document to a file. As an example, let's load an XML file that contains symbols and units, increase the units by 1, and store the updated content back into another XML file. Let's first tackle the step of loading the file.

Here's a sample file stocks.xml that we'll use:

```
UsingScala/stocks.xml
<symbols>
  <symbol ticker="AAPL"><units>200</units></symbol>
  <symbol ticker="ADBE"><units>125</units></symbol>
  <symbol ticker="ALU"><units>150</units></symbol>
  <symbol ticker="AMD"><units>150</units></symbol>
  <symbol ticker="CSCO"><units>250</units></symbol>
  <symbol ticker="HPQ"><units>225</units></symbol>
  <symbol ticker="IBM"><units>215</units></symbol>
  <symbol ticker="INTC"><units>160</units></symbol>
  <symbol ticker="MSFT"><units>190</units></symbol>
  <symbol ticker="NSM"><units>200</units></symbol>
  <symbol ticker="ORCL"><units>200</units></symbol>
  <symbol ticker="SYMC"><units>230</units></symbol>
  <symbol ticker="TXN"><units>190</units></symbol>
  <symbol ticker="VRSN"><units>200</units></symbol>
  <symbol ticker="XRX"><units>240</units></symbol>
</symbols>
```

The load() method of the XML singleton object in the scala.xml package will help load the file, as shown here:

```
UsingScala/ReadWriteXML.scala
import scala.xml._

val stocksAndUnits = XML load "stocks.xml"
println(stocksAndUnits.getClass())
println(s"File has ${(stocksAndUnits \\ "symbol").size} symbol elements")
```

The load() method returns an scala.xml.Elem instance. A quick XPath-like query on the instance shows the number of symbol elements in the file:

```
class scala.xml.Elem
File has 15 symbol elements
```

You already know how to parse the content of this document and store the symbols and the corresponding units in a Map. Here's the code that does just that:

```
UsingScala/ReadWriteXML.scala
val stocksAndUnitsMap =
  (Map[String, Int]() /: (stocksAndUnits \ "symbol")) { (map, symbolNode) =>
    val ticker = (symbolNode \ "@ticker").toString
    val units = (symbolNode \ "units").text.toInt
    map + (ticker -> units) //return new map, with one additional entry
  }

println(s"Number of symbol elements found is ${stocksAndUnitsMap.size}")
```

As we processed each symbol element, we accumulated the symbol and the corresponding units into a new Map. In the following output, you can see the number of symbols we loaded into the Map from the document:

```
Number of symbol elements found is 15
```

We have a few steps left: increase the units value, create an XML representation of the data, and store it into a file.

You know that Scala doesn't require you to stuff XML elements into a string. But, you may wonder, how do you generate dynamic content into an XML document? This is where the smarts of the Scala XML library go beyond what you've seen so far.

You can embed Scala expressions within any XML fragment. If we write <symbol ticker={tickerSymbol}/>, then Scala will replace {tickerSymbol} with the value of the variable tickerSymbol, which results in an element like <symbol ticker="AAPL"/>, for example. You can place any Scala code in between the {}, and that block can result in a value, an element, or a sequence of elements. Let's put this feature to use to create an XML representation from the Map we created previously. When done, we'll save the content into a file using the save() method of the XML object. Let's look at the code for this:

```
UsingScala/ReadWriteXML.scala
val updatedStocksAndUnitsXML =
<symbols>
  { stocksAndUnitsMap map updateUnitsAndCreateXML }
</symbols>

def updateUnitsAndCreateXML(element : (String, Int)) = {
  val (ticker, units) = element
  <symbol ticker={ticker}>
    <units>{units + 1}</units>
  </symbol>
}

XML save ("stocks2.xml", updatedStocksAndUnitsXML)

val elementsCount = (XML.load("stocks2.xml") \\ "symbol").size
println(s"Saved file has ${elementsCount} symbol elements")
```

Let's run the code and take a look at the output:

```
Saved file has 15 symbol elements
```

Let's examine the code that produced the output. We first created an XML document with symbols as the root element. The data for the child elements (symbol) we want to embed within this root element resides in stocksAndUnitsMap, which is a Map we created earlier. We iterate over each element of this map and create an XML representation using the function updateUnitsAndCreateXML(). The result of this operation is a collection of elements (since we used the map() method). Remember that in the closure attached to the map() method, Scala is implicitly sending the parameters we receive within the closure (an element of the Map) to the updateUnitsAndCreateXML() method.

Now, let's look at the updateUnitsAndCreateXML() method. It accepts an element of the Map as a parameter and creates an XML fragment of the format <symbol ticker="sym"><units>value</units></symbol>. While processing each symbol, we took care of the objective to increase units by 1.

In last step we save the generated document using the save() method. We read back the saved document from the file stocks2.xml to take a look at the content we generated.

The save() method simply saved the XML document without any bells and whistles. If you'd like to add an XML version, add doctypes, and specify encoding, use one of the variations of the save() method on the XML singleton object.

Getting Stock Prices from the Web

As the final step to complete our net asset application, we have to get the stock price from the web. We have the list of ticker symbols and the units in the file stocks.xml we saw earlier. For each of these symbols, we need to fetch the closing price. Thankfully, Yahoo provides a web service that we can use to get stock data. To find the latest closing price for Google stocks, for example, we can visit the following URL:

```
http://ichart.finance.yahoo.com/table.csv?s=GOOG&a=00&b=01&c=2015
```

The parameters s, a, b, and c represent the ticker symbol, start month (January is 0), start day, and start year, respectively. If you don't specify the end dates using the parameters d, e, and f, the service returns all prices from the given start date until the most recent available date. When you visit the previous URL, you'll get a comma-separated value (CSV) file to download.

A sample of the file is shown here:

```
Date,Open,High,Low,Close,Volume,Adj Close
2015-03-20,561.65,561.72,559.05,560.36,2585800,560.36
2015-03-19,559.39,560.80,556.15,557.99,1191100,557.99
2015-03-18,552.50,559.78,547.00,559.50,2124400,559.50
...
```

To get the latest closing price, we have to skip the first header line and step to the second line, containing the data for the most recent date. From among the comma-separated values, simply grab the fifth element—the element at index 4 starting the count with the traditional 0. Grab the 5th element if you want the closing price or grab the 7th element if you want the adjusted closing price.

Let's put the Yahoo service to work. We'll open our stocks.xml file, grab each symbol, and fetch the latest closing price for that ticker. We multiply the closing price we fetched by the number of units we have, and we get the total value for that stock. Total all those values, and we get to know the total worth of our investments.

Let's write the code that populates a map with the ticker symbols and units present in the XML file. We'll also write the code to fetch data from the Yahoo service into a singleton object named StockPriceFinder:

UsingScala/StockPriceFinder.scala
```
import java.util.Calendar

object StockPriceFinder {
  def getLatestClosingPrice(symbol: String) : Double = {
    val url = "http://ichart.finance.yahoo.com/table.csv?s=" +
        symbol + "&a=00&b=01&c=" + Calendar.getInstance().get(Calendar.YEAR)
    val data = scala.io.Source.fromURL(url).mkString
    val mostRecentData = data.split("\n")(1)
    val closingPrice = mostRecentData.split(",")(4).toDouble
    closingPrice
  }
  def getTickersAndUnits() = {
    val stocksAndUnitsXML = scala.xml.XML.load("stocks.xml")
    (Map[String, Int]() /: (stocksAndUnitsXML \ "symbol")) {
      (map, symbolNode) =>
        val ticker = (symbolNode \ "@ticker").toString
        val units = (symbolNode \ "units").text.toInt
        map + (ticker -> units)
    }
  }
}
```

In the getLatestClosingPrice() method, given a symbol, we go out to the Yahoo service and get the price data. Since the data is in CSV format, we split the data to extract the closing price. The closing price is finally returned from this method.

Since our ticker symbols and units are in stocks.xml, the getTickersAndUnits() method reads this file and creates a map of ticker symbols and units. We saw in earlier sections how to accomplish this. It is the same code moved into the singleton object. Now we're all set to fetch the data and compute the results. The code for that is shown here:

UsingScala/FindTotalWorthSequential.scala

```scala
object FindTotalWorthSequential extends App {
  val symbolsAndUnits = StockPriceFinder.getTickersAndUnits

  println("Ticker  Units  Closing Price($) Total Value($)")

  val startTime = System.nanoTime()
  val valuesAndWorth = symbolsAndUnits.keys.map { symbol =>
    val units = symbolsAndUnits(symbol)
    val latestClosingPrice = StockPriceFinder getLatestClosingPrice symbol
    val value = units * latestClosingPrice

    (symbol, units, latestClosingPrice, value)
  }

  val netWorth = (0.0 /: valuesAndWorth) { (worth, valueAndWorth) =>
    val (_, _, _, value) = valueAndWorth
    worth + value
  }
  val endTime = System.nanoTime()

  valuesAndWorth.toList.sortBy { _._1 }.foreach { valueAndWorth =>
    val (symbol, units, latestClosingPrice, value) = valueAndWorth
    println(f"$symbol%7s  $units%5d  $latestClosingPrice%15.2f  $value%.2f")
  }

  println(f"The total value of your investments is $$$netWorth%.2f")
  println(f"Took ${(endTime-startTime)/1000000000.0}%.2f  seconds")
}
```

Let's run the code and take a look at the output:

```
Ticker  Units  Closing Price($) Total Value($)
   AAPL    200           125.90  25180.00
   ADBE    125            77.36  9670.00
   ALU     150             3.84  576.00
    :       :               :     :
   TXN     190            59.28  11263.20
   VRSN    200            64.75  12950.00
   XRX     240            13.18  3163.20
The total value of your investments is $146473.80
Took 11.13  seconds
```

We first get the map of ticker symbols and units from the XML file using the StockPriceFinder's getTickersAndUnits() method, and store it in the variable symbolsAndUnits. Then, for each symbol, we request the StockPriceFinder's getLatestClosingPrice() method to get the latest price. The result of the map() operation is a collection of tuples with four values each: symbol, units, latestClosingPrice, and value of the stock. We then use the foldLeft() method's alternate method /:() to reduce the collection of tuples to a single value of netWorth. This concludes the computation part of the code and we're ready to print the results after this. To ensure the output appears in a sorted order by the ticker symbols, we convert the collection of tuples into a list using toList() and sort it by the symbol names—this is the first value in the tuple, indicated by the ._1 indexed property. We print the units, price, and value for each symbol, then the net worth, and finally the time the code took to run.

We didn't need much code to accomplish the task. The example took about 11 seconds to run. In the next section, we'll make it respond faster.

Making the Net Asset Application Concurrent

The sequential implementation of the net asset application looked up the latest price for each symbol one at a time. The major delay is the time spent waiting for the responses from the web—the network delay. Let's refactor the previous code so we can make the requests for the latest prices for all the symbols concurrently. When done, we should see a faster response from our net asset application.

To make this application concurrent, well, it's effortless. Since the ticker symbols are all in a collection, all we have to do is turn the collection into a parallel collection and we're done! We need to change only one line. In the previous code, change

```
val valuesAndWorth = symbolsAndUnits.keys.map { symbol =>
```

to

```
val valuesAndWorth = symbolsAndUnits.keys.par.map { symbol =>
```

All we did is insert a call to par() in between the calls to the keys() and map() method. Now compile and run the modified code to see the output:

```
Ticker  Units  Closing Price($) Total Value($)
   AAPL    200            125.90  25180.00
   ADBE    125             77.36  9670.00
    ALU    150              3.84  576.00
     :      :                 :     :
    TXN    190             59.28  11263.20
   VRSN    200             64.75  12950.00
    XRX    240             13.18  3163.20
The total value of your investments is $146473.80
Took 1.98  seconds
```

All the stock prices and values are the same between the two versions of the program. The concurrent version took considerably less time compared to the sequential code—big gain, little effort.

Wrapping Up

In this chapter, you saw firsthand the conciseness and expressiveness of Scala in building the net asset application. We used quite a number of features in this program: interaction with standard input and output; reading and writing files; loading, parsing, creating and saving XML documents; extracting values from XML documents using XPath-like query and powerful pattern matching; and getting data from a web service. As a final step we made the program concurrent and got faster response with almost no additional effort.

You've learned how to program with Scala, but our discussion can't be complete without learning about unit testing. Let's get to that next.

CHAPTER 16

Unit Testing

Your code always does what you type—unit tests will assert that it does what you actually meant. As you develop your application, unit testing further helps ensure your code continues to meet your expectations.

Learning to write unit tests in Scala will benefit you in a number of ways:

- It's a nice way to introduce Scala on your current projects. Even though your production code may be in Java, you can write the test code in Scala.

- It's a good way to learn Scala itself. As you learn the language, you can experiment with the language and its API by writing test cases.

- It improves your design. It's very hard to unit test large and complex code. In order to test it, you'd end up making the code smaller. This will lead to a better design by making the code more cohesive, loosely coupled, easier to understand, and easier to maintain.

You have a few options for unit testing in Scala; you can use Java-based tools like JUnit or use ScalaTest. ScalaTest has changed quite a bit in recent years —when tools evolve quickly, any attempt to provide a detailed example will run the risk of the code becoming obsolete very soon. Thus, this chapter provides a short introduction and some recommendations. Refer to the tutorials[1] for an extensive coverage of ScalaTest.

Using JUnit

Using JUnit to run tests written in Scala is really simple. Since Scala compiles to Java bytecode, you can write your tests in Scala, use scalac to compile your code into bytecode, and then run your tests like you normally run JUnit test

---

cases. Remember to include the Scala library in your classpath. Let's look at an example of writing a JUnit test in Scala:

UnitTesting/UsingJUnit.scala

```scala
import java.util.ArrayList
import org.junit.Test
import org.junit.Assert._

class UsingJUnit {
  @Test
  def listAdd() {
    val list = new ArrayList[String]
    list.add("Milk")
    list add "Sugar"
    assertEquals(2, list.size)
  }
}
```

We imported java.util.ArraryList and then org.junit.Test. We also included all the methods of org.junit.Assert. This serves as a static import, popularized in Java 5. Our test class, UsingJUnit, has one test method, listAdd(), decorated by the JUnit 4.0 Test annotation. Within the test method, we created an instance of ArrayList and first added the String "Milk" to it. That is pure Java syntax without the semicolon at the end. On the other hand, the next addition of "Sugar" illustrates some syntax sugar in Scala—it allowed us to drop the . and the parentheses. You can enjoy such lightweight syntax when writing your unit tests in Scala—for testing both Java code and Scala code. Finally, we assert that the ArrayList instance has two elements in it.

We can compile this code using scalac and run the code like we'd typically run any JUnit test. Here are the commands to do that:

```
scalac -d classes -classpath $JUNIT_JAR:$HAMCREST_JAR UsingJUnit.scala
java -classpath $SCALALIBRARY:$JUNIT_JAR:$HAMCREST_JAR:classes \
  org.junit.runner.JUnitCore UsingJUnit
```

Set up $JUNIT_JAR, $HAMCREST_JAR, and $SCALALIBRARY environmental variables on your machine to point to the location of the appropriate JARs for JUnit, Hamcrest, and the Scala library, respectively. Here's the result of the command to execute the test:

```
JUnit version 4.12
.
Time: 0.003

OK (1 test)
```

See how simple it is to write a JUnit test in Scala? You benefit further by taking advantage of familiar Scala idioms to clarify your code. It's pretty straightforward to use JUnit in Scala to test Java code, Scala code, or any code written for the Java platform, for that matter. Next we'll see what advantage ScalaTest provides over using JUnit.

Using ScalaTest

JUnit is a good starting point for unit testing Scala code. However, as you get more familiar with Scala, you'll want to take advantage of Scala's conciseness and idioms for unit testing as well. When you're ready for that, you may want to graduate to using ScalaTest. ScalaTest is a testing framework written in Scala by Bill Venners, with contribution from many other developers. It provides concise syntax for assertions and functional style for testing both Scala and Java code.

ScalaTest doesn't ship with Scala, so first you need to download it.[2] Once you download the JAR, set an environment variable, SCALA_TEST_JAR, to refer to the full path of that JAR.

Now that you've downloaded ScalaTest, let's write a test, similar to the one we wrote using JUnit, but this time using ScalaTest.

UnitTesting/UsingScalaTest.scala
```
import org.scalatest._
import java.util.ArrayList

class UsingScalaTest extends FlatSpec with Matchers {
  trait EmptyArrayList {
    val list = new ArrayList[String]
  }

  "a list" should "be empty on create" in new EmptyArrayList {
    list.size should be (0)
  }

  "a list" should "increase in size upon add" in new EmptyArrayList {
    list.add("Milk")
    list add "Sugar"

    list.size should be (2)
  }
}
```

---

2.   http://www.scalatest.org

We mixed ScalaTest's FlatSpec and Matcher traits into the UsingScalaTest class. ScalaTest promotes RSpec-like syntax for writing tests with the *should* syntax. In the test, we first created a trait named EmptyArrayList. You can create multiple traits, one for each setup of test instances you'd like to use in tests. For instance, if you want to prepopulate the list with sample data, you can do that in yet another trait.

We mixed the EmptyArrayList trait into the two tests using the new EmptyArrayList. This readily makes the variable named list, that we created in the trait, available within the tests. The code in the tests is fairly self-descriptive.

Compile and run the test using the following commands:

```
scalac -d classes -classpath $SCALA_TEST_JAR UsingScalaTest.scala
scala -classpath $SCALA_TEST_JAR:classes org.scalatest.run UsingScalaTest
```

ScalaTest will mix in the traits as directed and exercise the test methods we wrote in the test to produce the following output:

```
Run starting. Expected test count is: 2
UsingScalaTest:
a list
- should be empty on create
a list
- should increase in size upon add
Run completed in 181 milliseconds.
Total number of tests run: 2
Suites: completed 1, aborted 0
Tests: succeeded 2, failed 0, canceled 0, ignored 0, pending 0
All tests passed.
```

ScalaTest is quite versatile. It comes with a number of built-in traits to facilitate mocking using multiple different tools. For example, if you use Mockito to create stubs, mocks, or spies, you'll thoroughly enjoy the ease of use from Scala. Let's take a look at that next.

Using Mockito

It's better to eliminate, or at least reduce dependencies, as much as possible. You can then temporarily replace essential intrinsic dependencies with stubs or mocks to get rapid feedback from unit tests.

If you're used to EasyMock, JMock, or Mockito with JUnit, you can readily use them with ScalaTest as well. Let's explore an example that will illustrate the use of Mockito with ScalaTest.

Tests with Functional Style

Let's start with a series of tests for a score() method that's used in a guessing game. This method will return a total score based on the number of vowels—each vowel will receive one point whereas other characters will earn two points.

In the previous example we used a trait to hold the instance being tested. ScalaTest also provides a BeforeAndAfter mixing that will invoke a before and a after method for each test method. There's yet another technique we could use —one that's functional in style—as in this test:

```scala
import org.scalatest.{FlatSpec, Matchers}

class WordScorerTest extends FlatSpec with Matchers {

  def withWordScorer(test: WordScorer => Unit) = {
    val wordScorer = new WordScorer()

    test(wordScorer)
  }

  "score" should "return 0 for an empty word" in {
    withWordScorer { wordScorer => wordScorer.score("") should be (0) }
  }

  "score" should "return 2 for word with two vowels" in {
    withWordScorer { _.score("ai") should be (2) }
  }

  "score" should "return 8 for word with four consonants" in {
    withWordScorer { _.score("myth") should be (8) }
  }

  "score" should "return 7 for word with a vowel and three consonants" in {
    withWordScorer { _.score("that") should be (7) }
  }
}
```

The withWordScorer() method is a helper and not a test. It accepts a test function as its parameter and passes an instance of a WordScorer, the class under test, to the test function.

In the first test, we call the method withWordScorer() and pass a function value to it. The function value is essentially the test code; it receives an instance of WordScorer and asserts that its score() method returns a 0 when an empty String is passed.

In the remaining tests we use the withWordScorer() method in the same way, with one difference. Instead of the more verbose explicit name wordScorer, we use an underscore (_) to refer to the parameter that the function value receives.

Let's implement the score() method to satisfy these tests.

```
class WordScorer() {
  private val VOWELS = List('a', 'e', 'i', 'o', 'u')

  def score(word: String) = {
    (0 /: word) { (total, letter) =>
                      total + (if (VOWELS.contains(letter)) 1 else 2) }
  }
}
```

To compile and run the tests, use the following commands:

```
scalac -d classes -classpath $SCALA_TEST_JAR \
  WordScorer.scala WordScorerTest.scala
scala -classpath $SCALA_TEST_JAR:classes org.scalatest.run WordScorerTest
```

Let's ensure all tests are passing by running the tests:

```
Run starting. Expected test count is: 4
WordScorerTest:
score
- should return 0 for an empty word
score
- should return 2 for word with two vowels
score
- should return 8 for word with four consonants
score
- should return 7 for word that with a vowel and three consonants
Run completed in 181 milliseconds.
Total number of tests run: 4
Suites: completed 1, aborted 0
Tests: succeeded 4, failed 0, canceled 0, ignored 0, pending 0
All tests passed.
```

We have some basic features for the method being tested. Now let's now take it to the next level by bringing in a dependency.

Creating a Mock

Let's add a new requirement to the problem on hand. If the spelling of the given word is incorrect the score() method should return a 0; otherwise it will return a valid score.

Now we need to change the method to use a spell checker, but which one? A quick Google search for "Java Spell Checkers" should convince you that it's not a decision you want to make so quickly—there are that many out there. Our solution is to mock away the spell checker to keep the focus on the score() method while getting the rapid feedback from the tests.

Before we work on an incorrect spelling, we want to ensure the current tests will continue to pass with the inclusion of a spell checker. Let's make a series of small changes for that.

First, we need an interface—a trait in Scala, of course—to abstract a spell checker:

```
trait SpellChecker {
  def isCorrect(word: String): Boolean
}
```

Now, let's modify the withWordScorer() method in the test class to create a mock for the SpellChecker.

```
import org.scalatest.{FlatSpec, Matchers}
import org.mockito.Mockito._
import org.mockito.Matchers.anyString

class WordScorerTest extends FlatSpec with Matchers {

  def withWordScorer(test: WordScorer => Unit) = {
    val spellChecker = mock(classOf[SpellChecker])
    when(spellChecker.isCorrect(anyString)).thenReturn(true)
    val wordScorer = new WordScorer(spellChecker)

    test(wordScorer)

    verify(spellChecker, times(1)).isCorrect(anyString())
  }

  //No change to the tests, same as in the previous version
}
```

Using the mock() method of *Mockito* we create a mock object for the SpellChecker interface. All the current tests have words that are spelled correctly. To satisfy these tests, we instruct the mock, using the when() method, to return true for any word that's given as an argument to the isCorrect() method. Then we pass the mock instance of SpellChecker to the constructor of WordScorer. Once we return from the test call, to which the instance of WordScorer is passed, we ask Mockito to verify that the isCorrect() method on the mock was called exactly once, no matter what the string argument was.

We only changed the withWordScorer() method; the tests remain the same as in the previous version. Since we're passing an argument to the constructor of

WordScorer now, we have to change the class accordingly. Also, for the tests to pass, the score() method has to use the SpellChecker's isCorrect() method. Let's make the minimum code change to make the tests pass.

```scala
class WordScorer(val spellChecker: SpellChecker) {
  private val VOWELS = List('a', 'e', 'i', 'o', 'u')

  def score(word: String) = {
    spellChecker.isCorrect(word)
    (0 /: word) { (total, letter) =>
                    total + (if (VOWELS.contains(letter)) 1 else 2) }
  }
}
```

The WordScorer class receives and stores a reference to an instance of SpellChecker. The score() method merely invokes the isCorrect() method to satisfy the tests.

We need to include the Mockito library to successful compile and run the tests. Download Mockito[3] and set up the environment variable $MOCKITO_JAR to refer to the appropriate JAR file. Then run the following commands:

```
scalac -d classes -classpath $SCALA_TEST_JAR:$MOCKITO_JAR \
  WordScorer.scala SpellChecker.scala WordScorerTest.scala
scala -classpath $SCALA_TEST_JAR::$MOCKITO_JAR:classes \
  org.scalatest.run WordScorerTest
```

Now that we've added the mock and modified the class, let's ensure all tests are still passing by running them:

```
Run starting. Expected test count is: 4
WordScorerTest:
score
- should return 0 for an empty word
score
- should return 2 for word with two vowels
score
- should return 8 for word with four consonants
score
- should return 7 for word that with a vowel and three consonants
Run completed in 316 milliseconds.
Total number of tests run: 4
Suites: completed 1, aborted 0
Tests: succeeded 4, failed 0, canceled 0, ignored 0, pending 0
All tests passed.
```

As the final step, let's write the test for an incorrect spelling.

---

3. http://mockito.org

```
"score" should "return 0 for word with incorrect spelling" in {
  val spellChecker = mock(classOf[SpellChecker])
  when(spellChecker.isCorrect(anyString)).thenReturn(false)
  val wordScorer = new WordScorer(spellChecker)

  wordScorer.score("aoe") should be (0)
  verify(spellChecker, times(1)).isCorrect(anyString())
}
```

Since we need the SpellChecker mock's isCorrect() method to return false, in this newly added test we create a new mock instead of reusing the mock created in withWordScorer(). Running the tests now will result in a failure since the score() method of WordScorer is currently ignoring the result of the call to isCorrect(). Let's change that.

```
def score(word: String) = {
  if(spellChecker.isCorrect(word))
    (0 /: word) { (total, letter) =>
                    total + (if (VOWELS.contains(letter)) 1 else 2) }
  else
    0
}
```

The score() method now returns a valid score only if the spelling for the given word is correct; otherwise it returns 0. Let's run the tests once more, using the same commands as used before, and see all tests, including the newly added one pass.

```
Run starting. Expected test count is: 5
WordScorerTest:
score
- should return 0 for an empty word
score
- should return 2 for word with two vowels
score
- should return 8 for word with four consonants
score
- should return 7 for word that with a vowel and three consonants
score
- should return 0 for word with incorrect spelling
Run completed in 208 milliseconds.
Total number of tests run: 5
Suites: completed 1, aborted 0
Tests: succeeded 5, failed 0, canceled 0, ignored 0, pending 0
All tests passed.
```

You saw how easy it is to use the Java mocking libraries from ScalaTest. Now there's nothing to stop you from benefiting from the rapid feedback of unit tests.

Wrapping Up

Even though Scala has sensible static typing and quite a few errors will be caught at compile time, unit testing is still important. It can greatly help to get quick feedback that the evolving code continues to work as expected. You could use JUnit to test Scala code, but ScalaTest is a nice tool for testing both Scala code and Java code. In addition to providing fluency of tests, ScalaTest makes it quite easy to use the mocking libraries popular in Java.

We've come to the end of this journey and reached a beautiful shore. You're now ready to apply the concepts you've learned. Enjoy Scala's concise and expressive power as you begin to create real-world projects in Scala. I sincerely hope you benefit from this book and will be able to apply the concepts for greater good. Thank you for reading it.

Installing Scala

Installing Scala is quite easy. You most likely have found the instructions to install it on your system. Read through this appendix if you need some extra help.

Downloading

To get started, first download the most recent stable version of Scala.[1] Get the appropriate version for the platform you're on.

The examples in this book were tested with the following version of Scala:

```
Scala code runner version 2.11.7 -- Copyright 2002-2013, LAMP/EPFL
```

In addition to Scala, you'll need the JDK version 1.6 or newer. Take a moment to check which version of Java is installed and active on your system.

Once the download is complete, let's proceed to getting Scala installed on the system.

Installing

I'll assume you've downloaded the binary distribution of Scala and also have verified your Java installation. The installation steps vary depending on the platform you're on—refer to the relevant section.

Installing Scala on Windows

On Windows, the *msi* package nicely walks us through the installation steps; follow along with the instructions as they appear during installation. Choose the appropriate location to place the Scala binaries. If you have no particular location preference I suggest placing the distribution under C:\programs\scala

---

1.   http://www.scala-lang.org

directory. Choose a directory name with no whitespace in it, since path names with whitespace often cause trouble.

Let's make sure the setup went as expected. Close any open command-line windows because changes to the environment variables won't take effect until you reopen the windows. In a new command-line window, type scala -version, and make sure it reports the right version of Scala you just installed. If you got that working, you're all set to use Scala!

Installing Scala on Unix-like Systems

There are a couple of options to install Scala on Unix-like systems. On Mac OS X, you can use brew install scala. On other flavors of Unix-like systems, use the appropriate installation or package manager.

Alternately, directly download the distribution file and untar it. Move the unbundled directory to the appropriate location. For example, on my system, I copied the unbundled directory to the /opt/scala directory. Finally, set up the path to the bin directory of the Scala distribution.

As a final step, let's run Scala to ensure the setup went smoothly. Technically, we can source the profile file to bring in the changes to the environment variables, but it's less trouble to open a new terminal window. In it, type scala -version, and ensure it reports the version of Scala you expect. Now you're all set to use Scala!

Web Resources

A Brief History of Scala —— http://www.artima.com/weblogs/viewpost.jsp?thread=163733
Martin Odersky talks about creating Scala.

Command Query Separation —— http://www.martinfowler.com/bliki/CommandQuerySeparation.html
In this blog, Martin Fowler discusses the term *command query separation*.

Discussion Forum for This Book —— https://forums.pragprog.com/forums/346/topics/13475
This is the discussion forum for this book, where readers share their opinions, ask questions, respond to questions, and interact with each other.

Essence vs. Ceremony —— http://blog.thinkrelevance.com/2008/4/1/ending-legacy-code-in-our-lifetime
In this blog titled "Ending Legacy Code in Our Lifetime," Stuart Halloway discusses essence vs. ceremony.

Loan Pattern ———————————————— https://wiki.scala-lang.org/display/SYGN/Loan
This is the Scala wiki page describing the Loan pattern—a pattern to dispose of nonmemory resources automatically.

Mockito ———————————————————— http://mockito.org
This is the website for the popular mocking library that can be used in both Java and Scala.

Polyglot Programming —— http://memeagora.blogspot.com/2006/12/polyglot-programming.html
Neal Ford talks about polyglot programming.

Scala Language Website ———————————— http://www.scala-lang.org
This is the official website for the Scala programming language.

Scala Language Download _____ http://www.scala-lang.org/download
This is the official website for downloading the Scala compiler and libraries.

The Scala Language API _____ http://www.scala-lang.org/api
This is the online version of the Scala Language API.

ScalaTest _____ http://www.scalatest.org
This is a testing framework written in Scala to test Scala and Java code.

Website for this book _____ http://www.pragprog.com/titles/vsscala2
This the official website for this book, where you'll find code samples, forums, and errata.

Bibliography

[AS96]   Harold Abelson and Gerald Jay Sussman. *Structure and Interpretation of Computer Programs*. MIT Press, Cambridge, MA, 2nd, 1996.

[Bec96]   Kent Beck. *Smalltalk Best Practice Patterns*. Prentice Hall, Englewood Cliffs, NJ, 1996.

[Blo08]   Joshua Bloch. *Effective Java*. Addison-Wesley, Reading, MA, 2008.

[Fri97]   Jeffrey E. F. Friedl. *Mastering Regular Expressions*. O'Reilly & Associates, Inc., Sebastopol, CA, 1997.

[GHJV95]   Erich Gamma, Richard Helm, Ralph Johnson, and John Vlissides. *Design Patterns: Elements of Reusable Object-Oriented Software*. Addison-Wesley, Reading, MA, 1995.

[Goe06]   Brian Goetz. *Java Concurrency in Practice*. Addison-Wesley, Reading, MA, 2006.

[HT00]   Andrew Hunt and David Thomas. *The Pragmatic Programmer: From Journeyman to Master*. Addison-Wesley, Reading, MA, 2000.

[Sub11]   Venkat Subramaniam. *Programming Concurrency on the JVM*. The Pragmatic Bookshelf, Raleigh, NC, and Dallas, TX, 2011.

[Sub14]   Venkat Subramaniam. *Functional Programming in Java*. The Pragmatic Bookshelf, Raleigh, NC, and Dallas, TX, 2014.

Index

The Joy of Mazes and Math

Rediscover the joy and fascinating weirdness of mazes and pure mathematics.

Mazes for Programmers

A book on mazes? Seriously?

Yes!

Not because you spend your day creating mazes, or because you particularly like solving mazes.

But because it's fun. Remember when programming used to be fun? This book takes you back to those days when you were starting to program, and you wanted to make your code do things, draw things, and solve puzzles. It's fun because it lets you explore and grow your code, and reminds you how it feels to just think.

Sometimes it feels like you live your life in a maze of twisty little passages, all alike. Now you can code your way out.

Jamis Buck
(286 pages) ISBN: 9781680500554. $38
https://pragprog.com/book/jbmaze

Good Math

Mathematics is beautiful—and it can be fun and exciting as well as practical. *Good Math* is your guide to some of the most intriguing topics from two thousand years of mathematics: from Egyptian fractions to Turing machines; from the real meaning of numbers to proof trees, group symmetry, and mechanical computation. If you've ever wondered what lay beyond the proofs you struggled to complete in high school geometry, or what limits the capabilities of the computer on your desk, this is the book for you.

Mark C. Chu-Carroll
(282 pages) ISBN: 9781937785338. $34
https://pragprog.com/book/mcmath

Seven in Seven

You need to learn at least one new language every year. Here are fourteen excellent suggestions to get started.

Seven Languages in Seven Weeks

You should learn a programming language every year, as recommended by *The Pragmatic Programmer*. But if one per year is good, how about *Seven Languages in Seven Weeks*? In this book you'll get a hands-on tour of Clojure, Haskell, Io, Prolog, Scala, Erlang, and Ruby. Whether or not your favorite language is on that list, you'll broaden your perspective of programming by examining these languages side-by-side. You'll learn something new from each, and best of all, you'll learn how to learn a language quickly.

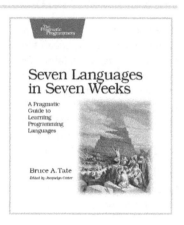

Bruce A. Tate
(330 pages) ISBN: 9781934356593. $34.95
https://pragprog.com/book/btlang

Seven More Languages in Seven Weeks

Great programmers aren't born—they're made. The industry is moving from object-oriented languages to functional languages, and you need to commit to radical improvement. New programming languages arm you with the tools and idioms you need to refine your craft. While other language primers take you through basic installation and "Hello, World," we aim higher. Each language in *Seven More Languages in Seven Weeks* will take you on a step-by-step journey through the most important paradigms of our time. You'll learn seven exciting languages: Lua, Factor, Elixir, Elm, Julia, MiniKanren, and Idris.

Bruce Tate, Fred Daoud, Jack Moffitt, Ian Dees
(320 pages) ISBN: 9781941222157. $38
https://pragprog.com/book/7lang

Seven in Seven

From Web Frameworks to Concurrency Models, see what the rest of the world is doing with this introduction to seven different approaches.

Seven Web Frameworks in Seven Weeks

Whether you need a new tool or just inspiration, *Seven Web Frameworks in Seven Weeks* explores modern options, giving you a taste of each with ideas that will help you create better apps. You'll see frameworks that leverage modern programming languages, employ unique architectures, live client-side instead of server-side, or embrace type systems. You'll see everything from familiar Ruby and JavaScript to the more exotic Erlang, Haskell, and Clojure.

Jack Moffitt, Fred Daoud
(302 pages) ISBN: 9781937785635. $38
https://pragprog.com/book/7web

Seven Concurrency Models in Seven Weeks

Your software needs to leverage multiple cores, handle thousands of users and terabytes of data, and continue working in the face of both hardware and software failure. Concurrency and parallelism are the keys, and *Seven Concurrency Models in Seven Weeks* equips you for this new world. See how emerging technologies such as actors and functional programming address issues with traditional threads and locks development. Learn how to exploit the parallelism in your computer's GPU and leverage clusters of machines with MapReduce and Stream Processing. And do it all with the confidence that comes from using tools that help you write crystal clear, high-quality code.

Paul Butcher
(296 pages) ISBN: 9781937785659. $38
https://pragprog.com/book/pb7con

Pragmatic Programming

We'll show you how to be more pragmatic and effective, for new code and old.

Your Code as a Crime Scene

Jack the Ripper and legacy codebases have more in common than you'd think. Inspired by forensic psychology methods, this book teaches you strategies to predict the future of your codebase, assess refactoring direction, and understand how your team influences the design. With its unique blend of forensic psychology and code analysis, this book arms you with the strategies you need, no matter what programming language you use.

Adam Tornhill
(218 pages) ISBN: 9781680500387. $36
https://pragprog.com/book/atcrime

The Nature of Software Development

You need to get value from your software project. You need it "free, now, and perfect." We can't get you there, but we can help you get to "cheaper, sooner, and better." This book leads you from the desire for value down to the specific activities that help good Agile projects deliver better software sooner, and at a lower cost. Using simple sketches and a few words, the author invites you to follow his path of learning and understanding from a half century of software development and from his engagement with Agile methods from their very beginning.

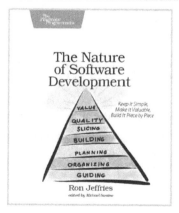

Ron Jeffries
(178 pages) ISBN: 9781941222379. $24
https://pragprog.com/book/rjnsd

The Pragmatic Bookshelf

The Pragmatic Bookshelf features books written by developers for developers. The titles continue the well-known Pragmatic Programmer style and continue to garner awards and rave reviews. As development gets more and more difficult, the Pragmatic Programmers will be there with more titles and products to help you stay on top of your game.

Visit Us Online

This Book's Home Page
https://pragprog.com/book/vsscala2
Source code from this book, errata, and other resources. Come give us feedback, too!

Register for Updates
https://pragprog.com/updates
Be notified when updates and new books become available.

Join the Community
https://pragprog.com/community
Read our weblogs, join our online discussions, participate in our mailing list, interact with our wiki, and benefit from the experience of other Pragmatic Programmers.

New and Noteworthy
https://pragprog.com/news
Check out the latest pragmatic developments, new titles and other offerings.

Save on the eBook

Save on the eBook versions of this title. Owning the paper version of this book entitles you to purchase the electronic versions at a terrific discount.

PDFs are great for carrying around on your laptop—they are hyperlinked, have color, and are fully searchable. Most titles are also available for the iPhone and iPod touch, Amazon Kindle, and other popular e-book readers.

Buy now at *https://pragprog.com/coupon*

Contact Us

Online Orders:	*https://pragprog.com/catalog*
Customer Service:	*support@pragprog.com*
International Rights:	*translations@pragprog.com*
Academic Use:	*academic@pragprog.com*
Write for Us:	*http://write-for-us.pragprog.com*
Or Call:	+1 800-699-7764